GILBERT & GEORGE

LONDON PICTURES

2011

With lots of love from
Gilbert and George x
x

GILBERT & GEORGE

LONDON PICTURES

2011

GALERIE THADDAEUS ROPAC

PARIS
14 APRIL – 26 MAY 2012

SALZBURG
24 NOVEMBER – 28 DECEMBER 2012

GILBERT & GEORGE

LONDON PICTURES 2011

" ...gazing fearfully at the huge town before them, as if foreboding that their misery there would be but as a drop of water in the sea, or as a grain of sea-sand on the shore... Food for the hospitals, the churchyards, the prisons, the river, fever, madness, vice, and death – they passed on to the monster, roaring in the distance, and were lost."

Charles Dickens – *Dombey and Son,* 1847

Throughout their art, with unwavering constancy, the vision and presence of Gilbert & George have seemed to permeate the very pores of London – the city in which they have lived and worked together since 1967. So intense is their empathy, as artists, with the streets and buildings and atmosphere, the sleepless thoroughfares and anonymous presences, the institutions and detritus and imprints of history, the strangeness and newness and dereliction of London, that they seem in their art to both haunt the city – as tireless themselves as ghosts – and to be a living part of its fabric, melding or drifting or watching, through shabby streets, polished concrete or soot-blackened brick.

In the two hundred and ninety-two 'LONDON PICTURES', their extent created from the meticulous sifting and classification, by subject, of 3712 newspaper posters, produced daily and weekly by various London newspapers, the presence of Gilbert & George has now become overtly and determinedly spirit-like – as though the artists were psychic manifestations of the city itself, its sense of place and history. The 'LONDON PICTURES' comprise both a directory of quotidian urban human behaviour – revealing and shocking and violent, in all its sluggish or volatile momentum – and as such the city's moral portrait: an unflinching audit of modern western society's relationship to itself, stripped of rhetoric or intellectual disguise.

For these newspaper posters – this assault on reason and calm by announcements of violence, passion, misery and greed – articulate what might be termed London's nervous system: the impulses, instincts, reflexes, tics, surges and sensitivities of an illimitable torrent of human existence. Such naked feelings have always been both the subject and temper of the art of Gilbert & George, just as those same emotions and sensations, their actions and their historical consequences, have shaped the city's body, and kept its sentience alert. The 'LONDON PICTURES', therefore, can be seen as containing the cumulative force and intensity of the art of Gilbert & George to date. They might also mark a point when Gilbert & George, through the transformative agency of their art, become like spirits of London – a state achieved, in their art and its creations, through their intense immersion in the stuff of the city, and their identification, as witnesses and moral seers, with the cycles of life and death that it contains.

Gilbert: "All the posters that we collected are from London – that is how these 'LONDON PICTURES' began. And all the subjects are from London, and around the world."

George: "We always thought that we were trying to do London pictures with 'RED MORNING' and so forth – but they never became specifically about London in that way; it was always edging around the subject. But then these posters enabled us to address those subjects that one connects with London: the city of murder and sex and disaster and burning buildings."

Gilbert: "For years we have said that we never want to be anywhere else. London is the most important part of our inspiration. It is all that surrounds us. And so we have been able to include all this remarkable surface of thoughts and feelings that we find in these posters – you wouldn't be able to paint a picture like that. There are so many layers in these new pictures, which you wouldn't be able to do in a painting."

George: "We can address those subjects that otherwise would be almost impossible. To make a big picture called 'Pervert', for instance – to be able to address that subject."

Gilbert: "It feels like Dickens – he walked London and saw these things: the suicides, the rape… These posters show the western world inside us all: it's like taking London and putting it inside an MRI scanner. And it is also like a universal diary of London. We have always felt that it takes a while for a subject, or even a building, to really speak to us. It may take years even; but then it is as though these things come to life and speak to us - and we can make art from it."

The 'LONDON PICTURES' seem to consolidate a vision and a journey that the artists began nearly fifty years ago. The cyclone of feelings that they convey with such force – as though the low roar of an angry storm, rising and falling, could be felt through the newspaper media of words and images – seems summoned from the depths of an ancient and exhausted restlessness; that from the actuality of news headlines, brutal, blunt, absurd, there resonates a vision of the city as Gilbert & George have known and traversed it, drawing upon its energy, dreams and trauma as though from a palette of human feeling – recognized and employed since the beginnings of their art.

It is not that the acts and events announced by these posters are sensational and unusual; rather, the opposite: it is their regularity that shocks – the routine of horror and misery, its turbulence all-pervading, its reliability known; but its reality usually unseen. How did Gilbert & George come to know this city, and enable themselves to merge with its torpor, vexed energy, battered streets and magnificence?

Having met at St Martin's School of Art in 1967, on London's busy Charing Cross Road, the two young artists chose to become separate from their teachers and peers, preferring to explore the vastness and mystery of the city around them. Here lay the inspiration for their life's work as one artist, Gilbert & George. Almost immediately they knew and declared that they were Living Sculptures – that they, Gilbert & George, were their art. They dressed soberly and correctly, as smartly as their circumstances allowed. They were polite and friendly to all whom they met. They worked from dawn until dusk, every day, to turn the intensity of their feelings and their experiences into art, and to make a place where they could live. They roamed the city and London absorbed them – in exact proportion to the manner in which they absorbed London.

Gilbert: "It is to do with our loneliness – our loneliness when we started our art. The feeling of 'SIDE BY SIDE' (1971), and going into the 'DARK SHADOW' (1974) of loneliness in a different way – all this stuff is there, already, I really believe it: broken bottles; postcards of unhappy landscapes. And then with 'DUSTY CORNERS' (1975) and 'DEAD BOARDS' (1976) – this atmosphere… It was not the street, but it was the loneliness of the world. And with these new 'LONDON PICTURES' we are able to show an extraordinary townscape of London."

George: "Bleak and empty and desolate…"

Gilbert: "Even the trees in our pictures are yearning for something. And even when we made the 'COSMOLOGICAL PICTURES' (1989), it was like a yearning for an ideal dream world. You never see the world for what it is, you see it through your own brain – different for everyone: happy, unhappy, the struggle of life. And with these 'LONDON PICTURES', it's all real, not fake – that's what we like."

Gilbert & George had settled in the East End of London, first in Wilkes Street, and then Fournier Street – at that time a dangerous and derelict district, hard by Liverpool Street Station. To the west of them, the old City of London maintained its enclosed, medieval world – Italianate banks and counting houses, dim courtyards, smoky dining rooms and dark pubs; a district that between the 1980s and the present would suddenly accelerate its modernity – becoming ultra-modern and stateless, the hub of the biggest and wealthiest financial centre in the world; and around which, like a dirty tide, the renovation encrusted buildings of Edwardian and Victorian London retained their cowed and battered air.

Around Spitalfields, where the artists lived, the darkling eighteenth century streets seemed to lie densely scattered, like bleached and broken bones; and in the tall, high-windowed houses, beyond their dismal or portentous front doors, could be found little workshops, furriers' rooms, obscure offices and businesses, store rooms, artisan studios or solitary tenants. Alternately bustling and desolate, it was a place of working men's cafes and poor families; their neighbours were market porters, tramps, immigrant workers and worshippers, and 'the meths men' – alcoholics who drank themselves to blindness and death on industrial ethanol, fumous and mauvish. It was the lingering twilight of this society that Gilbert & George would later create in their film, made in 1980, 'THE WORLD OF GILBERT & GEORGE'.

But within these surroundings, Gilbert & George discovered an aspect of London that might have seemed unchanged for a hundred years. Always researching the history of London, the artists would read that in 1869, J. Ewing Richie had pronounced:

"The swells in the park, the millers in Mark Lane, the graziers in the new cattle market, the Jews in Houndsditch or Holywell Street, the prim pale lads in the City; the sailors at Shadwell, and Deptford and Wapping, the German sugar bakers in Whitechapel, the Chinese opium smokers in Tiger Bay – really form as distinct a community as any Red Indians dwelling beyond the sunset, and the bars of all the western stars. A large book might be written about the east of London…" And so this East end of the city would be for Gilbert & George the crucible of human feelings and behaviour – the place in which the local becomes the universal:

George: "We have always said that when you see the church in one of our pictures, it is not the church in Fournier Street - it's the church inside you. Because for or against the church, we all know what it means."

Gilbert: "And in every interview we ever gave, we always said that the centre of the universe is Liverpool Street Station."

George: "And that if a space ship was arriving from outer space, and they had five minutes to interview people about life on Earth, the city that they would go to is London. There would be no use going to Zurich – that's typical planet Earth circa 1937. Whereas London is Today."

Historically, the East End of London had not only been poor, to the point of destitute, but also home to society's outcasts, victims and criminal classes. Those who slipped beneath the surface of London's brutally strong currents and rip tides could find themselves dragged under, to the shabby streets and missions and hostels to be found around Shoreditch and Whitechapel. The houses and streets were both sanctuary and prison, an enclosed universe, to many of their inhabitants – and daily witness to the extremes of life as much as its drear momentum: intoxication, struggle and violence, prayer and hope and work and misery were the commonplace heaving and groaning of this dank section of the urban machine.

Gilbert: "There is something of our art from 1980 in these 'LONDON PICTURES' – when we made pictures such as 'ALDGATE','SPITALFIELDS' and 'FOURNIER STREET'."

George: "The general educated opinion on these pictures at that time was 'Why on Earth would you bring these wretched disgusting subjects of this vile part of London into the gallery? We know what goes on down there. We don't need to see pictures of it…' We were accused of 'snooping on low-life' when we made 'THE DIRTY WORDS' (1977) pictures. But Dickens did that, didn't he? And we're living in the middle of it here anyway – to call it 'snooping' is absurd."

The 'LONDON PICTURES' derive a great part of their impact and intensity from the directness and unchanged immediacy of the newspaper posters within all but one panel of each picture. In each remaining panel, as though adding the Royal Warrant to each forensic pronouncement of outrage – for example: 'STAB', 'STAB DEATH', 'STABBED' – can be found a different image of HM Queen Elizabeth II, taken from a coin, her countenance and profile changing with age, dented and worn through the usage of currency. There is a stark and arresting juxtaposition of this iconic likeness, potent with pomp and authority, and the alphabetical index of outrage, by subject, refined by the 'LONDON PICTURES'. Her Majesty appears to endorse the title of each picture, providing a state colophon to their vision of modern London; and by doing so become implicated in the society and morality that they describe. The words 'IT'S WRITTEN ALL OVER THEM' beneath the legend, 'A LONDON PICTURE', propose that these headlines cannot help but reveal what we as a society have become capable of, and have allowed to happen. Behind modern urban society's veneer of respectability and order, volatility and suffering is constant.

The great Victorian visionary and critic, John Ruskin, also reported on the lives of East London's suffering, direct from their own testaments, in his three lectures 'Sesame and Lilies', written in 1867. The atmosphere of the supernatural is present – not in Ruskin's thesis or prose, but in the intensity of atmosphere and strangeness within the reported testaments. Taken from a Daily Telegraph newspaper of that year, Ruskin recounts the coroner's court hearing of the case of a deceased workman – first blinded by close work in poor light, and finally starving to death. Like Dickens, in his accusatory political essay 'The Parish', Ruskin was appalled by the callousness of the Parish as a social service. These abject conditions are matched by the surrealism of the witness's language – as he confesses to preferring starvation and death, rather than entering the Parish Workhouse:

"A Juror: 'You are dying of starvation yourself, and you ought to go into the house [workhouse] until summer.' Witness: 'If we went in we should die. When we come out in the summer we should be like people dropped from the sky. No one would know us, and we would not even have a room.' "

As seems to lie behind the posters of the contemporary

London newspapers, it is the routine and regularity of this suffering within the metropolis that both appals and gives rise to a form of semantic strangeness. Beyond the statistic and the legal investigation of the death, there stretch the sensitivities of a human life, and the inter-connectedness of that life to others. And yet the monumental significance of that life and its death becomes absorbed into the bureaucratic, daily flow of the city's workings. It is the acknowledgement of such an assimilation, the moral drama that exists beneath the typographical shorthand of a newspaper poster, that the 'LONDON PICTURES' reveal – the 'moral dimension' that Gilbert & George must feel within a subject, in order to transpose that dimension into their art, and make it available to the viewer.

Such has always been their mission. Early on, in their neat suits, the best that they could manage, Gilbert & George worked tirelessly at their art – walking the streets, day and night, to the furthest edges and deepest recesses of London, always discovering and experiencing new feelings and new impressions. And soon they knew that in the few streets around Fournier Street – this urban whirlpool - they could find all of the qualities, good and bad, that comprise the modern human condition. The voice of London became, for the artists, what they called its 'moral dimension' – sometimes made eloquent through the traces, records, detritus and excreta left behind by the passage and lives of anonymous strangers; on other occasions newly found in familiar sites, buildings or trees. To reveal and explore this moral dimension has been the subject and main purpose of all of the art of Gilbert & George.

George: "We always say that we take images of a subject again and again, until we find the moral dimension – and then it speaks to us. Like we took images outside buildings of lace curtains – and we didn't know why. Then we took more, and we suddenly realized that these curtains were like the house's burka; they serve the same function – the people in the house can look out, but we can't look in. And in that moment we were able to use these images in the new 'LONDON PICTURES'. We wouldn't have been able to use them until we knew what they mean to us."

Gilbert: "These posters are amazing realism – an amazingly intense vision of a city. London is the most on-edge city in the world – people want to come here from all over the world. I am sure that we are part of the dark side of East London – we wouldn't go to the West End to take an image. We know that misery is fascinating. That's human life – hidden suffering. And in some ways we are exposing what is going on inside people's minds. We have to fill our brains with a density of a particular image, in order to work out what it means to us, and what it might mean to the viewer. And sometimes, very rarely, a single image might take us off on a whole new direction."

George: "I am sure that when we made the picture 'News', in 2004, which includes images of a newspaper poster, we didn't know or plan or think that one day we would make a whole group of pictures based on newspaper posters."

Gilbert: "It was later that we became interested in that whole world of subjects like suicide, rape, killing, murder, OAP [old age pensioners]… It became like a new world – subjects that you wouldn't normally be able to use in art; how would we use this stuff in art? Only because it is written down and combined with these layers: of brick walls, and us melting into them or into trees… It becomes like a vision of London – a certain London that exists…"

The scope of the 'LONDON PICTURES' is epic, and derives from the manner in which each picture, to a greater extent, automatically 'creates itself' as a consequence of the means by which Gilbert & George have classified and catalogued the newspaper headline posters that comprise each text-based panel. Thus the two hundred and ninety-two 'LONDON PICTURES' have been determined in size and title by the mathematical and alphabetical refinement, by subject, of the 3712 posters that were stolen and accumulated by the artists over many years. As they were collecting these posters, Gilbert & George had no inkling or premonition as to what their eventual purpose would be.

Gilbert: "At first we just had posters, which we had stolen over the years – a massive amount. We would walk each day over to Liverpool Street, and one of us would buy a Mars Bar while the other stole the poster."

George: "We didn't realize how many we had collected – we thought it was just a couple of hundred posters."

Gilbert: "When we counted them, there were 3712. Then, just before Christmas 2010, we started laying them down by subject on the studio floor – and it was amazing."

George: "Many of the posters have more than one subject; so it was like a 'four layer' sort-out. For instance, within the subject heading 'KILL', there is 'boy', 'girl', 'woman', 'man' – so we had to adjust the piles. Subjects such as 'STAB' and 'DEATH' have too many variants, and so we had to make a decision as to which to keep. And so for instance there is a picture called 'STAB' and a picture called 'STAB DEATH' – within the larger subject area of stabbings."

Gilbert: "We had to be able to break it down into a system – beginning alphabetically by subject. For those subject groups which were too big, we looked to see what other words occurred, and whether we could make a picture from those –secondary subjects. We also have to leave one panel free, bottom right, for the title – so to make an eight-part picture we needed seven posters that included the word referring to its subject. So from the posters themselves, sorted in this system by word and subject, we knew the title of a picture and how big it was. For each picture we made a folder, with the title, and all the images relating to that picture."

George: "This system is also very revealing. For instance, when we isolate the word 'LONDON' we find that the other frequent words within that subject area are 'MONEY'. For 'LOVER', we have fifteen posters, and within those headlines we also find: 'KILLED', 'MURDER', 'MONEY', 'DIES', 'HACKED TO DEATH'... Whereas you would have thought that 'LOVER' would be quite a nice list, wouldn't you?

The simple system when we were first sifting the posters was: nothing pleasant. And a friend said that surely there must be plenty of pleasant subjects – but they must be invisible to us, because I don't remember seeing any."

And thus, from the 3712 stolen posters, the alphabetical list of 'LONDON PICTURES' began to create itself through an almost automatic process: 'ACCUSED', 'ADDICT', 'ADDICTS', 'ANGEL', 'ARMED', 'ARREST', 'ARREST STRAIGHT'... A further nuance was added to the composition and titling of the 'LONDON PICTURES' by the distinction between those posters printed in a thicker, cursive script (like hand-written capital letters) and those printed in more etiolate sans serif capital letters. The latter were always denoted, as a suffix to the title, 'STRAIGHT'. In this, Gilbert & George were both distinguishing the two typefaces, but also making a play on the use of 'straight' as slang for 'heterosexual'.

Their point was that the continued highlighting of 'gay' society was irrelevant, outmoded and divisive; for example, why distinguish between 'gay' and 'straight' marriage, rather than simply referring to 'marriage'? The inclusive aspect of the subjects described by the 'LONDON PICTURES' – its democracy of events and social types - was a feature that they found particularly interesting.

The viewer's experience of each picture begins, perhaps, with the manner in which the images of Gilbert & George – stern, impassive, staring, or glimpsed on a street as though photo-journalistically – take their places within the back-ground of poster-based panels. They are always depicted in a figurative, un-manipulated form, and yet their presence is otherworldly and ghost-like. They seem to stare towards the viewer in a manner that is simultaneously accusatory and mute, knowing and impassive, sentient and vacant. Elsewhere they are seen as though from afar – even the sunlight on a street adding somehow to their strangeness and solitude, their sense of being both within the present and a visitor to it.

In this the artists consolidate, artistically, what might be seen as their 'psychic' constitution as Living Sculptures and the authors of 'SIDE BY SIDE' (1971) and 'DARK SHADOW' (1974) – their place as eternal outsiders, sleepless wanderers of the city, urban seers, 'super-tramps', isolated, dispossessed, solitary: finding a spiritual home (as young artists) beneath a railway arch; later, becoming monstrous versions of themselves, crazed and gesticulating like mad sentinels. Within the 'LONDON PICTURES' they appear as fragments, reflections or transparent versions of themselves: their edges are sometimes blurred, or their bodies merge into whiteness; at times their heads are distorted, but not as mutants – rather, as presences just glimpsed on the street by chance, that disappear as soon as they are recognized. There is neither sadness nor anger about their presence: rather a sense of eternal patience or impassive watchfulness – a quality that has also been constant through the art of Gilbert & George.

In relation to the 'LONDON PICTURES', the artists had also, serendipitously, come across the writings of Lord Dowding – Air Chief Marshall and Commander-in-Chief of the Royal Air Force during the Battle of Britain. Subsequent to winning the Battle of Britain, Dowding – perhaps traumatized by strain and exhaustion, perhaps not – became increasingly interested in spiritualism, and in the induction of spirits into the afterlife. From these interests he wrote several books, all of which have been of great interest to Gilbert & George. His particular concept of ghosts and spirits, therefore, informed an aspect of the artists' depiction of themselves within the 'LONDON PICTURES'. But it is the manner in which the presence of Gilbert & George, within these pictures, becomes synonymous with the intense and particular atmosphere of the city, that is paramount: how they depict themselves as ghost-like extensions of London's dark, brooding or near electrical sentience – emanations from a numinous geography.

Gilbert: "The layers in the 'LONDON PICTURES' melt together – it's extraordinary. It is like spirits of London – walking the streets. But it is also by accident; we noticed that some of the images looked like spirits, and then we started to read Lord Dowding's books about ghosts. Spirits can be in your brain, too – memories and dreams can be three dimensional, as can the very intense atmosphere on a street or from a building.

George: "We like to think that we, along with the viewer, are all complicit in how we have made the world. We wanted each picture to 'decide itself' – the same way that a day decides itself."

George: "We always liked the idea of Dowding, because, like Bomber Harris, he divides opinion. He won the Battle of Britain, which stopped a Nazi invasion of this country, which would have changed the course of history. But there are still people who think that there shouldn't be a statue to him. We also liked the idea that he had parties in his headquarters with the killed pilots, who were dressed as they were when they were killed – he wrote at great length about that. You can argue about this forever, but he certainly wasn't a liar."

Gilbert: "He was so unhappy and obsessed that these young people were dead – after just one flight maybe – that he started seeing them coming back alive..."

George: "We were taking pictures of ourselves in the yard, and then blanked out with white everything except the figure and a bit of yard, or holes in us... And so you saw aspects of us. It is not an obvious thing, which we like as well – but more mysterious, like the Dowding boys."

Gilbert: "It made us as though we were melting into the surroundings – a 'spirit image'; or like the wartime Powell & Pressburger film ['A Matter of Life and Death'] about the young airman caught between life and death."

The remaining visual elements of the 'LONDON PICTURES' are pared down and literal: streets, house-fronts, bricks, net curtains, car window reflections. The colours are refined to black and white, red and flesh colour. This palette is also the consequence of the automatic formulation of the pictures, and the removal by the artists of any conscious compositional process or decision-making.

George: "We knew we wanted them to be black and white, and that red is the most expressive colour for the title. And the only other thing in all of the pictures is the human presence, so we added flesh colour."

Gilbert: "A black and white image can just speak more. And the accident of the aesthetic, we like very much. In some ways, we have taken the process of composition away. We didn't change anything."

George: "And we decided that we would not violate the posters in the 'LONDON PICTURES' in any way. We didn't want the images we took and used to be consciously 'good', technically. They should just be like something you see on your way to breakfast in the morning, or on your way home in the evening. They are automatic in the sense that they are not concentrated – no thinking or planning at all."

Gilbert: "We simply needed an atmosphere to complete the picture."

George: "If someone comes down the street, you maybe don't know who they are, where they've come from or where they're going. And the images can be like that, also. They will make their own life."

Gilbert: "We create a visual spirit – like an atmosphere from a time or day; it is not composed... We wanted to be taken over by the spirit of it."

George: "But strangely, we think that we have made very moving images. We only realized that at the end. We lived the process of making these pictures, more than any others we have made: of being with them, alone, in them."

The 'LONDON PICTURES' can be seen as the incendiary conflation of an automatic, classification based process, and a deep excursion into the psychic and emotional territory that has been pioneered by the art of Gilbert & George. In the past, the artists have spoken of how in order to create they must maintain an absolute balance, in themselves, between technical control and 'crazed' or 'dead headed' psychology. The 'LONDON PICTURES' can be seen as a monumental testament to this creative dichotomy: wherein the 'self-deciding' compositional process of the pictures is matched by a deeper and deeper advance, by the artists, into the gravitational field of atmosphere, place, time and feelings. It is the territory of Dickens's 'Night Walks' – in which the secrets of all London must seem to lie bare before his undefended, vulnerable but all-seeing gaze: a place beyond sadness, or death or event, where the only continuum is the life energy of the city, flowing without pause or emotion, eternally, indifferent to individual human destiny.

George: "This is the great adventure of the Greco/Romano Judaeo/Christian Secularist society, always trying to move forward, always under attack. Everything playing its part in an onward and ongoing gradual improvement."

Gilbert: "Trying to understand one another – that is surely the most important thing? I think it is the balance to survive. The skies don't change because we have murders in the street."

George: "Maybe the 'LONDON PICTURES' are the local version of that."

Gilbert: "They tell an amazing story. That is what we love – they are the cries of London: the street cries of London."

George: "And they are also the doorway into this amazing world – of misery, unhappiness and shame."

Michael Bracewell

292 LONDON PICTURES 2011

ACCUSED
ADDICT
ADDICTS
ANGEL
ARMED
ARREST
ARREST STRAIGHT
ARRESTED
ARRESTED STRAIGHT
ARSON
ATTACK
ATTACK STRAIGHT
ATTACKER
ATTACKS
ATTACKS STRAIGHT
AXE
BABIES
BABY
BABY STRAIGHT
BANKER
BATTERED
BATTLE
BATTLE STRAIGHT
BEATEN TO DEATH
BEATEN TO DEATH STRAIGHT
BIKER
BLAZE
BODY
BOMB
BOMB STRAIGHT
BOMBEY
BOMBEY STRAIGHT
BOY
BOY AGED
BOY AGED STRAIGHT

BOY STRAIGHT
BOYS
BRAWL
BROTHEL
BURGLAR
BURGLAR STRAIGHT
BURGLARY
CABBIE
CAGED
CEMETERY
CHILD
CHILD STRAIGHT
CHILDREN
CHILDREN STRAIGHT
CHURCH
CITY
CITY MONEY
CITY STRAIGHT
CRACK
CRIME
CUTE KIDS
CYCLIST
CYCLIST STRAIGHT
DEAD
DEAD STRAIGHT
DEATH CRASH
DEATH LEAP
DEATH PLUNGE
DEATH PLUNGE STRAIGHT
DEATH SOMETHING
DEATH STRAIGHT
DEATH
DEATHS
DEATHS STRAIGHT
DIE

DIE STRAIGHT
DIED
DIED STRAIGHT
DIES
DIES STRAIGHT
DOG
DRIVER
DRUG
DRUG STRAIGHT
DRUGS
DRUGS STRAIGHT
DRUNK
DYING
FAMILY
FAMILY STRAIGHT
FOUND
FURY
GANG STRAIGHT
GANG
GANGS
GANGS STRAIGHT
GAY
GAY STRAIGHT
GIRL
GIRL AGED
GIRL AGED STRAIGHT
GIRL STRAIGHT
GRANDAD
GUN
GUN STRAIGHT
GUNMAN
GUNMAN STRAIGHT
GUNMEN
GUNNED DOWN
GUNPOINT

GUNS
HANGED
HANGING
HATE
HELL
HOLIDAY
HOODIES
HOOKER
HORROR
HUNT
HUNTED
HURT
ISLAM
ISLAM STRAIGHT
JAIL
JAIL STRAIGHT
JAILED
JAILED STRAIGHT
KERB
KIDNAP
KIDS
KILL
KILL STRAIGHT
KILLED
KILLED STRAIGHT
KILLER
KILLER STRAIGHT
KILLERS
KILLERS STRAIGHT
KILLING
KILLING STRAIGHT
KILLINGS
KILLS
KILLS STRAIGHT
KNIFE

KNIFE MURDER
KNIFE STRAIGHT
KNIFED
KNIFED TO DEATH
KNIFEMAN
LADPALMATE
LIFE
LIFE STRAIGHT
LONDON
LONDON BOMB
LONDON CRIME STRAIGHT
LONDON CRIME
LONDON STRAIGHT
LONDON'S
LOVER
MACHETE
MAN
MAN AGED
MAN DIES
MAN STABBED
MAN STRAIGHT
MISSING
MONEY FIRST
MONEY
MONEY STRAIGHT
MONEY LAST
MOSQUE
MOTHER
MOTHER STRAIGHT
MUGGER
MUGGER STRAIGHT
MUGGERS
MUGGING
MUGGY
MUM
MURDER
MURDER STRAIGHT
MURDERED

MURDERED STRAIGHT
MURDERS
MUSLIM
MUSLIM STRAIGHT
MYSTERY
OAP
OAPS
PAEDO
PARK
PENSIONER
PERVERT
PLAYBOY
PLOT
PLUNGE
POLICE
POLICE STRAIGHT
PORN
PREACHER
PRISON
PUPIL
PUPILS
RACE
RACE HATE
RACIST
RAID
RAID STRAIGHT
RAIDERS
RAPE
RAPE STRAIGHT
RAPED
RAPIST
RAPIST STRAIGHT
RAT
ROBBED
ROBBER
ROBBERS
ROBBERY
ROBBERY STRAIGHT

SCHOOL STRAIGHT
SCHOOL
SCHOOLBOY
SCHOOLS
SEX
SEX & MONEY
SEX ATTACKER
SEX BEAST
SEX PEST
SEX STRAIGHT
SHOOT OUT
SHOOTING
SHOOTING STRAIGHT
SHOOTINGS
SHOP
SHOT
SHOT DEAD
SHOT GUN
SHOT STRAIGHT
SHOTS
SOCCER
SOCCER STRAIGHT
STAB
STAB DEATH
STABBED
STABBED STRAIGHT
STABBED TO DEATH
STABBED TO DEATH STRAIGHT
STABBING
STABBING STRAIGHT
STABBINGS
STAR
STRANGLED
STRANGLER
STUDENT
STUDENT STRAIGHT
STUDENTS
SUICIDE

SUICIDE STRAIGHT
TEACHER
TEACHER STRAIGHT
TEEN
TEEN STRAIGHT
TEEN'S
TEENAGE
TEENAGE STRAIGHT
TEENAGER
TEENAGER STRAIGHT
TEENS
TERROR
TERROR BOMB
TERROR STRAIGHT
TERROR PLOT
THIEF
THIEVES
THUG
THUGS
THUGS STRAIGHT
TODDLER
TOP TOTS
TOT
TOTS
TUBE
TUBE STRAIGHT
VANDALS
VICE
VICTIM
VICTIM STRAIGHT
WAR
WOMAN
WOMAN AGED
WOMAN STRAIGHT
WOMEN
YOB
YOBS
YOUTH

THE 292 **LONDON PICTURES**
ARE REPRODUCED HERE IN
ALPHABETICAL ORDER

COP ACCUSED OF SEX ATTACK
LIFE-SAVERS ACCUSED OF STEALING FROM PATIENTS
PAKISTANI MURDER TRIANGLE : LOVERS ACCUSED
ARCHWAY COUPLE ACCUSED OF MURDER BID
N1 COUPLE ACCUSED OF BABY MURDER
PARENTS ACCUSED OF KILLING BABY SON
MUM AND BOYFRIEND ACCUSED OF BABY'S MURDER
ACCUSED 'SEX COP' TRIAL: RESULT
MAN, 46, ACCUSED OF KILLING HIS MUM
LOVE LETTER CLAIM OF JET TERROR ACCUSED
WOMAN ACCUSED OF KILLING MAN, 91
ACCUSED
2011
A LONDON PICTURE
IT'S WRITTEN ALL OVER THEM

ACCUSED. 2011. 226 x 254 cm

CRACK ADDICT DWARF BATTERED
TV CHEF SAVES CRACK ADDICT FROM JAIL
CRAZED ADDICT KILLED TEACHER WITH SCISSORS
ADDICT
2011
A LONDON PICTURE
IT'S WRITTEN ALL OVER THEM
Gilbert & George

ADDICT. 2011. 151 x 127 cm

ADDICTS
CRACK
DEAL
BACKFIRES
ADDICTS
THROWN
LIFELINE
BOROUGH
BAN FOR
DRUG
ADDICTS
ADDICTS
2011
A LONDON PICTURE
IT'S WRITTEN ALL OVER THEM

ADDICTS. 2011. 151 x 127 cm

ANGEL
POSTMAN
ROBBED
OF MAIL
ANGEL
DOUBLE
STABBING
HORROR
ANGEL
RAPE:
MAN IS
CHARGED
HUNT FOR
ANGEL SEX
ATTACKER
ANGEL
BAR
THIEVES
BLITZ
ANGEL
2011
A LONDON PICTURE
IT'S WRITTEN ALL OVER THEM

ANGEL. 2011. 151 x 190 cm

ARMED
POLICE
ARREST
BOMB
SUSPECT
ARMED
GANG
SNATCH
CASE FULL
OF CASH
ARMED
COPS TO
TACKLE
GUN
GANGS
ARMED
ROBBER
JAILED
SEVEN
YEARS
ARMED
SEIGE
ON
DLR
VAN THIEF
RAMS
ARMED
COPS
ARMED
MUGGER
WALLPAPER
LATEST
ARMED
POLICE
SIEGE
HORROR
ARMED
2011
A LONDON PICTURE
IT'S WRITTEN ALL OVER THEM

ARMED. 2011. 226 x 190 cm

MILLY DOWLER MURDER ARREST
HOLLOWAY BUS MURDER ARREST
CITY CHIEF MURDER: DRAMATIC ARREST
WPC MURDER: LONDON ARREST DETAILS
BARRYMORE MURDER ARREST SENSATION
ARREST
2011
A LONDON PICTURE
IT'S WRITTEN ALL OVER THEM

ARREST. 2011. 151 x 190 cm

ARREST OF YOUNG ARSENAL STAR
ELECTION FRAUD: ARREST
TV GIRL'S DRINK DRIVE ARREST
NAKED MAN'S ARCHWAY ARREST
SUFFOLK STRANGLER: SECOND ARREST
ARREST STRAIGHT
2011
A LONDON PICTURE
IT'S WRITTEN ALL OVER THEM

ARREST STRAIGHT. 2011. 151 x 190 cm

CELEBRITY CHEF ARRESTED
SUN EDITOR ARRESTED
TORY PEER ARRESTED
TOP COMEDIAN ARRESTED
ROCK STAR ARRESTED OVER ASSAULT
'WORLD'S WORST HACKER' ARRESTED IN LONDON
'CASH FOR PEERAGES' -MAN ARRESTED
HISTORIAN ARRESTED BY GUN COPS -PICTURE
SOCCER STARS ARRESTED
SPORTINGBET BOSS ARRESTED IN U.S.
LAW CHIEF'S CLEANER ARRESTED
SHANNON: STEPDAD ARRESTED
BATTERED TODDLER: MILLIONAIRE FATHER ARRESTED
LONDON SEX ATTACKS: MAN ARRESTED
HACKNEY JOGGER MURDER: MAN ARRESTED
POLICE MARKSMEN ARRESTED FOR 'MURDER'
NURSE MURDER: MAN ARRESTED
ARRESTED
2011
A LONDON PICTURE
IT'S WRITTEN ALL OVER THEM

ARRESTED. 2011. 226 x 381 cm

JUNKIE ROCKER ARRESTED OVER PHOTO
MULLER MURDER SUSPECT ARRESTED
£40m GEMS RAID: MAN ARRESTED
MAN IS ARRESTED OVER DOUBLE MURDER
MOLEMAN ARRESTED AFTER DEFYING COURT
CURRY KING ARRESTED
CHELSEA BOSS MOURINHO ARRESTED
ENGLAND FOOTBALL STAR ARRESTED
ISLINGTON BABY DEATH: MOTHER ARRESTED
PRIEST ARRESTED AFTER GRAVE PROTEST
ASBO ALCOHOLIC ARRESTED ON ROUTE TO HOSPITAL
ONION THROWING GANG ARRESTED
ARRESTED DAD'S DEATH TRAGEDY
FATHER STABBED: MAN ARRESTED
THREE ARRESTED OVER FATAL SHOOTING
ARRESTED STRAIGHT
2011
A LONDON PICTURE
IT'S WRITTEN ALL OVER THEM

ARRESTED
STRAIGHT

2011

302 x 254 cm

ARSON ATTACK ON DISABLED MAN'S FLAT
ARSON ATTACKS: SHOCK RISE
ARSON MURDER TRIAL LATEST
'ARSON MURDER' TRIAL OPENS
FAMILY ESCAPES ARSON ATTACK
TWO DENY 'ARSON' MURDER
TEENAGERS FACE ARSON MURDER CHARGE
ARSON MANIAC LINKED TO 30 BLAZES
GIRL AND GRAN DIE IN ARSON ATTACK
ARSONIST JAILED AFTER PETROL BOMBING
NIGHT CLUB ARSON ATTACK
ARSON
2011
A LONDON PICTURE
IT'S WRITTEN ALL OVER THEM

ARSON. 2011. 226 x 254 cm

LONDON HALLOWEEN MACHINE GUN ATTACK
CITY TEACHER'S ATTACK ON OXFORD
HORROR ACID ATTACK ON LOVER
CAMERON ATTACK ON SEXY CLOTHES FOR KIDS
DRAMATIC TV ATTACK ON MET CHIEF
ANIMAL RIGHTS ACTIVISTS ATTACK CITY BOSS
HACKNEY PARK ATTACK VICTIM DIES
TV CHEF DIES OF HEART ATTACK
ATTACK
2011
A LONDON PICTURE
IT'S WRITTEN ALL OVER THEM

ATTACK. 2011. 226 x 190 cm

RAPIST'S 71 SEX ATTACK VICTIMS
MAJOR TERROR ATTACK FOILED
MINISTER HIT IN GREEN CUSTARD ATTACK
COUNCIL FACES 'RACISM' ATTACK
BUS IS HIT IN AIR RIFLE ATTACK
MEDICS SAVE MAN'S EYESIGHT AFTER N1 ATTACK
N1 CENTRE GANG ATTACK ARRESTS
BROTHERS CLEARED OF COURT ATTACK
ATTACK VICTIM FIGHTS FOR LIFE
CRUEL BLEACH ATTACK ON CAT
ATTACK VICTIM'S STRUGGLE FOR NEW LIFE
MAN DRAGGED ALONG STREET IN ATTACK
ATTACK VICTIM'S NOSE BITTEN
SHOVEL ATTACK REVENGE PAIR ARE JAILED
WILD GEESE ATTACK FEARS
GLASS ATTACK AT CLUB
FOOTBALLER CLEARED OF REVENGE ATTACK
'HUMAN TORCH' ATTACK HORROR
MAN HELD AFTER VIGILANTE ATTACK
MYSTERY OF ATTACK VICTIM FOUND IN PARK
B'DESHI MOB ATTACK TRIAL HALTED
MAN IN DAYLIGHT BASEBALL BAT ATTACK
THREATS AGAINST FOX ATTACK FAMILY
GLASS ATTACK ON PUB DRINKER
METAL BAR ATTACK ON HOLLOWAY MAN
BOTTLE ATTACK ON RAP STAR
SHOE STABBER FACES JAIL OVER ATTACK
TV STAR SPARED JAIL OVER N5 ATTACK
HIGHBURY STATION ATTACK ON COP
FOOTBALLER ORDERED ATTACK ON MANAGER
BAND SAVES FAN FROM GIG ATTACK
HOODIE GANG IN TERRIFYING N1 CENTRE ATTACK
BRUTAL ATTACK AT UNSTAFFED STATION
VICIOUS RACISTS ATTACK BUS PASSENGER
ATTACK STRAIGHT
2011
A LONDON PICTURE
IT'S WRITTEN ALL OVER THEM

ATTACK STRAIGHT. 2011. 377 x 444 cm

POLICE HUNT FOR BRICK ATTACKER
ARCHWAY SEX ATTACKER JAILED
HERO COP TACKLES HOSPITAL SCISSORS ATTACKER
NIGHT BUS KNIFE ATTACKER JAILED
ATTACKER 'POSSESSED' BY SATANIST CLAIM
BATTERED GRAN ATTACKER ADMITS GUILT
ATTACKER JAILED FOR BRUTAL ASSAULTS
HUNT FOR BUS SEX ATTACKER
NIGHTCLUB BOTTLE ATTACKER HUNTED
STATION SEX ATTACKER HUNTED
TUFNELL PARK RAPE BID ATTACKER HUNTED
ATTACKER
2011
A LONDON PICTURE
IT'S WRITTEN ALL OVER THEM

ATTACKER. 2011. 226 x 254 cm

ATTACKS ON NURSES AND DOCTORS SOAR
STRESSED CITY BOSS ATTACKS DAUGHTER AGED TWO
YARD ACTS ON G20 ATTACKS
ATTACKS RISE ON LONDON BUS DRIVERS
FIFTH BOMBER ADMITS PLOTTING 21/7 ATTACKS
ATTACKS
2011
Gilbert & George
A LONDON PICTURE
IT'S WRITTEN ALL OVER THEM

ATTACKS. 2011. 151 x 190 cm

BLACK CAB SEX ATTACKS TRIAL: VERDICTS
FEARS OVER ATTACKS ON GAYS
PARK MENACE ATTACKS 7 WOMEN IN A DAY
RISE IN ISLINGTON ATTACKS ON GAYS
PARKING WARDENS FACE 170 ATTACKS A DAY
150 ATTACKS ON PARKING WARDENS
ATTACKS UP ON POLICE
BOTTLE ATTACKS IN WAVE OF STREET VIOLENCE
DANGER DOGS ATTACKS ALERT
SCANDAL OF HOSPITAL ATTACKS ON STAFF
HACKNEY TOP FOR DRUNK SEX ATTACKS
SHOCKING INCREASE IN SEX ATTACKS
BOY, 15, IN CANAL KNIFE ATTACKS
TEENAGE GIRLS BLAMED FOR 170 ATTACKS
KNIFEMAN HUNTED AFTER 2 ATTACKS
ATTACKS STRAIGHT
2011
A LONDON PICTURE
IT'S WRITTEN ALL OVER THEM

ATTACKS STRAIGHT

2011

302 x 254 cm

HORROR OF AXE KILLING
AXE GANG IN BRUTAL ROBBERY RAID
AXE FALLS ON OLD FOLK'S DAY CENTRE
NURSES FACE THE AXE AT BART'S
AXE KILLING MYSTERY
AXE
2011
A LONDON PICTURE
IT'S WRITTEN ALL OVER THEM

AXE. 2011. 151 x 190 cm

TOTTENHAM WOMAN IN MIRACLE BABIES SCANDAL
DESIGNER BABIES -NEW LAWS
LONDON WOMAN'S 'DESIGNER BABIES'
BABIES
2011
A LONDON PICTURE
IT'S WRITTEN ALL OVER THEM

BABIES. 2011. 151 x 127 cm

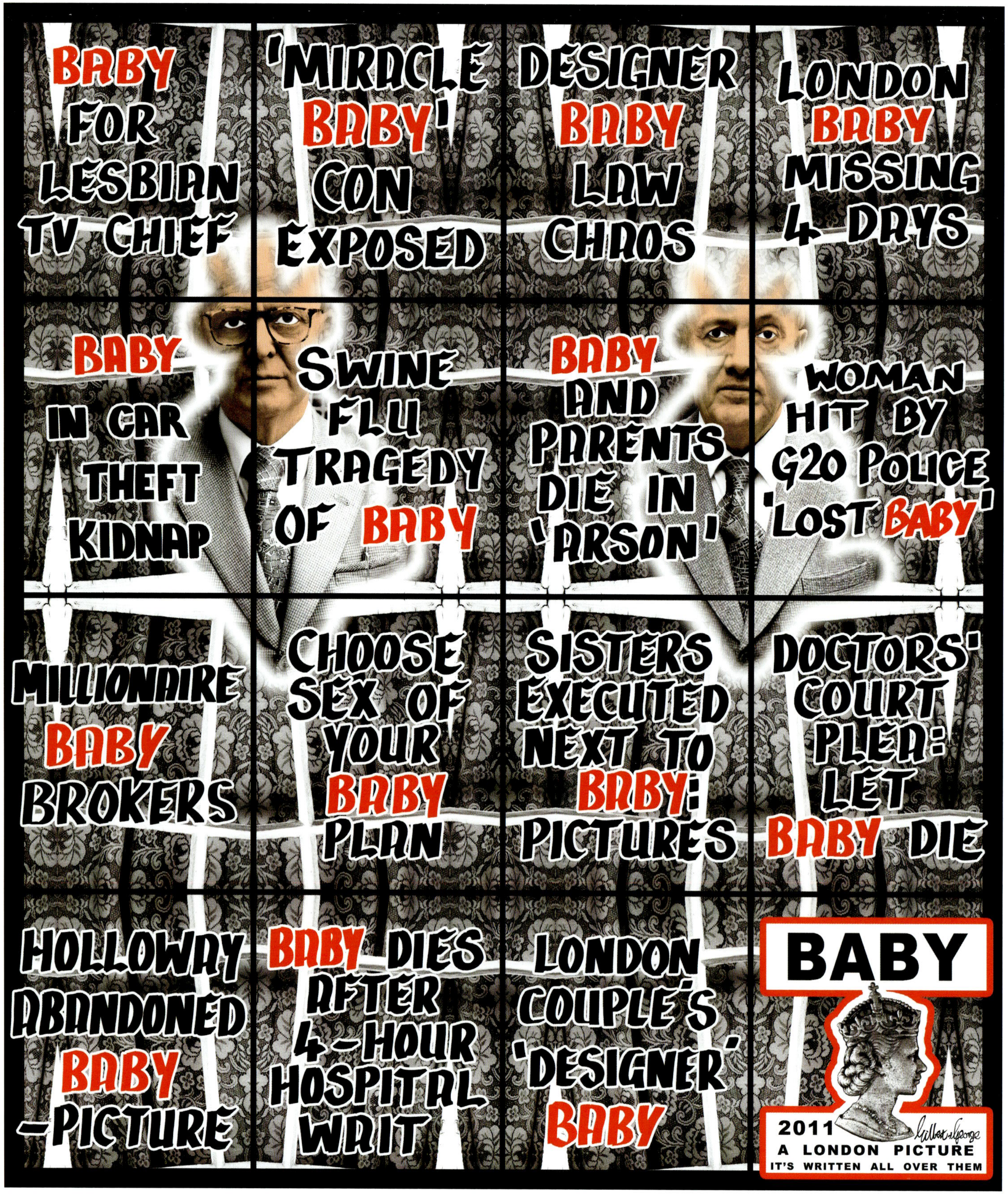
BABY FOR LESBIAN TV CHIEF
'MIRACLE BABY' CON EXPOSED
DESIGNER BABY LAW CHAOS
LONDON BABY MISSING 4 DAYS
BABY IN CAR THEFT KIDNAP
SWINE FLU TRAGEDY OF BABY
BABY AND PARENTS DIE IN 'ARSON'
WOMAN HIT BY G20 POLICE 'LOST BABY'
MILLIONAIRE BABY BROKERS
CHOOSE SEX OF YOUR BABY PLAN
SISTERS EXECUTED NEXT TO BABY: PICTURES
DOCTORS' COURT PLEA: LET BABY DIE
HOLLOWAY ABANDONED BABY -PICTURE
BABY DIES AFTER 4-HOUR HOSPITAL WAIT
LONDON COUPLE'S 'DESIGNER' BABY
BABY
2011
A LONDON PICTURE
IT'S WRITTEN ALL OVER THEM

BABY

2011

302 x 254 cm

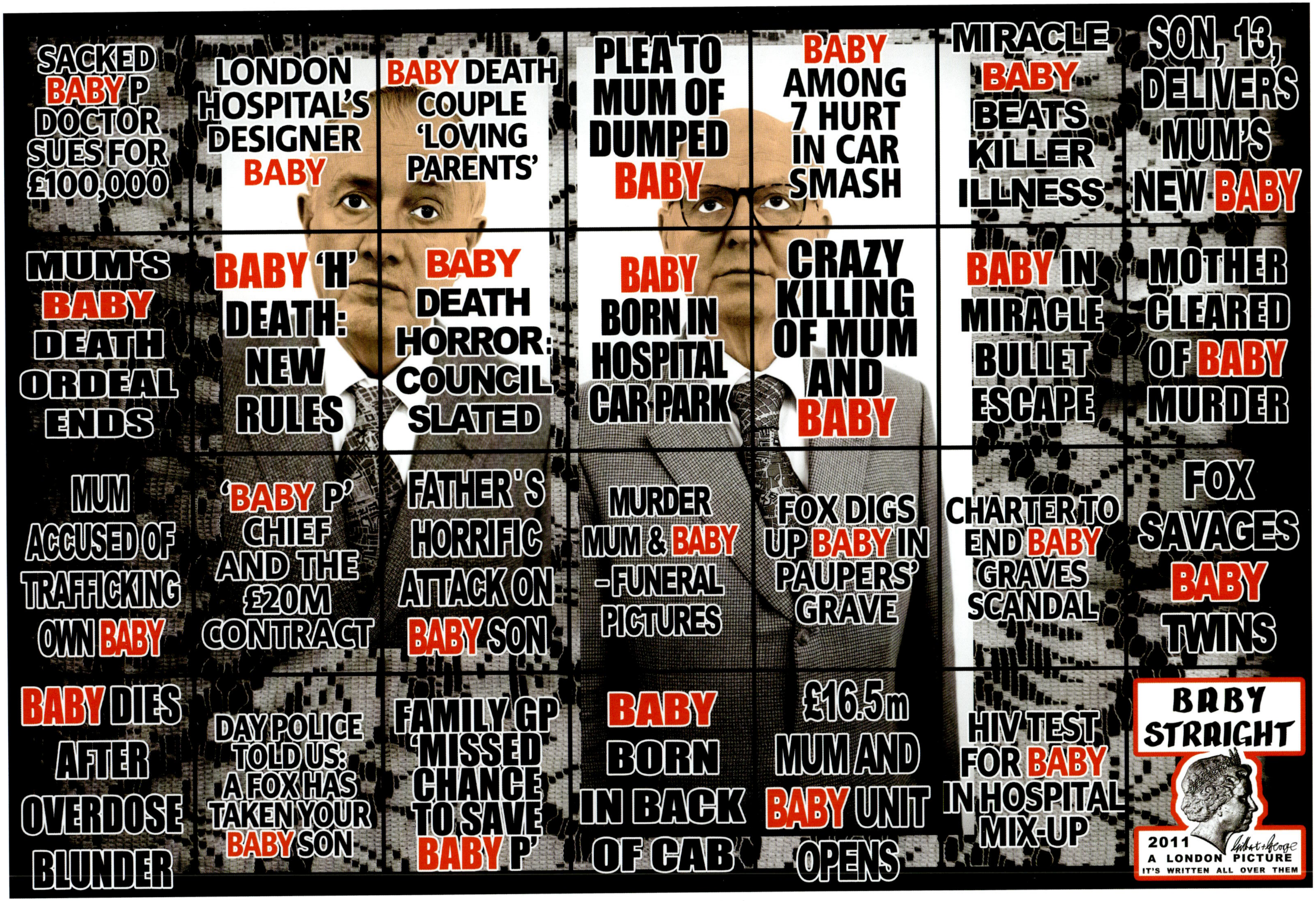
SACKED BABY P DOCTOR SUES FOR £100,000
LONDON HOSPITAL'S DESIGNER BABY
BABY DEATH COUPLE 'LOVING PARENTS'
PLEA TO MUM OF DUMPED BABY
BABY AMONG 7 HURT IN CAR SMASH
MIRACLE BABY BEATS KILLER ILLNESS
SON, 13, DELIVERS MUM'S NEW BABY
MUM'S BABY DEATH ORDEAL ENDS
BABY 'H' DEATH: NEW RULES
BABY DEATH HORROR: COUNCIL SLATED
BABY BORN IN HOSPITAL CAR PARK
CRAZY KILLING OF MUM AND BABY
BABY IN MIRACLE BULLET ESCAPE
MOTHER CLEARED OF BABY MURDER
MUM ACCUSED OF TRAFFICKING OWN BABY
'BABY P' CHIEF AND THE £20M CONTRACT
FATHER'S HORRIFIC ATTACK ON BABY SON
MURDER MUM & BABY -FUNERAL PICTURES
FOX DIGS UP BABY IN PAUPERS' GRAVE
CHARTER TO END BABY GRAVES SCANDAL
FOX SAVAGES BABY TWINS
BABY DIES AFTER OVERDOSE BLUNDER
DAY POLICE TOLD US: A FOX HAS TAKEN YOUR BABY SON
FAMILY GP 'MISSED CHANCE TO SAVE BABY P'
BABY BORN IN BACK OF CAB
£16.5m MUM AND BABY UNIT OPENS
HIV TEST FOR BABY IN HOSPITAL MIX-UP
BABY STRAIGHT
2011
A LONDON PICTURE
IT'S WRITTEN ALL OVER THEM

BABY STRAIGHT. 2011. 302 x 444 cm

CHELSEA BANKER MURDER HORROR
BANKER VANISHES WITH 2 SHOTGUNS
'TERROR BANKER' FREE IN LONDON: PICTURE
CHELSEA BANKER MURDER TRIAL
STABBED BANKER: THE LAST MINUTES
BANKER MURDER: FULL STORY REVEALED
BANKER ACCUSED OF RAPING DAUGHTER
CHELSEA BANKER MURDER: VERDICT
BANKER
2011
A LONDON PICTURE
IT'S WRITTEN ALL OVER THEM

BANKER. 2011. 226 x 190 cm

BATTERED. 2011. 151 x 190 cm

BATTLE OF BRICK LANE: SPECIAL REPORT
WOMAN'S BATTLE TO USE FROZEN EMBRYO
PENNILESS' HUSBAND IN £400M DIVORCE BATTLE
CITY SUPERWOMAN -MY BATTLE WITH GUNMAN
MOTHER'S COURT ABORTION BATTLE
BATTLE
2011
Gilbert & George
A LONDON PICTURE
IT'S WRITTEN ALL OVER THEM

BATTLE. 2011. 151 x 190 cm

BATTLE
TO SAVE
'TOO OLD'
CARETAKER
3AM
KEBAB
SHOP
BATTLE
HEIRESS'
£100m
DIVORCE
BATTLE
STABBING
BATTLE
CLOSES
MARKET
ARSENAL
£50M
TAKEOVER
BATTLE
BATTLE FOR
ROBIN
HOOD
GARDENS
POLICE
STATION
BATTLE
HOTS UP
BATTLE
STRAIGHT
2011
Gilbert+George
A LONDON PICTURE
IT'S WRITTEN ALL OVER THEM

BATTLE STRAIGHT. 2011. 151 x 254 cm

INNOCENT LONDON DRIVER BEATEN TO DEATH
BARCLAYS BANKER BEATEN TO DEATH
BACKPACK GIRL BEATEN TO DEATH
BEATEN TO DEATH
2011
Gilbert & George
A LONDON PICTURE
IT'S WRITTEN ALL OVER THEM

BEATEN TO DEATH. 2011. 151 x 127 cm

BEGGAR BEATEN TO DEATH AT HIGHBURY STATION
SON OF TOP CRICKETER 'BEATEN TO DEATH'
BANKER BEATEN TO DEATH
BEATEN TO DEATH STRAIGHT
2011
A LONDON PICTURE
IT'S WRITTEN ALL OVER THEM

BEATEN TO DEATH STRAIGHT. 2011. 151 x 127 cm

BIKER HURT IN CLOTHES LINE PRANK
BIKER DEATH: MAN ARRESTED
TEEN BIKER KILLED IN CRASH
HIT & RUN BIKER KILLED IN ACCIDENT
ISLINGTON BIKER, 20, KILLED IN CRASH
CROSSING DEATH BIKER WALKS FREE
BIKER DIES IN HORROR SMASH
BIKER
2011
A LONDON PICTURE
IT'S WRITTEN ALL OVER THEM

BIKER. 2011. 151 x 254 cm

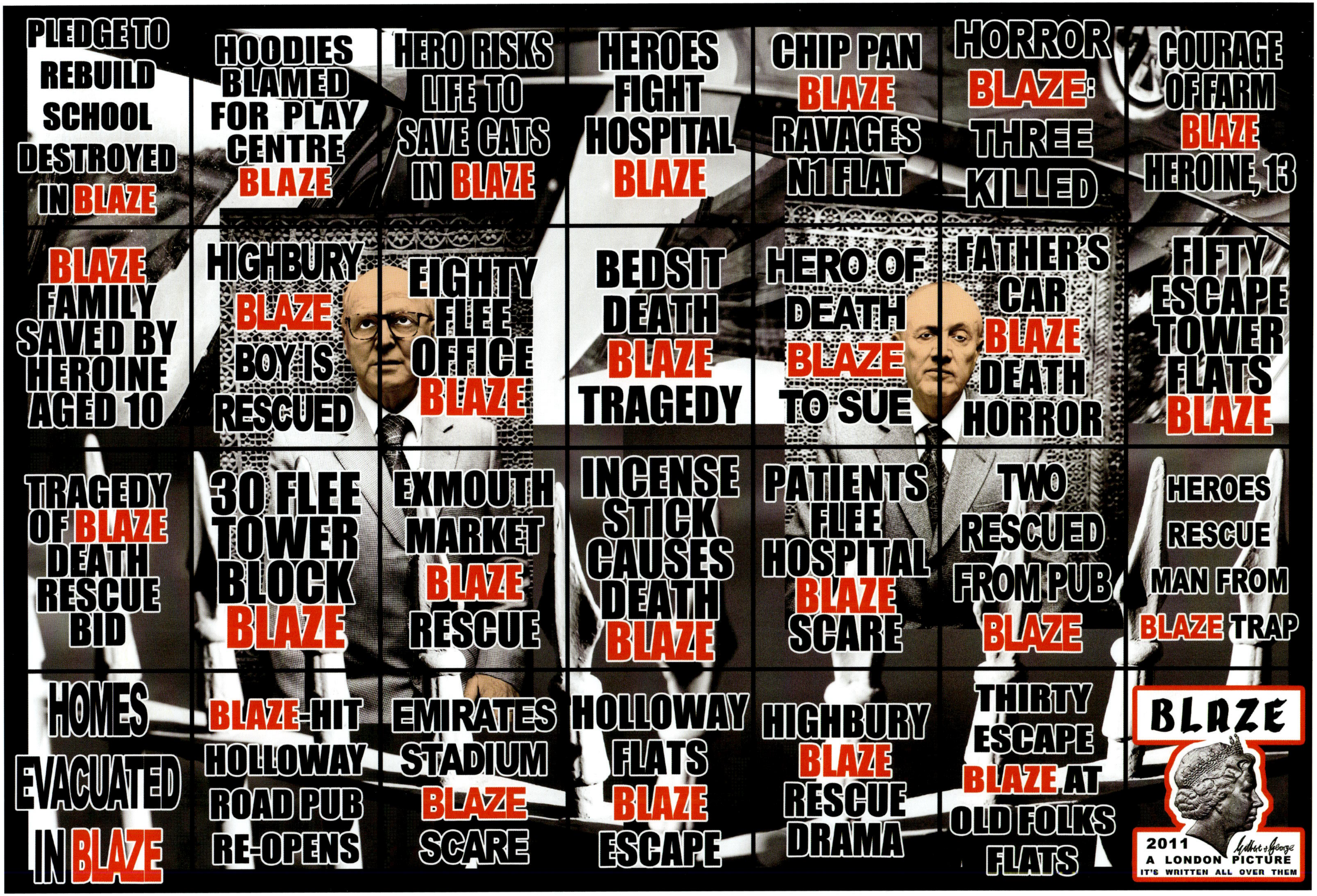

PLEDGE TO REBUILD SCHOOL DESTROYED IN BLAZE
HOODIES BLAMED FOR PLAY CENTRE BLAZE
HERO RISKS LIFE TO SAVE CATS IN BLAZE
HEROES FIGHT HOSPITAL BLAZE
CHIP PAN BLAZE RAVAGES N1 FLAT
HORROR BLAZE: THREE KILLED
COURAGE OF FARM BLAZE HEROINE, 13
BLAZE FAMILY SAVED BY HEROINE AGED 10
HIGHBURY BLAZE BOY IS RESCUED
EIGHTY FLEE OFFICE BLAZE
BEDSIT DEATH BLAZE TRAGEDY
HERO OF DEATH BLAZE TO SUE
FATHER'S CAR BLAZE DEATH HORROR
FIFTY ESCAPE TOWER FLATS BLAZE
TRAGEDY OF BLAZE DEATH RESCUE BID
30 FLEE TOWER BLOCK BLAZE
EXMOUTH MARKET BLAZE RESCUE
INCENSE STICK CAUSES DEATH BLAZE
PATIENTS FLEE HOSPITAL BLAZE SCARE
TWO RESCUED FROM PUB BLAZE
HEROES RESCUE MAN FROM BLAZE TRAP
HOMES EVACUATED IN BLAZE
BLAZE-HIT HOLLOWAY ROAD PUB RE-OPENS
EMIRATES STADIUM BLAZE SCARE
HOLLOWAY FLATS BLAZE ESCAPE
HIGHBURY BLAZE RESCUE DRAMA
THIRTY ESCAPE BLAZE AT OLD FOLKS FLATS
BLAZE
2011
A LONDON PICTURE
IT'S WRITTEN ALL OVER THEM

BLAZE. 2011. 302 x 444 cm

MYSTERY BODY IN BURNED OUT CAR
DEALER ADMITS DUMPING BODY
POLICE DIVERS RECOVER BODY
NEWBORN BABY'S BODY DUMPED
BODY IN SUITCASE: MAN ACCUSED
BODY FOUND IN RIVER
BODY OF ANTHRAX VICTIM RELEASED
BODY IN FOREST MURDER TRIAL
DRUGS DEALER JAILED FOR DUMPING MURDERED MAN'S BODY
DEALER FACES JAIL FOR KILLING BODY BUILDER
DEATH MYSTERY OF BODY IN FLAT
MYSTERY OF BODY IN CANAL
BODY FOUND IN CANAL
BODY IN CANAL - MAN CHARGED
TEENAGER CLEARED OF BODY IN WOODS MURDER
WOMAN'S BODY FOUND ON HEATH
MAGGOTS INVASION HITS HOMES AFTER BODY IS FOUND
MYSTERY STILL SURROUNDS BODY 35 YEARS ON
HORROR OF 'BODY IN SUITCASE' KILLING
BODY
2011
A LONDON PICTURE
IT'S WRITTEN ALL OVER THEM

BODY. 2011. 302 x 317 cm

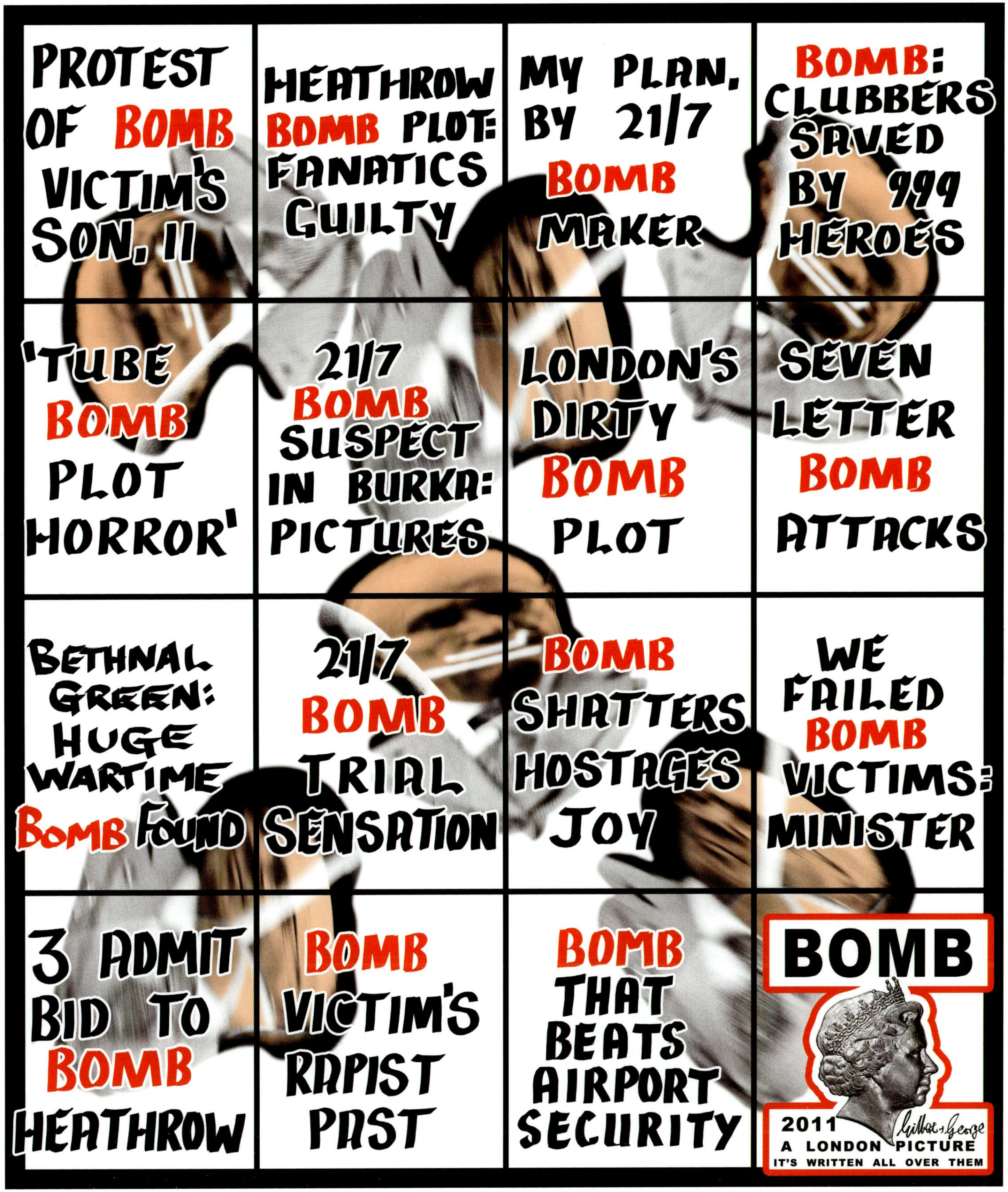
PROTEST OF BOMB VICTIM'S SON, 11
HEATHROW BOMB PLOT: FANATICS GUILTY
MY PLAN, BY 21/7 BOMB MAKER
BOMB: CLUBBERS SAVED BY 999 HEROES
'TUBE BOMB PLOT HORROR'
21/7 BOMB SUSPECT IN BURKA: PICTURES
LONDON'S DIRTY BOMB PLOT
SEVEN LETTER BOMB ATTACKS
BETHNAL GREEN: HUGE WARTIME BOMB FOUND
21/7 BOMB TRIAL SENSATION
BOMB SHATTERS HOSTAGES JOY
WE FAILED BOMB VICTIMS: MINISTER
3 ADMIT BID TO BOMB HEATHROW
BOMB VICTIM'S RAPIST PAST
BOMB THAT BEATS AIRPORT SECURITY
BOMB
2011
A LONDON PICTURE
IT'S WRITTEN ALL OVER THEM

BOMB

2011

302 x 254 cm

POLICE SMASH JET BOMB PLOT
SACKED 7/7 BOMB VICTIM SUES
ALDGATE BOMB: 'TALEBAN LINK'
100 EVACUATED IN FIRE 'BOMB' DRAMA
TOWER BLOCK BOMB SCARE
PETROL BOMB FLATS TERROR
UNEXPLODED WARTIME BOMB CHAOS
FAMILIES FLEE HOMES IN BOMB SCARE
WW2 BOMB SURVIVORS' REUNION
MEMORIAL TO BOMB VICTIMS AFTER 60 YEARS
BUS BOMB TRIAL VERDICT
CAMERAS CAPTURED BUS BOMB BID
JET BOMB PLOT SUSPECT CLEARED
JULY 21 BUS BOMB SUSPECT IN COURT
WARTIME BOMB SCARE
TERROR SUSPECT BOMB MANUAL CLAIM
FAMILY ESCAPES PETROL BOMB ATTACK
TERROR PLOT TO BOMB JETS
SHOEBOX BOMB SCARE ON BUS
BOMB STRAIGHT
2011
A LONDON PICTURE
IT'S WRITTEN ALL OVER THEM

BOMB STRAIGHT. 2011. 302 x 317 cm

MINISTERS CONFESS OVER LOCKERBIE BOMBER
BOMBER'S WIFE GUILTY OF SHIELDING HUSBAND
AIRLINE BOMBERS JAILED 100 YEARS
RUSSIAN BOMBERS HEAD FOR BRITAIN
40 YEARS FOR 21/7 LONDON BOMBERS
LOCKERBIE BOMBER 'CLOSE TO DEATH'
INSULT TO THE VICTIMS OF 7/7 BOMBINGS
EIGHT 'SUICIDE BOMBERS' CHARGED
BOMBEY
2011
A LONDON PICTURE
IT'S WRITTEN ALL OVER THEM

BOMBEY. 2011. 226 x 190 cm

JET BOMB PLOTTER JAILED
ALDGATE BOMBING FOUR YEARS ON
BOMB SCARE HAVOC IN BRICK LANE
ARSONIST JAILED AFTER PETROL BOMBING
BOMBING TRAGEDY INSPIRED FIRST AID WORKER
JULY BOMBINGS FIVE YEARS ON
BOMBING FEARS HIT BRICK LANE
NEW CCTV IMAGE OF 7/7 BUS BOMBER
BOMBEY STRAIGHT
2011
A LONDON PICTURE
IT'S WRITTEN ALL OVER THEM

BOMBEY STRAIGHT. 2011. 226 x 190 cm

LYNCHED BOY: MOTHER'S TORMENT
ARSENAL HAILS IT'S BOY WONDER
BOY HELD OVER RAIL SABOTAGE
QPR BOY: MURDER TRIAL DECISION
BACKPACK BOY TOLD OFF BY DAD
LONDON BOY SHOT DEAD IN BEDROOM
QPR BOY MURDER TRIAL -LATEST
CHASED BOY IN DEATH PLUNGE
BOY
2011
A LONDON PICTURE
IT'S WRITTEN ALL OVER THEM

BOY. 2011. 226 x 190 cm

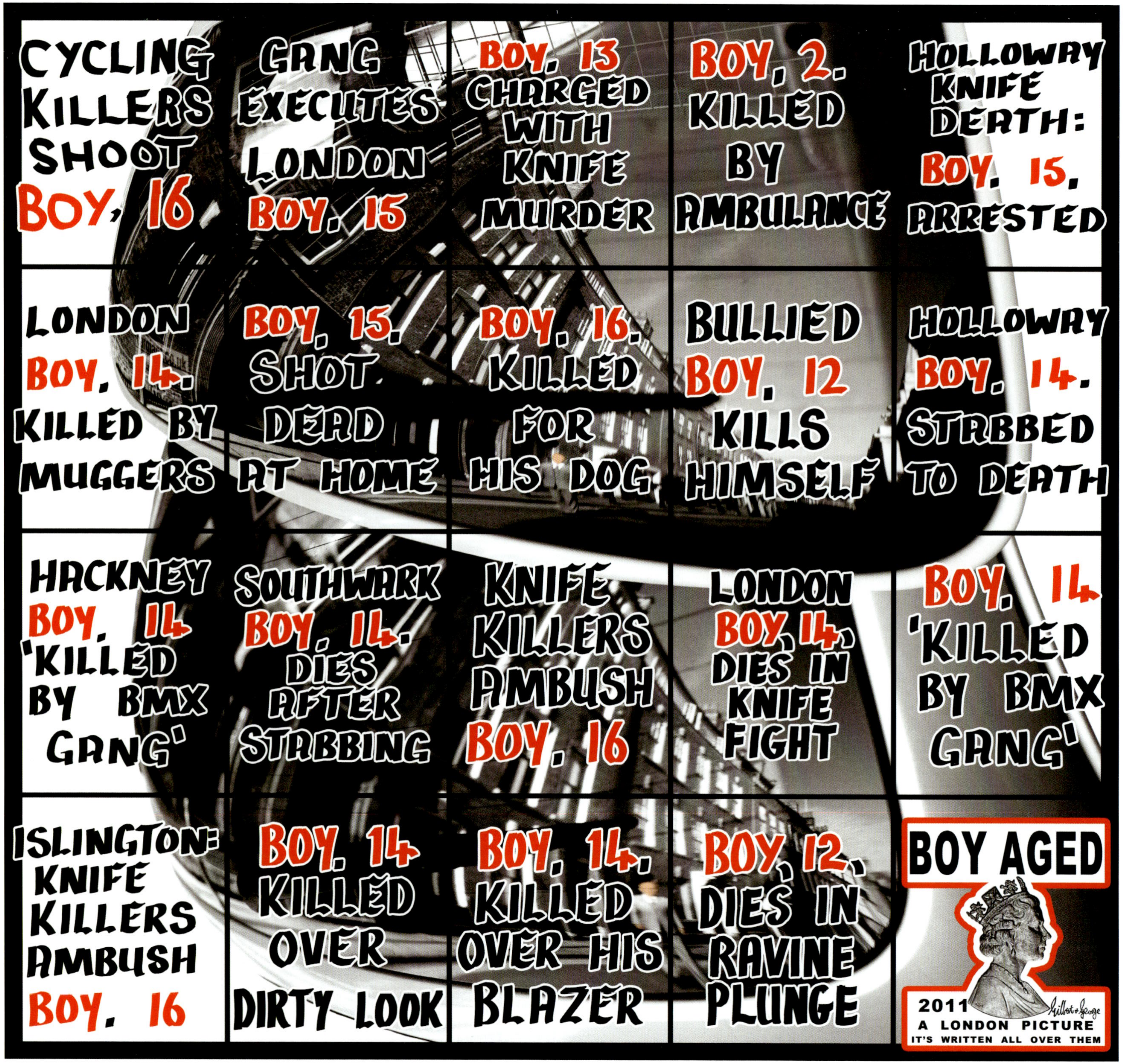
CYCLING KILLERS SHOOT BOY, 16
GANG EXECUTES LONDON BOY, 15
BOY, 13 CHARGED WITH KNIFE MURDER
BOY, 2, KILLED BY AMBULANCE
HOLLOWAY KNIFE DEATH: BOY, 15, ARRESTED
LONDON BOY, 14, KILLED BY MUGGERS
BOY, 15, SHOT DEAD AT HOME
BOY, 16, KILLED FOR HIS DOG
BULLIED BOY, 12 KILLS HIMSELF
HOLLOWAY BOY, 14, STABBED TO DEATH
HACKNEY BOY, 14 'KILLED BY BMX GANG'
SOUTHWARK BOY, 14, DIES AFTER STABBING
KNIFE KILLERS AMBUSH BOY, 16
LONDON BOY, 14, DIES IN KNIFE FIGHT
BOY, 14 'KILLED BY BMX GANG'
ISLINGTON: KNIFE KILLERS AMBUSH BOY, 16
BOY, 14 KILLED OVER DIRTY LOOK
BOY, 14, KILLED OVER HIS BLAZER
BOY, 12, DIES IN RAVINE PLUNGE
BOY AGED
2011
A LONDON PICTURE
IT'S WRITTEN ALL OVER THEM

BOY AGED. 2011. 302 x 317 cm

HOTEL SEX ATTACK ORDEAL OF BOY, 12
KNIFE BOY, 16, FACES LONG JAIL SENTENCE
MOVIE STARDOM FOR SCHOOL BOY, 13
BOY OF 13 BECOMES A DAD
THUGS ATTACK BIRTHDAY BOY, 4
FATHER STABS BOY, 4 TO DEATH
BOY, 14, ADMITS KILLING
BOY, 13 CHARGED WITH MURDER
BOY, 5 DIES IN ROAD HORROR
BOY, 14, STABBED TO DEATH
BOY, 13 IN GBH ARREST
BOY, 2 DIES IN FAIR GROUND TRAGEDY
BOY, 5, KILLED IN CRASH TRAGEDY
BOY, 15, DIES IN MOTORBIKE CRASH
BOY, 4, SCOOPS GOLDEN TICKET
BOY, 10, ACCUSED OF RAPE
BOY 14 IN DOCK OVER KILLING
BOY, 4, TOWER BLOCK FALL HORROR
BOY, 13 CHARGED WITH KNIFE MURDER
BOY, 11, SHOT DEAD – FIRST PICTURE
BOY, 2 DIES IN FUNFAIR HORROR
BOY, 15, IN MOPED CRASH HORROR
BOY OF 15 IN STABBING HORROR
BOY, 14, STABBED OUTSIDE SHOPS
BULLIES JAILED OVER ATTACK ON BOY, 13
DOORSTEP KILLING: BOY, 16 ON TRIAL
BOY, 15 STABBED ON WAY TO SCHOOL
BOY AGED STRAIGHT
2011 A LONDON PICTURE
IT'S WRITTEN ALL OVER THEM

BOY AGED STRAIGHT. 2011. 302 x 444 cm

MOB KNIFE BOY AT SCHOOL BUS STOP
MYSTERY DONOR GIVES BOY LIFE
SCHOOL RAMPAGE BOY KILLS 15
BOY GANG 'SHOOTS BROTHERS FOR iPODS'
CHANTING GANG KILLS BOY IN STREET
LONDON BOY SHOT DEAD AT HOME
'BOY SLAVE' WOMAN FACES JAIL
HOSPITAL BOY DIES HOURS AFTER SENT HOME
MODEL BOY IS SCARRED FOR LIFE
MACHINE GUN BOY JAILED
DISABLED BOY A PRISONER IN OWN HOME
POLICE SWOOP ON GUN BOY OUTSIDE SCHOOL
N1 BOY IS SAVAGED BY BULL TERRIRER
ARCHWAY BIKE STUNT BOY IS AIRLIFTED TO HOSPITAL
'BIN BOY' COP ESCAPES CHARGES
'BIN BOY' HIT BY BUS
BULLIES TERRORISE BOY AT COLLEGE
'ROVING GANG' KILLED INNOCENT BOY
BOY GEORGE TRIAL LATEST
14-YEAR OLD BOY STABBED BY GANG
SCHOOL TRIP BOY GOES MISSING
BOY HAD MURDER GUN IN SCHOOLBAG
CANCER BOY FULFILS HIS DREAM
BOY STRAIGHT
2011
A LONDON PICTURE
IT'S WRITTEN ALL OVER THEM

BOY STRAIGHT. 2011. 302 x 381 cm

PAIR ACCUSED OF BOYS TORTURE
BOYS OF 10 AND 11 ON SCHOOL RAPE BID CHARGE
BOYS STABBED IN STREET FIGHTS
SUICIDE OF MAN ACCUSED OF SEX WITH 300 BOYS
EXAMS LEAP BY BOYS SCHOOL
BOYS
2011
Gilbert + George
A LONDON PICTURE
IT'S WRITTEN ALL OVER THEM

BOYS. 2011. 151 x 190 cm

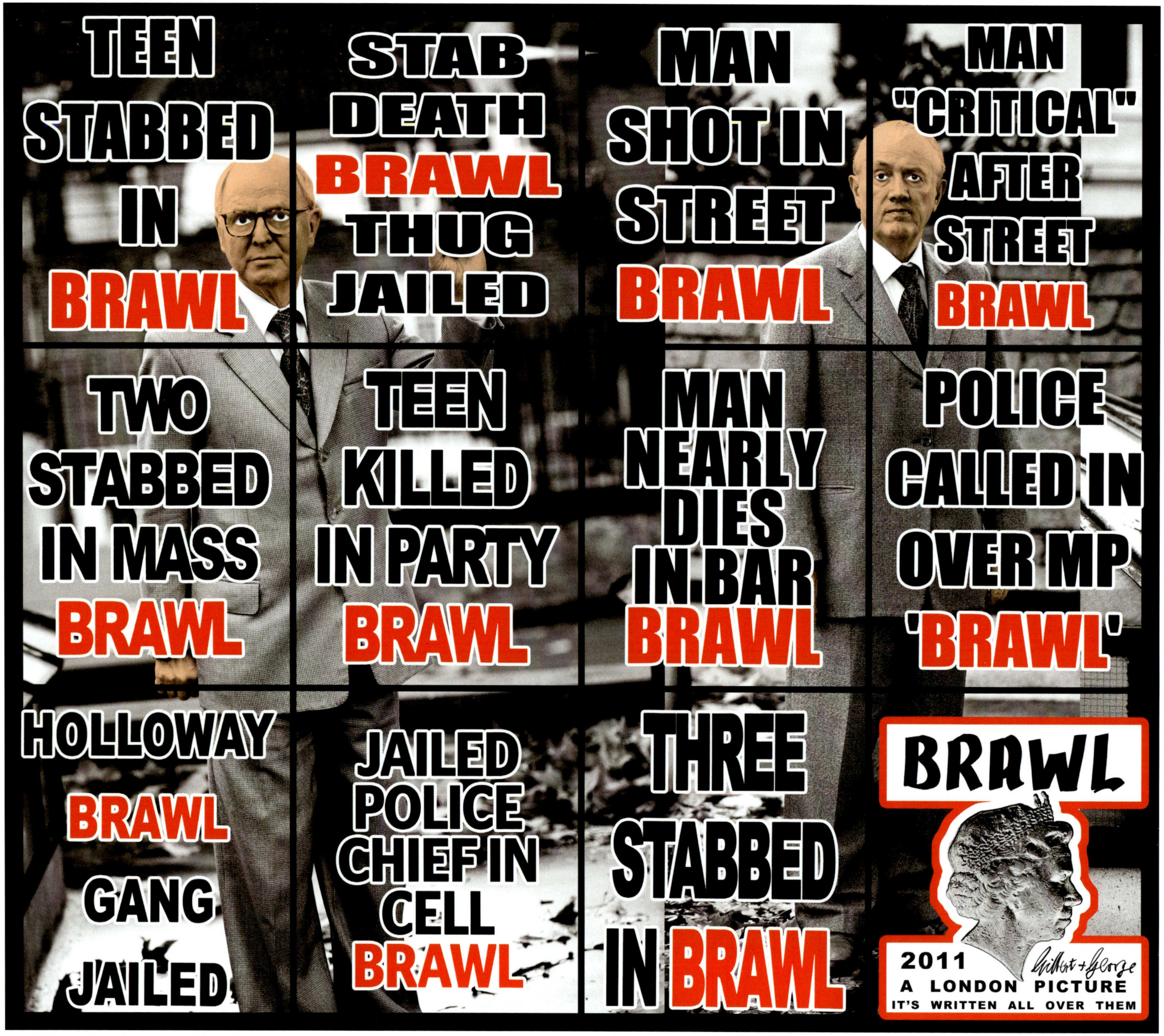
TEEN STABBED IN BRAWL
STAB DEATH BRAWL THUG JAILED
MAN SHOT IN STREET BRAWL
MAN "CRITICAL" AFTER STREET BRAWL
TWO STABBED IN MASS BRAWL
TEEN KILLED IN PARTY BRAWL
MAN NEARLY DIES IN.BAR BRAWL
POLICE CALLED IN OVER MP 'BRAWL'
HOLLOWAY BRAWL GANG JAILED
JAILED POLICE CHIEF IN CELL BRAWL
THREE STABBED IN BRAWL
BRAWL
2011
A LONDON PICTURE
IT'S WRITTEN ALL OVER THEM

BRAWL. 2011. 226 x 254 cm

VICAR FIGHTS BROTHEL CLOSURE
THREE JAILED OVER BROTHEL RAPES
BROTHEL OUTRAGE OVER SQUARE RELAUNCH
BROTHEL BOSSES TO KEEP FORTUNE
POLICE CLOSE BROTHEL IN RAID
BROTHEL SHUT AFTER N19 RAID
£500,000 BROTHEL FORTUNE OF VICE BOSS
POLICE RAID BROTHEL
BROTHEL
2011
A LONDON PICTURE
IT'S WRITTEN ALL OVER THEM

BROTHEL. 2011. 226 x 190 cm

BURGLAR
RAPES
PREGNANT
WOMAN
BANKER'S
FIGHT FOR
LIFE WITH
BURGLAR
HUSBAND
ESCAPES
CHARGE FOR
KILLING
'BURGLAR'
BURGLAR
2011
A LONDON PICTURE
IT'S WRITTEN ALL OVER THEM

BURGLAR. 2011. 151 x 127 cm

BURGLAR CAUGHT ON SPY CAMERA
BURGLAR STEALS WADS OF FAKE CASH
'SORRY' BURGLAR CAUGHT RETURNING TV SET
HOLLOWAY CAT BURGLAR CAUGHT
BUNGLING 'BURGLAR' STUCK IN WINDOW
POLICE 'DECOY' HOME TRAPS BURGLAR
BIG BUMMED BURGLAR BANGED UP
BURGLAR STRAIGHT
2011
A LONDON PICTURE
IT'S WRITTEN ALL OVER THEM
Gilbert+George

BURGLAR STRAIGHT. 2011. 151 x 254 cm

ISLINGTON: TRAGEDY OF 105 YEAR OLD BURGLARY VICTIM
FRANK LAMPARD: MY BURGLARY NIGHTMARE
BIGGEST EVER HOUSE BURGLARY
BURGLARY
2011
A LONDON PICTURE
IT'S WRITTEN ALL OVER THEM

BURGLARY. 2011. 151 x 127 cm

CABBIE MOWED DOWN TRAFFIC WARDEN
CHEF WHO STABBED CABBIE ESCAPES JAIL
ROBBED CABBIE IN DEATH CRASH
CABBIE FOUND DEAD BY PREGNANT WIFE
CABBIE KILLED IN ROW OVER FARE
'RAPIST CABBIE DRUGGED 14 VICTIMS'
CABBIE DENIES MURDER OF MUM, 100
CABBIE FORGOES XMAS TO AID HOSPICE
CABBIE
2011
A LONDON PICTURE
IT'S WRITTEN ALL OVER THEM

CABBIE. 2011. 226 x 190 cm

'BITE THE BLANKET' BOUNCER CAGED
FIREBOMB TERROR GANG CAGED
'WILD ANIMAL' GANG CAGED
RAHMAN KILLER CAGED
HUMAN FIREBALL FIEND CAGED
CAMERA PHONE RAPIST CAGED
KETCHUP ROW KILLER CAGED
TEEN GUNMAN CAGED
CRYSTAL METH DRUG BARON CAGED
MUM &SON CAGED FOR SHOTGUN
SCHOOLBOY RAPE GANG CAGED
CAGED
2011
A LONDON PICTURE
IT'S WRITTEN ALL OVER THEM

CAGED. 2011. 226 x 254 cm

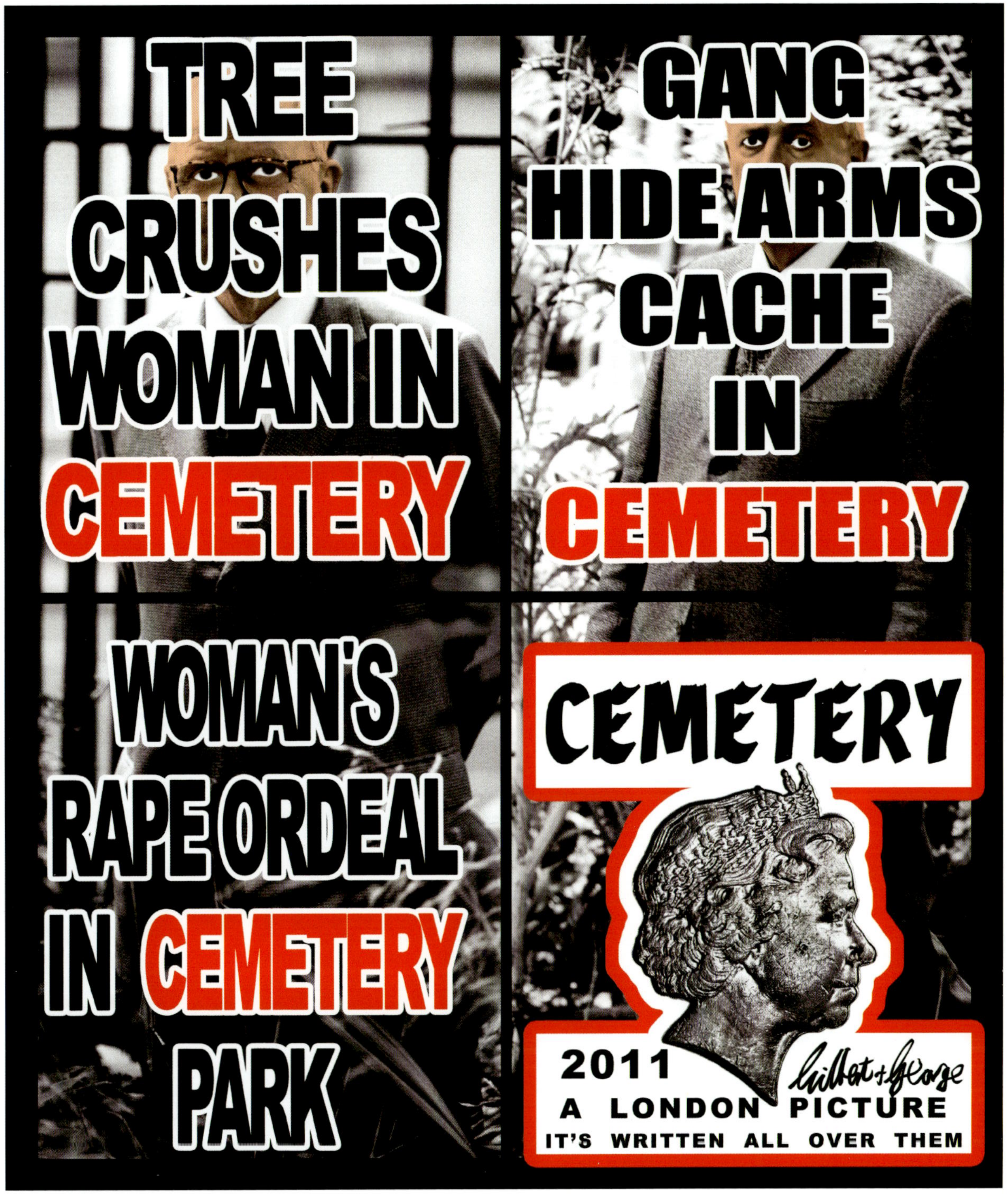
TREE
CRUSHES
WOMAN IN
CEMETERY
GANG
HIDE ARMS
CACHE
IN
CEMETERY
WOMAN'S
RAPE ORDEAL
IN CEMETERY
PARK
CEMETERY
2011
A LONDON PICTURE
IT'S WRITTEN ALL OVER THEM

CEMETERY. 2011. 151 x 127 cm

GEORGE BEST CHILD SEX CLAIM
SECRET LOVE CHILD OF 'LOST' STAR
CHILD DEATH DOCTOR: MAJOR RULING
HORROR OF CHILD FAILED BY COUNCIL
LONDON CHILD SLAVES FREED
FACEBOOK MOTHERS' CHILD SEX 'BRUTALITY'
ACTOR DENIES CHILD SEX CHARGES
LONDON CHILD KILLER JAILED
TV COMIC ON CHILD PORN CHARGE
SEX TRIAL TV STAR: I SUFFERED CHILD ABUSE
LANGHAM CHILD PORN VERDICT
CHILD
2011
A LONDON PICTURE
IT'S WRITTEN ALL OVER THEM

CHILD. 2011. 226 x 254 cm

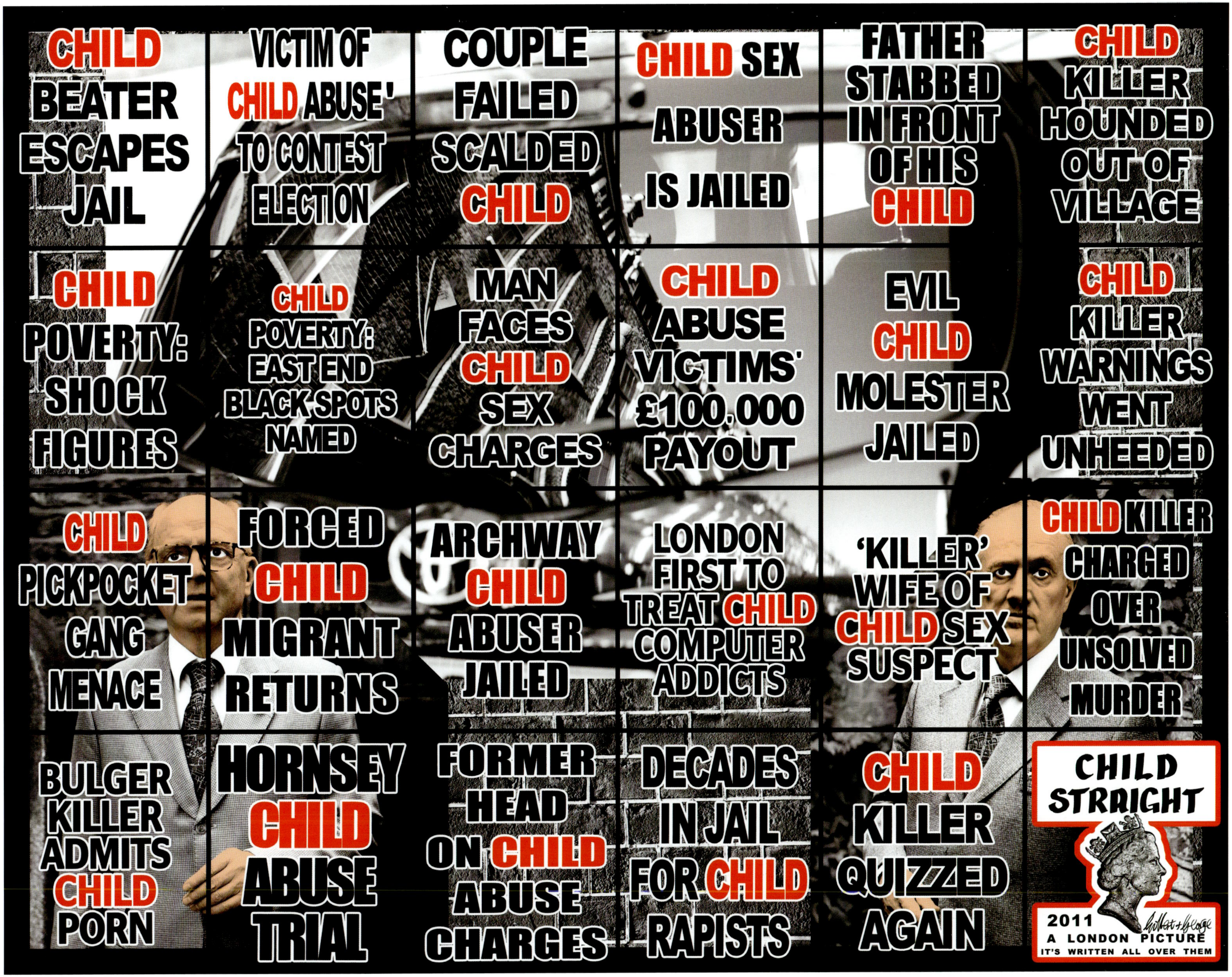
CHILD BEATER ESCAPES JAIL
VICTIM OF 'CHILD ABUSE' TO CONTEST ELECTION
COUPLE FAILED SCALDED CHILD
CHILD SEX ABUSER IS JAILED
FATHER STABBED IN FRONT OF HIS CHILD
CHILD KILLER HOUNDED OUT OF VILLAGE
CHILD POVERTY: SHOCK FIGURES
CHILD POVERTY: EAST END BLACK SPOTS NAMED
MAN FACES CHILD SEX CHARGES
CHILD ABUSE VICTIMS' £100,000 PAYOUT
EVIL CHILD MOLESTER JAILED
CHILD KILLER WARNINGS WENT UNHEEDED
CHILD PICKPOCKET GANG MENACE
FORCED CHILD MIGRANT RETURNS
ARCHWAY CHILD ABUSER JAILED
LONDON FIRST TO TREAT CHILD COMPUTER ADDICTS
'KILLER' WIFE OF CHILD SEX SUSPECT
CHILD KILLER CHARGED OVER UNSOLVED MURDER
BULGER KILLER ADMITS CHILD PORN
HORNSEY CHILD ABUSE TRIAL
FORMER HEAD ON CHILD ABUSE CHARGES
DECADES IN JAIL FOR CHILD RAPISTS
CHILD KILLER QUIZZED AGAIN
CHILD STRAIGHT
2011
A LONDON PICTURE
IT'S WRITTEN ALL OVER THEM

CHILD STRAIGHT. 2011. 302 x 381 cm

CHILDREN IN VOODOO KILLINGS IN HACKNEY CHURCHES
CHILDREN KILLED IN NEW BLITZ
CHILDREN MUST NOT USE MOBILES: REPORT
MOTHER KILLS CHILDREN ON RAIL LINE
WOMAN'S COURT BATTLE TO HAVE CHILDREN
CHILDREN LOSE FREE DENTISTS
HORROR OF MISSILE ATTACK CHILDREN
HERO KNIFED SAVING CHILDREN
ANIMAL RIGHTS FANATICS TARGET CHILDREN
MOTHER, CHILDREN DIE IN RIVER TRAGEDY
CHILDREN IN VOODOO KILLINGS IN LONDON CHURCHES
CHILDREN
2011
A LONDON PICTURE
IT'S WRITTEN ALL OVER THEM

CHILDREN. 2011. 226 x 254 cm

HOSPITAL LEFT SICK CHILDREN WITHOUT WATER
ROCK CLUB BIDS TO LET IN CHILDREN
500,000 CHILDREN OFF SCHOOL AGAIN
HAITI: FEARS FOR TWO MILLION CHILDREN
HALF OF CHILDREN LIVE IN POVERTY
COUPLE CASHED IN ON DEAD CHILDREN
CHILDREN AS YOUNG AS 12 HOOKED ON CANNABIS
CHILDREN ESCAPE ABDUCTION ATTEMPTS
CHILDREN HELD OVER RUSH-HOUR MURDER OF BOY, 15
100,000 CHILDREN CANNOT WRITE AT 7
CHILDREN PAY PRICE OF E.COLI FAILURES
CHILDREN STRAIGHT
2011
Gilbert + George
A LONDON PICTURE
IT'S WRITTEN ALL OVER THEM

CHILDREN STRAIGHT. 2011. 226 x 254 cm

COUNCIL CRUCIFIED OVER CHURCH SCHOOL
CHURCH HIT BY ARSON ATTACK
GIANT TREE CRASHES ON CHURCH
SWAP KNIFE FOR A BIBLE IN CHURCH
CHURCH SERVICE HAMMER TERROR
CHURCH PLUNGE 'MIRACLE' ESCAPE
CHURCH LEADER JAILED FOR SEX ASSAULTS
CHURCH SCHOOLS TOP OF THE CLASS
CHURCH
2011
A LONDON PICTURE
IT'S WRITTEN ALL OVER THEM

CHURCH. 2011. 226 x 190 cm

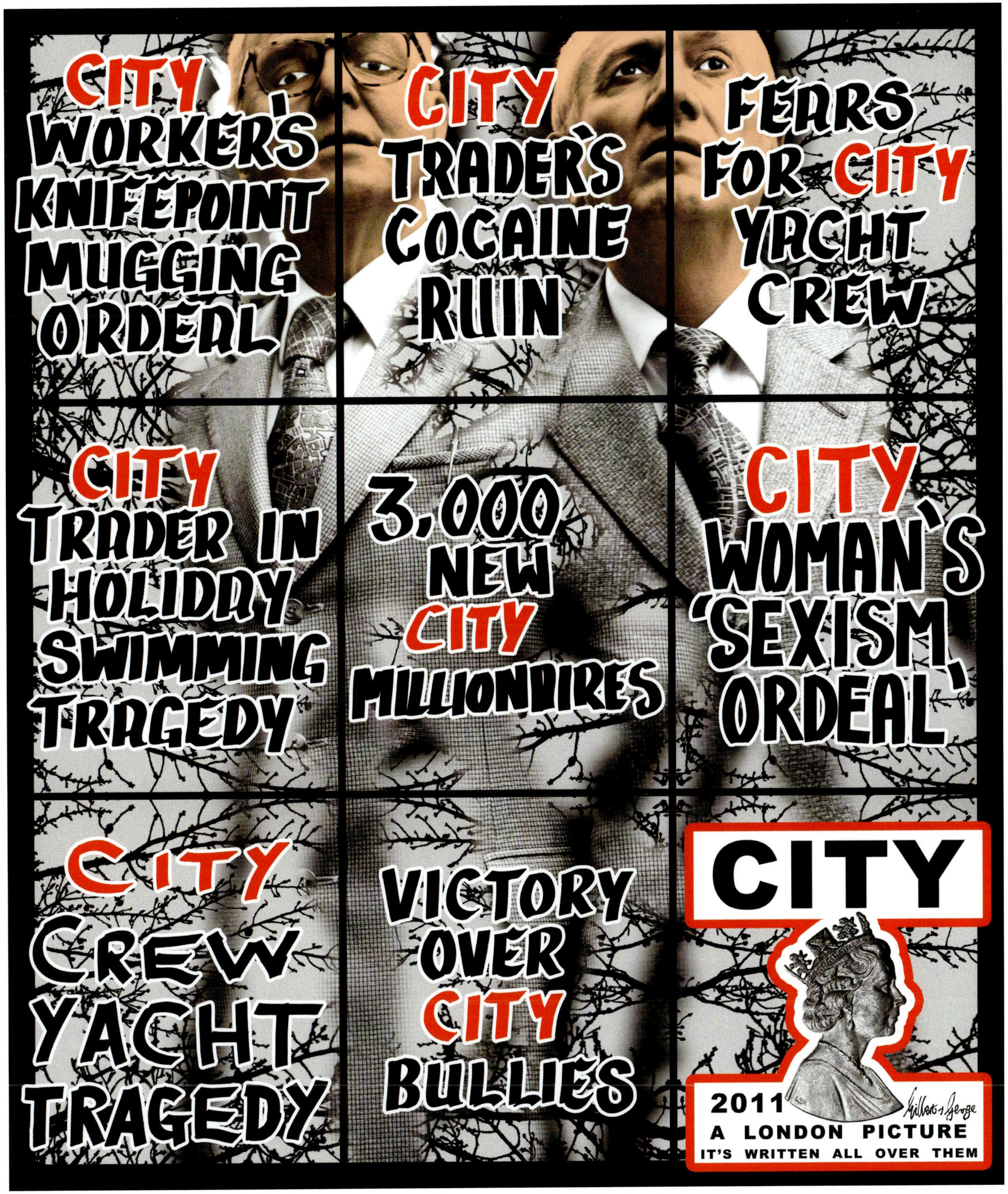
CITY WORKER'S KNIFEPOINT MUGGING ORDEAL
CITY TRADER'S COCAINE RUIN
FEARS FOR CITY YACHT CREW
CITY TRADER IN HOLIDAY SWIMMING TRAGEDY
3,000 NEW CITY MILLIONAIRES
CITY WOMAN'S 'SEXISM' ORDEAL
CITY CREW YACHT TRAGEDY
VICTORY OVER CITY BULLIES
CITY
2011
A LONDON PICTURE
IT'S WRITTEN ALL OVER THEM

CITY. 2011. 226 x 190 cm

£220M
CITY
BANK RAID
PLOT
CITY
BANKERS'
£14bn
PAYDAY
'LIES' OF
£19M
CITY
LAWYER
CITY
STAR'S
£160M
GAMBLE
CITY
TRADERS
LOSE
£1.5BN
CITY
TRADER'S
£100,000
SPACE
TRIP
CITY:
£700 m
CRYSTAL
BUILDING-
PICTURES
£800,000
FOR
BULLIED
CITY
WOMAN
CITY MONEY
2011
Gilbert & George
A LONDON PICTURE
IT'S WRITTEN ALL OVER THEM

CITY MONEY. 2011. 226 x 190 cm

CITY FIRM SUED FOR £40M OVER 'SEX SLURS'
CITY BANKER'S £50,000 BAR BILL
CITY BOSS TREATED BROKER 'LIKE PROSTITUTE'
CITY WOMAN WINS 'SEX PEST' CASE
CITY LIFT DEATH FIRMS FACE COURT
CITY BAR MURDER: POLICEMAN CHARGED
24-HOUR DRINKING BOOM HITS CITY
£365M CITY FRAUD-6 HELD
CITY STRAIGHT
2011
A LONDON PICTURE
IT'S WRITTEN ALL OVER THEM

CITY STRAIGHT. 2011. 226 x 190 cm

CRACK HOUSE MUM JAILED
FEARS OVER 'CRACK BABIES'
CRACK RAIDS REVEAL HIDDEN DRUGS DANGER
170th CRACK HOUSE CLOSED
CRACK IN THE CRYPT
Addicts using old church
POLICE IN CRACKHOUSE CRACKDOWN
CRACK DENS HIT AS POLICE SWOOP
CRACK
2011
A LONDON PICTURE
IT'S WRITTEN ALL OVER THEM

CRACK. 2011. 151 x 254 cm

ESCAPED PRISONER GOES ON CRIME SPREE
CAR CRIME SOARS
GREEN LANES CRIME DYNASTY SMASHED
GOSWELL RD PLAGUED BY PHONE BOX CRIME
CRIME & GRIME CLEAN - UP IN DALSTON CRACKDOWN
I QUIT, SAYS ACTOR HIT BY CRIME SPREE
SPY CAMS TURN A BLIND EYE TO CRIME
ISLINGTON CRIME IS WORST IN UK
CALL TO CUT CRIME WITH FEWER POLICE
KILLER CAUGHT 13 YEARS AFTER CRIME
TURKISH CRIME DYNASTY SMASHED
CRIME
2011
A LONDON PICTURE
IT'S WRITTEN ALL OVER THEM

CRIME. 2011. 226 x 254 cm

CUTE KIDS:
MAKE
YOUR VOTE
COUNT
12 PAGE
CUTE
KIDS
SUPPLEMENT
CUTE KIDS
COMPETITION
SEE INSIDE
FOR FULL DETAILS
CUTE
KIDS
2008:
VOTING
OPENS
NEXT WEEK!
VOTE
FOR
CUTE KIDS
LATEST
CUTE
KIDS
CUTE
KIDS
COMP
WINNER
NAMED
CUTE KIDS
SUPPLEMENT
INSIDE NEXT WEEK
GET READY
FOR CUTE
KIDS PHOTO
CONTEST
2005
ENTER
OUR
CUTE
KIDS
COMP
CUTE KIDS
20 - PAGE
PULL - OUT
SPECIAL
CUTE
KIDS
COMP
WINNERS
VOTING
STARTS
FOR CUTE
KIDS
CUTE KIDS
COMP
STARTS
NEXT WEEK
CUTE KIDS
NOW AT
KINGSLAND SHOPPING
CENTRE
26th JULY-7th AUGUST
CUTE KIDS
2011
A LONDON PICTURE
IT'S WRITTEN ALL OVER THEM

CUTE KIDS.

2011

302 x 254 cm

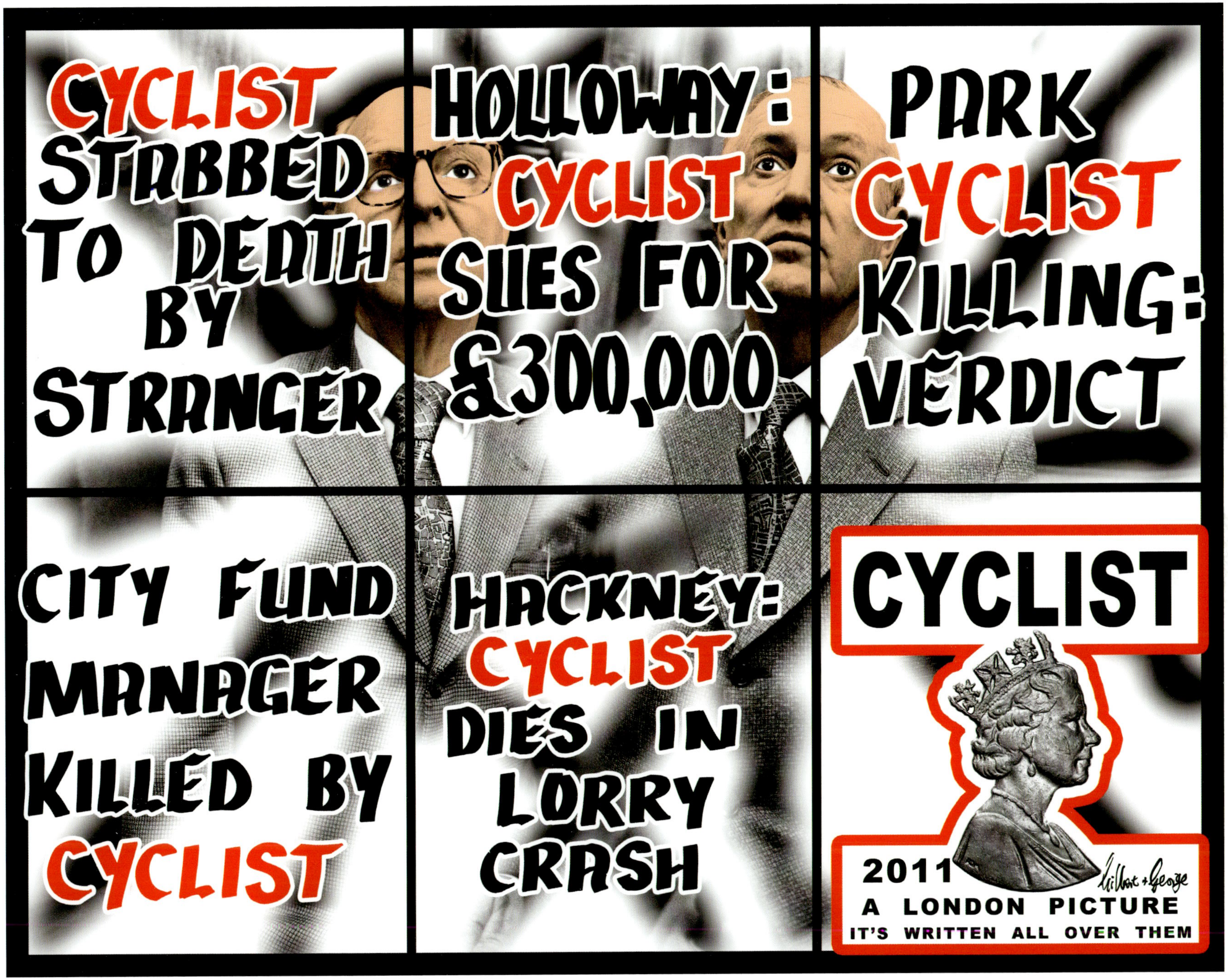
CYCLIST STABBED TO DEATH BY STRANGER
HOLLOWAY: CYCLIST SUES FOR £300,000
PARK CYCLIST KILLING: VERDICT
CITY FUND MANAGER KILLED BY CYCLIST
HACKNEY: CYCLIST DIES IN LORRY CRASH
CYCLIST
2011
A LONDON PICTURE
IT'S WRITTEN ALL OVER THEM

CYCLIST. 2011. 151 x 190 cm

BIKE THIEF PUSHES CYCLIST IN CANAL
CYCLIST DIES IN LORRY CRASH
CYCLIST KILLED IN LORRY HORROR
CYCLIST KILLED IN ROAD HORROR
HORROR CRASH CYCLIST LASTING MEMORIAL
CYCLIST DIES IN CRASH ON ICY ROAD
CYCLIST KILLED BY DRUG USER DRIVER
ANOTHER CYCLIST KILLED IN ROAD HORROR
CYCLIST DIES IN ROAD HORROR
WOMAN CYCLIST CRUSHED TO DEATH
CYCLIST ROAD DEATH HORROR
CYCLIST, 24 CRUSHED TO DEATH BY LORRY
CYCLIST HURT IN LORRY CRASH
CYCLIST HURT IN CRASH AT ARMY HQ
999 COPS IN HORROR SMASH WITH CYCLIST
CYCLIST INJURED IN BUS SMASH
WOMAN CYCLIST IN ROAD HORROR
CYCLIST HURT IN SNOWBALL ATTACK
CYCLIST KILLED IN N7 ROAD CRASH
CYCLIST STRAIGHT
2011
A LONDON PICTURE
IT'S WRITTEN ALL OVER THEM

CYCLIST STRAIGHT. 2011. 302 x 317 cm

WAVE TRAGEDY: 50 BRITONS DEAD
HUNDREDS FEARED DEAD IN FLOODS: DRAMATIC PICTURES
LONDON WOMAN LAY DEAD FOR 2 YEARS
HUNDREDS DEAD IN STAMPEDE
3 SHOT DEAD: GUNMAN ON RUN
CANOE WIFE'S EMAILS TO 'DEAD' HUSBAND
PLAYBOY PRINCE IS DEAD
POP LEGEND DEAD IN HOTEL
ENRON SCANDAL CHIEF DEAD
SEX SCANDAL MINISTER DEAD
QUAKE: 33,000 DEAD
2,000 DEAD IN TSUNAMI PANIC
MAN SHOT DEAD OUTSIDE BAR
LONDON RADIATION ALERT OVER DEAD SPY
TWO WOMEN SHOT DEAD
LONDON: MAN SHOT DEAD
SCORES DEAD IN MADRID PLANE CRASH
HOW TV MAN WAS SHOT DEAD
MISSING TEACHER FOUND DEAD
WOMAN MISSING ON DATE IS DEAD
GEORGE BEST DEAD
TIFFANY'S RAIDED: MAN DEAD
BROWN 'DEAD MAN WALKING'
DEAD
2011
A LONDON PICTURE
IT'S WRITTEN ALL OVER THEM
Gilbert & George

DEAD. 2011. 302 x 381 cm

'THOUSANDS DEAD' IN QUAKE HORROR
AIRPORT PLANE CRASH: 9 DEAD
MAN WHO 'CAME BACK FROM DEAD'
WOMAN FOUND DEAD ON ESTATE
MAN DEAD IN N1 FLAT FOR A WEEK
MYSTERY OF MAN DEAD IN FRONT OF TV
PRAYERS FOR 173 WARTIME DEAD
MAN IS FOUND DEAD IN PHONE BOX
MUM'S VIGIL FOR DEAD SON
ONE DEAD IN POLICE CHASE HORROR
HOLLOWAY MAN LEFT DEAD FOR WEEKS
MYSTERY OF MEN FOUND DEAD WITH BINS ON HEADS
EAST END HONOURS ITS WAR DEAD
FIRE CREW REMEMBER DEAD HEROES
RECORD CROWDS HONOUR WAR DEAD
DEAD KIDS' DAD DEMANDS PUBLIC INQUIRY
COUPLE FOUND DEAD IN HOUSE OF HORROR
NOWHERE LEFT TO BURY DEAD
HEIRESS FOUND DEAD IN FLAT
MYSTERY OF WALKER FOUND DEAD IN POND
'MOLEMAN' TUNNELLER FOUND DEAD
SHOP WORKER FOUND DEAD IN LAKE
MAN SHOOT DEAD IN PARK
DEAD STRAIGHT
2011
A LONDON PICTURE
IT'S WRITTEN ALL OVER THEM
Gilbert & George

DEAD STRAIGHT. 2011. 302 x 381 cm

HEAD-ON
DEATH
CRASH
TRAGEDY
PLEA FOR
ACTION
AT DEATH
CRASH
LIGHTS
TUFNELL
PARK
DEATH
CRASH
VERDICT
DEATH
CRASH
DRIVER
ADMITS
BLAME
ANGER
AT DEATH
CRASH
VERDICT
DEATH
CRASH
2011
Gilbert & George
A LONDON PICTURE
IT'S WRITTEN ALL OVER THEM

DEATH CRASH. 2011. 151 x 190 cm

'CRY FOR HELP' GIRL'S DEATH LEAP
CHARITY MAN IN TOWER DEATH LEAP
WOMAN IN TUBE DEATH LEAP
CITY STAR'S CHAMPAGNE DEATH LEAP
MUM'S DEATH LEAP TO ESCAPE DRUG DEALERS
DEATH LEAP
2011
Gilbert & George
A LONDON PICTURE
IT'S WRITTEN ALL OVER THEM

DEATH LEAP. 2011. 151 x 190 cm

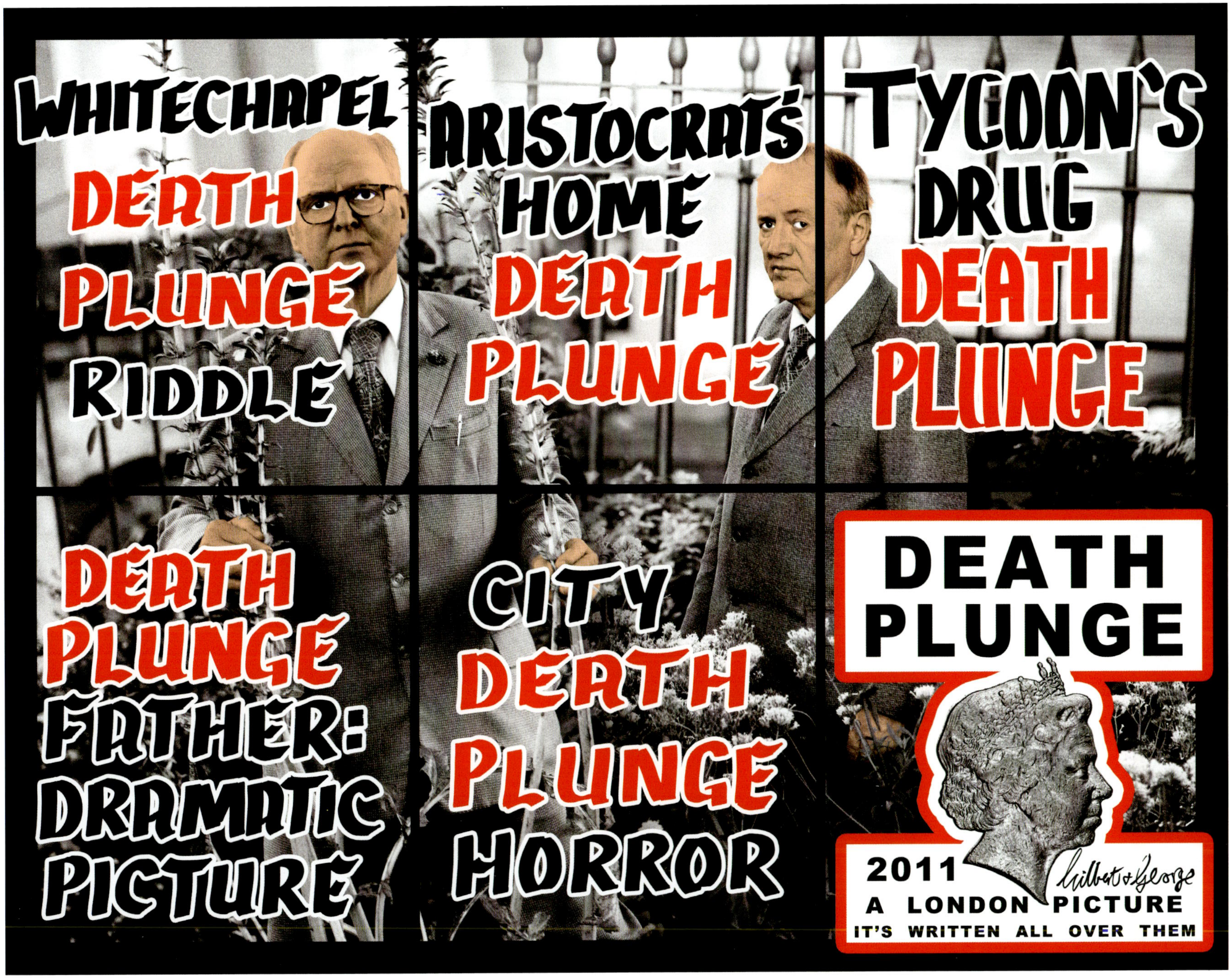
WHITECHAPEL
DEATH
PLUNGE
RIDDLE
ARISTOCRAT'S
HOME
DEATH
PLUNGE
TYCOON'S
DRUG
DEATH
PLUNGE
DEATH
PLUNGE
FATHER:
DRAMATIC
PICTURE
CITY
DEATH
PLUNGE
HORROR
DEATH
PLUNGE
2011
Gilbert & George
A LONDON PICTURE
IT'S WRITTEN ALL OVER THEM

DEATH PLUNGE. 2011. 151 x 190 cm

ACTOR IN DEATH PLUNGE RIDDLE
DALSTON DEATH PLUNGE MYSTERY
SON OF MARQUESS IN DEATH PLUNGE
TOWER BLOCK DEATH PLUNGE
MYSTERY OF N1 DEATH PLUNGE
SICK SNAPS OF DEATH PLUNGE VICTIM
MY GRIEF, BY DEATH PLUNGE WIDOW
100 FT DEATH PLUNGE HORROR
MUM-OF-THREE IN 100FT DEATH PLUNGE HORROR
TOWER DEATH PLUNGE TRAGEDY
HOSPITAL DEATH PLUNGE HORROR
SCAFFOLD DEATH PLUNGE MYSTERY
DEATH PLUNGE TRIAL VERDICT
COPS PROBE DEATH PLUNGE MYSTERY
COUNCIL FACESS DEATH PLUNGE INQUIRY
TOWER BLOCK DEATH PLUNGE
SINGER IN DEATH PLUNGE
ARCHWAY BRIDGE DEATH PLUNGE
MAN IN STATION DEATH PLUNGE
DEATH PLUNGE STRAIGHT
2011
A LONDON PICTURE
IT'S WRITTEN ALL OVER THEM

DEATH PLUNGE STRAIGHT. 2011. 302 x 317 cm

SOCCER STARS FACE DEATH CHARGES
CLEANER'S OVERDOSE DEATH MYSTERY
CARE HOME DEATH TRAGEDY
CARE HOME BLAZE DEATH 'FAILURE'
FAMILY TELL OF COURT DEATH HEARTACHE
BOUNCY CASTLE OF DEATH BANNED
GRANNY'S DEATH MYSTERY
ROAD CLOSURE 'DEATH THREATS'
HIT AND RUN CRASH DEATH TRAGEDY
OLYMPIC HOPEFUL'S DEATH MYSTERY
CABBIE'S ROPE DEATH HORROR
MYSTERY OF TEEN'S DEATH TRAGEDY
PRISON CELL DEATH VERDICT
ACTOR IN STATION DEATH TRAGEDY
BANKER IN LIFT DEATH HORROR
MOTHER WINS PRISON DEATH BATTLE
STATION TRAIN DEATH HORROR
CARE HOME DEATH SHOCK
40FT DEATH BLAZE PLUNGE
PICCADILLY DEATH CRASH: MODEL'S GRIEF
CHELSEA REF DEATH THREAT
ESTATE DOGS FACE 'DEATH SENTENCE'
CITY BANKER'S RAIL DEATH MYSTERY
DEATH SOMETHING
2011
A LONDON PICTURE
IT'S WRITTEN ALL OVER THEM

DEATH SOMETHING. 2011. 302 x 381 cm

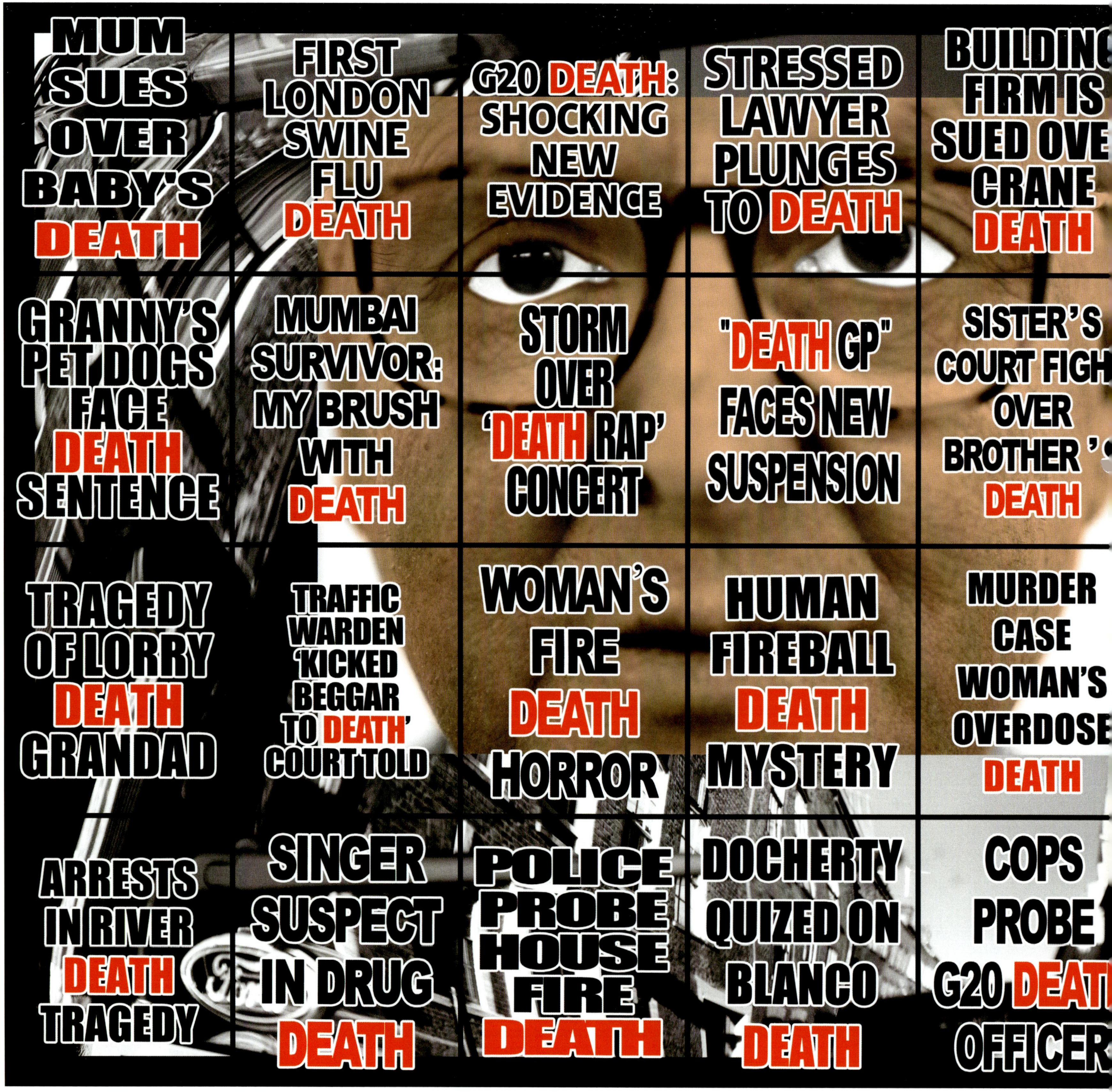
MUM SUES OVER BABY'S DEATH
FIRST LONDON SWINE FLU DEATH
G20 DEATH: SHOCKING NEW EVIDENCE
STRESSED LAWYER PLUNGES TO DEATH
GRANNY'S PET DOGS FACE DEATH SENTENCE
MUMBAI SURVIVOR: MY BRUSH WITH DEATH
STORM OVER 'DEATH RAP' CONCERT
"DEATH GP" FACES NEW SUSPENSION
TRAGEDY OF LORRY DEATH GRANDAD
TRAFFIC WARDEN 'KICKED BEGGAR TO DEATH' COURT TOLD
WOMAN'S FIRE DEATH HORROR
HUMAN FIREBALL DEATH MYSTERY
ARRESTS IN RIVER DEATH TRAGEDY
SINGER SUSPECT IN DRUG DEATH
POLICE PROBE HOUSE FIRE DEATH
DOCHERTY QUIZED ON BLANCO DEATH
MURDER CASE WOMAN'S OVERDOSE DEATH
COPS PROBE G20 DEAT OFFICER

DEATH STRAIGHT

2011

302 x 698 cm

DEATH STALKS CYCLONE AMILIES
FIREBALL DEATH 'TEXT THREATS'
FOX MAY HAVE CAUSED ROAD DEATH
'DEATH DOC' SAYS SORRY GIVING EVIDENCE
DOCTOR FACES DEATH PROBE INQUIRY
RIVERBOAT DEATH: TWO IN COURT
BAKER'S DEATH FALL RAGEDY
VIGIL FOR G20 DEMO DEATH
'DEATH SENTENCE' DOGS ARE SAVED
'DEATH JUNCTION' SAFETY BATTLE
'DEATH CROSSING' SAFETY CALL
BABY'S TRAGIC COT DEATH
PRISON LAMMED OVER NMATE'S DEATH
COPS PROBE WOMAN'S DEATH
MIDWIVES SLAMMED OVER BABY DEATH
CELL DEATH MUM'S INQUEST VICTORY
ARRESTS OVER SCOOTER CRASH DEATH
AREAS' 'HIGH DEATH RISK' RANKING
DEATH DDLE OF BOXING BOSS'S BROTHER
CHILD'S SWINE FLU DEATH
MAN IN DRESS 'PUSHED' TO HIS DEATH ON THE TUBE
EC1 FUGITIVE'S JAIL CELL DEATH MYSTERY
FAMILY CALL FOR HOSPITAL DEATH PROBE
DEATH STRAIGHT
2011 A LONDON PICTURE
Gilbert + George
IT'S WRITTEN ALL OVER THEM

DEATH LEAP FAMILY: FIRST PICTURE
HARROW SCHOOL DEATH: DRAMATIC NEW DETAILS
ASHES DEATH THREATS
TIFFANY'S DEATH RAID: LATEST
GIRL EATING HERSELF TO DEATH
BRITISH DEATH TOLL SOARS
BANKER'S S+M DEATH RIDDLE
GARY GLITTER 'FACES DEATH PENALTY'
TRAIN DEATH FAMILY: CCTV PICTURE
HOLIDAY CHILDREN POISONED TO DEATH
DIANA DEATH: THE WHOLE TRUTH
DEATH OF LONDON MARATHON RUNNER, 22
ENGLAND WORLD CUP HERO'S FIRE DEATH
LAWYER JUMPS 80FT TO DEATH
POISON SPY CLOSE TO DEATH
FIREWORKS DEATH BLAST: DRAMATIC PICTURE
CITY STAR JUMPS TO DEATH IN BEST SUIT
DEATH DRIVE PEER TO GO FREE
LONDON PC's 999 DEATH: MAN HELD
BBC STAR QUIZZED OVER LOVER'S DEATH
PHONE DEATH DRIVERS FACE 14 YEARS
BBC STAR HELD OVER DEATH OF PRESENTER
ESSEX NURSERY DEATH INQUIRY PLEA
DEATH OF THE FREE CITY LUNCH
DEATH OF CITY BONUS CULTURE
RAIL DEATH FAMILY'S NEW TRAGEDY
BEN'S CHILLING ESSAY ON VIOLENT DEATH
DEATH
2011 A LONDON PICTURE
IT'S WRITTEN ALL OVER THEM

DEATH. 2011. 302 x 444 cm

DOCTOR LINKED TO 40 DEATHS SUSPENDED
WOMEN'S DRINK DEATHS DOUBLE
CYCLE DEATHS -SPECIAL REPORT
LONDON HOSPITAL SUPERBUG DEATHS
DEEPCUT DEATHS: OFFICIAL REPORT
SWINE FLU: 12 MORE DEATHS
BABY DEATHS MOTHER CLEARED
SURGERY DEATHS PROBE AT TOP HOSPITAL
DEATHS
2011
A LONDON PICTURE
IT'S WRITTEN ALL OVER THEM

DEATHS. 2011. 226 x 190 cm

JUNKIE DEATHS INQUEST VERDICT
210 CHILD ABUSE DEATHS
SCULPTOR ACCUSED OVER DEATHS
A12 CAR DEATHS: TRIAL IS SET
ARSONIST JAILED FOR TRIPLE DEATHS
DEATHS SPELL DEER PARK'S END?
MAN JAILED OVER GAS DEATHS
BOY RACER IN DEATHS CASE IS SENTENCED
DEATHS STRAIGHT
2011
A LONDON PICTURE
IT'S WRITTEN ALL OVER THEM

DEATHS STRAIGHT. 2011. 226 x 190 cm

'DRIVERS LEFT CITY BANKER TO DIE'
FOUR GIRLS DIE IN VALENTINE MASSACRE
COPTER HORROR: CHELSEA FANS DIE
TWIN BABIES DIE IN FLOOD RESCUE
LONDON NURSES DIE ON MERCY MISSION
SUFFOLK STRANGLER TO DIE IN JAIL
BUS-STOP KILLER MUST DIE IN JAIL
BRITISH PARAS DIE IN AFGHAN AMBUSH
DIE
2011
A LONDON PICTURE
IT'S WRITTEN ALL OVER THEM

DIE. 2011. 226 x 190 cm

ELDERLY DIE ALONE: SHOCK FIGURES
MORE TROOPS DIE IN BLACKEST WEEK
FAMILY OF 3 DIE IN HOLIDAY TRAGEDY
THREE DIE IN CRASH HORROR
CHILD SURVIVES AS 150 DIE IN AIRBUS
MURDER BABE LEFT TO DIE
3 DIE IN CAR HORROR
'228 DIE' AS JET PLUNGES INTO SEA
CAR RAMS ROYAL PARADE: 2 DIE
CRASH VICTIMS GET RIGHT TO DIE
BRITISH PARAS DIE IN AFGHAN AMBUSH
DIE STRAIGHT
2011
A LONDON PICTURE
IT'S WRITTEN ALL OVER THEM

DIE STRAIGHT. 2011. 226 x 254 cm

WHY LONDON'S WHALE DIED
HOW WHITECHAPEL FIREMAN DIED IN BLAZE
MY WIFE DIED A WAR HERO
DIED
2011
Gilbert & George
A LONDON PICTURE
IT'S WRITTEN ALL OVER THEM

DIED. 2011. 151 x 127 cm

HOTEL WORKER DIED IN 999 CALL TRAGEDY
OAP DIED AFTER WART OPERATION
LONDON SOLDIER DIED IN HAIL OF 60 BULLETS
MAN DIED AFTER SEX ACT 'WENT WRONG'
MAN DIED AFTER DRINKING COCAINE LACED RUM
DIED STRAIGHT
2011
A LONDON PICTURE
IT'S WRITTEN ALL OVER THEM

DIED STRAIGHT. 2011. 151 x 190 cm

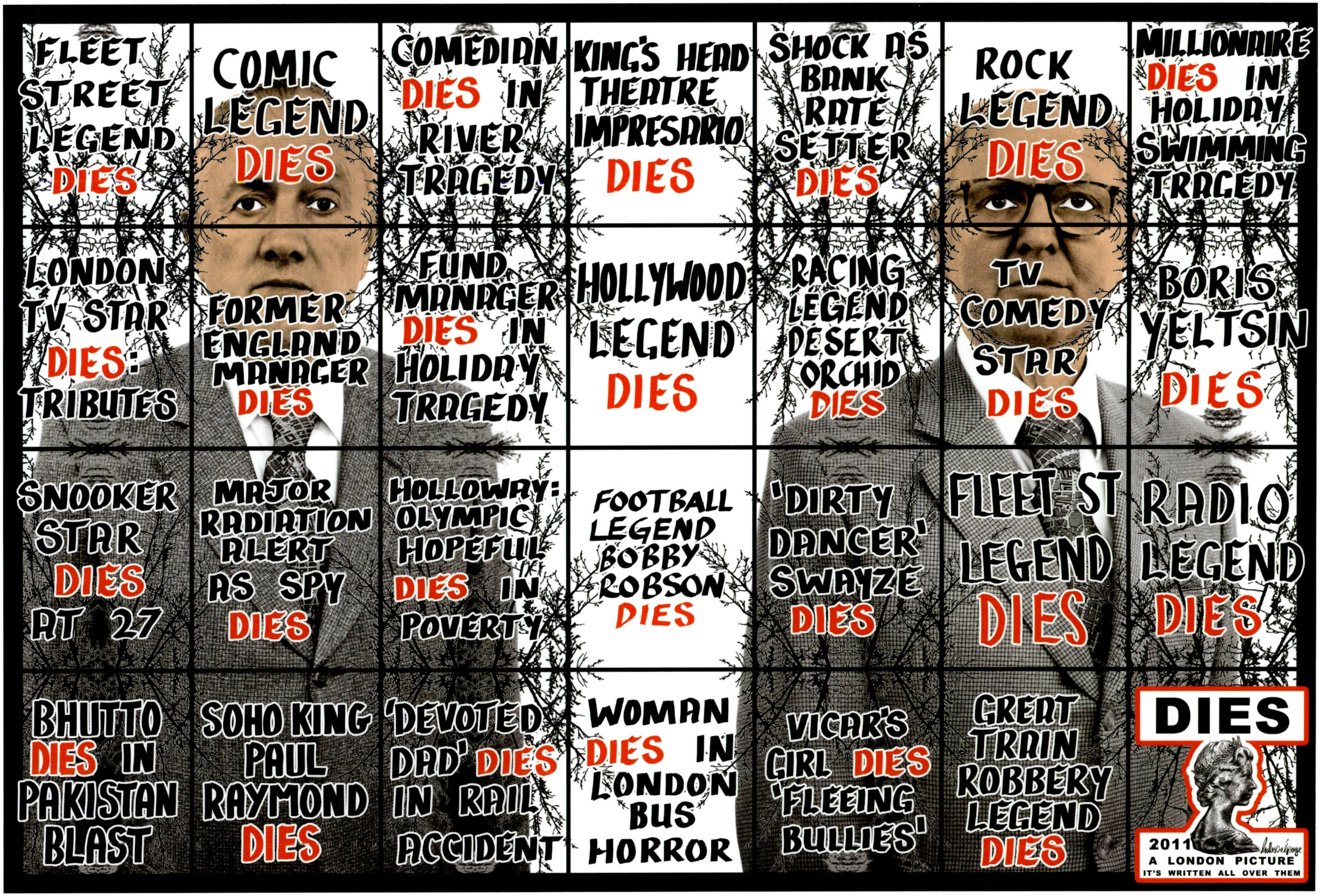
FLEET STREET LEGEND DIES
COMIC LEGEND DIES
COMEDIAN DIES IN RIVER TRAGEDY
KING'S HEAD THEATRE IMPRESARIO DIES
SHOCK AS BANK RATE SETTER DIES
ROCK LEGEND DIES
MILLIONAIRE DIES IN HOLIDAY SWIMMING TRAGEDY
LONDON TV STAR DIES: TRIBUTES
FORMER ENGLAND MANAGER DIES
FUND MANAGER DIES IN HOLIDAY TRAGEDY
HOLLYWOOD LEGEND DIES
RACING LEGEND DESERT ORCHID DIES
TV COMEDY STAR DIES
BORIS YELTSIN DIES
SNOOKER STAR DIES AT 27
MAJOR RADIATION ALERT AS SPY DIES
HOLLOWAY: OLYMPIC HOPEFUL DIES IN POVERTY
FOOTBALL LEGEND BOBBY ROBSON DIES
'DIRTY DANCER' SWAYZE DIES
FLEET ST LEGEND DIES
RADIO LEGEND DIES
BHUTTO DIES IN PAKISTAN BLAST
SOHO KING PAUL RAYMOND DIES
'DEVOTED DAD' DIES IN RAIL ACCIDENT
WOMAN DIES IN LONDON BUS HORROR
VICAR'S GIRL DIES 'FLEEING BULLIES'
GREAT TRAIN ROBBERY LEGEND DIES
DIES
2011
A LONDON PICTURE
IT'S WRITTEN ALL OVER THEM

DIES. 2011. 302 x 444 cm

QUAGLINO'S CLOSED AFTER DINER DIES
RADIO LEGEND DIES
SOAP STAR WENDY DIES
9/11 WIDOW DIES IN U.S. JET CRASH
TV COMEDY STAR DIES
LONDON OLYMPIC HOPEFUL DIES IN POVERTY
FOOTBALL LEGEND BOBBY ROBSON DIES
DAD DIES AFTER DRINKING FROM LAVA LAMP
BRAIN VICTIM DIES FIGHTING FIRE
BANKER DIES IN BIKE CRASH
EX-BOXER DIES IN BLAZE TRAGEDY
YOUNG MUM DIES AFTER EATING EGG ROLL
BETHNAL GREEN BOXING CHAMP DIES IN CRASH
CRASH DAD DIES AFTER HEART ATTACK
WOMAN DIES IN FIRE HORROR AT FLATS
DAD DIES AFTER 10TH FLOOR PLUNGE
PARENTS HELD AFTER BABY DIES
FATHER DIES IN DOORSTEP STABBING
BABY DIES IN HOUSE OF MURDER
'PERFECT SON' DIES AFTER ATTACK
WOMAN DIES IN RELIGIOUS FAST
YOUNG MUM DIES IN STABBING INCIDENT
WOMAN DIES IN FLAT BLAZE
TWIN DIES IN HIT & RUN TRAGEDY
TRIBUTES AS POP STAR ALF DIES AT 93
MAN DIES AFTER BREAKING NOSE
FAST FOOD BOSS DIES IN HORROR CRASH
BIKER DIES IN HORROR SMASH
BRITISH PILOT DIES IN SKI HORROR
DIES STRAIGHT
2011
A LONDON PICTURE
IT'S WRITTEN ALL OVER THEM

DIES STRAIGHT. 2011. 377 x 381 cm

PET DOG IS KILLED AS IT IS HIT BY TRAIN
CAT IS KILLED IN PARK DOG ATTACK
PET DOG LEFT TO STARVE TO DEATH
DANGER DOG STILL LOOSE AFTER PET ATTACK
DOG STABBED PROTECTING OWNER
PET IS MAULED TO DEATH IN DOG ATTACK
DOG SAVED FROM SAVAGE ATTACK
DOG
2011
A LONDON PICTURE
IT'S WRITTEN ALL OVER THEM

DOG. 2011. 151 x 254 cm

B'DESH FAMILIES FACE DRUG DILEMMA
PAYBACK TIME FOR DRUG RACKETEERS
DISUSED PUB FUELS DRUG FEARS
COPS TARGET BROCKLEY DRUG DEALERS
WHITECHAPEL MUM TELLS OF DRUG HELL TRAGEDY
OUR ESTATE DRUG HELL
N1 DRUG BARON JAILED FOR 18 YEARS
RAID SPARKS DRUG EPIDEMIC FEAR
'HEROES' STAND UP TO DRUG DEALERS
CHIP SHOP DRUG DEALERS JAILED
GRANDAD MURDERED FOR A DRUG FIX
N1 MAN ON £20 MILLION DRUG SMUGGLING CHARGE
£15,000 DRUG DEALER JAILED
ARCHWAY DRUG DEALER JAILED
DRUG DEN CLOSED AFTER SECOND RAID
SCHEME TO TACKLE GROWING DRUG ABUSE PROBLEM
DRUG SMUGGLER STYLIST JAILED
DRUG COPS SEIZE £2,500 IN FLAT RAID
TRAGIC FAMILY'S DRUG DEATH WARNING
DRUG STRAIGHT
2011
A LONDON PICTURE
IT'S WRITTEN ALL OVER THEM
Gilbert & George

DRUG STRAIGHT. 2011. 302 x 317 cm

DRUGS VICTIM LIKE 'ELEPHANT MAN'
DRUGS TEST SCANDAL REVEALED
FILM STAR'S DRUGS DEATH
PRINCE WILLIAM IN £40m DRUGS SWOOP
BRITISH GOLD MEDALLIST'S DRUGS BUST
DRUGS
2011
A LONDON PICTURE
IT'S WRITTEN ALL OVER THEM
Gilbert + George

DRUGS. 2011. 151 x 190 cm

MODEL VANISHES IN DRUGS TRAGEDY
DRUGS FLOW CUT BY HEROIN CASE WIN
DEALER THREW DRUGS OVER JAIL WALL
DRUGS DEALER JAILED
DRUGS & KNIVES SEIZED IN ESTATE RAID
MAJOR DRUGS RING BROKEN
POLICE DRUGS BLITZ ON STREETS
ESSEX RD TEENAGER'S 'DRUGS FARM'
COLUMBIAN DRUGS TRIAL: MAN IN DOCK
DRUGS 'MURDER BID': TRIAL OPENS
GIRLS OF 11 OFFER SEX TO PAY FOR DRUGS
5 HELD IN £20m DRUGS HAUL
LORRY BOSS CLEARED OF £8M DRUGS CHARGES
N1 GANG CAUGHT WITH £12 MILLION DRUGS HAUL
DRUGS BARON CLEARED OF MURDER
TRADER DEALT DRUGS FROM STALL
DRUGS SEIZED IN CAR BLITZ
COPS SWOOP ON DRUGS DEN
DRUGS BATCH LACED WITH GLASS
KNIVES & DRUGS SEIZED IN BLITZ
DODGY DRUGS DEATH TOLL RISES
DRUGS DEN FLAT SHUT DOWN
£5m DRUGS GANG JAILED
DRUGS STRAIGHT
2011
A LONDON PICTURE
IT'S WRITTEN ALL OVER THEM

DRUGS STRAIGHT. 2011. 302 x 381 cm

DRUNK. 2011. 151 x 127 cm

COUNCIL PUTS UP COST OF DYING
DYING GIRL'S TRAGIC LAST MOMENTS
DYING MAN WEDS LOST LOVE
GIRL, 14, COMFORTS DYING STAB VICTIM
MISSING THREE DAYS' OF DYING FATHER
DYING
2011
A LONDON PICTURE
IT'S WRITTEN ALL OVER THEM

DYING. 2011. 151 x 190 cm

TEEN GANG RAID W. END STORE
FOSTER CHILD SENT TO BOMBER'S HOME
BOMBED BUS DRIVER'S BRAVERY
ARSENAL STAR JAILED
LONDON STABBINGS CRISIS- SPECIAL REPORT
POLICE SHOOT AT CHELSEA RAIDER
ISLINGTON: SCHOOLBOY MARTIN'S KILLER GETS LIFE
ISLINGTON: TEENAGE SHOPPER STABBED TO DEATH
TOTTENHAM: GIRL SHOT DEAD -PICTURE
FAMILIES HIRE GUARDS TO BEAT MUGGERS
BULLIED PUPILS HAVE FACE SURGERY
STABBED SCHOOLBOY -DRAMATIC NEW DETAILS
HOODIES ON BIKES SHOOT BOY DEAD
ISLINGTON: BOY, 13 ACCUSED OF KNIFE MURDER
'RIPPER': TWO MORE BODIES FOUND
TORY 'DRINK TAX' TO CURB YOBS
MAN BEHEADED IN LONDON STREET
POP TYCOON SHOT BY SON
DRUGS HERO KNIFED: DRAMATIC PICTURE
TONI-ANN BYFIELD: MURDER VERDICT
ARSON MYSTERY: THIRD BODY FOUND
FINES FOR PARENTS OF UNRULY PUPILS
ESSEX: ROBBERS SHOOT HAVE-A-GO COMMUTER
PRINCE'S NIGHTCLUB AND THE 'DRUNK YOBS'
'MADDY DIED IN HOTEL ROOM' -POLICE
'MUGGERS' THROW MAN FROM TRAIN
KNIFE GANG MURDER FATHER
FAMILY
2011 A LONDON PICTURE
IT'S WRITTEN ALL OVER THEM

FAMILY. 2011. 302 x 444 cm

CHILD RAPIST GETS 10 YEARS
CHILD RAPIST JAILED
MISSING KIDS FOUND
FAMILY BLASTS CHILD KILLER SENTENCE
FEARS GROW OVER MISSING OAP
SWIM KIDS FLEE POOL BLAZE
PARTY DEATH: DAD'S ANGUIS
TEENAGER CONVICTED OF KARATE CHOP KILLING
FEARS OVER MISSING OAP
PAEDO'S KILLER WINS JAIL CUT
BOY, 13 HAMMER ATTACK HORROR
MARTIN KILLING: BROTHER SPEAKS OUT
FAMILY'S GRIEF AFTER PREGNANT MUM'S KILLING
GRANN RAPIST JAILE FOR 8 YEARS
FAGIN'S KITCHEN' THIEVES JAILED
MAN 'SERIOUS' AFTER HOODIES ATTACK
MISSING BOYS IN RITUAL SACRIFICE FEAR
VIOLENT DRUNK BANNED FROM 4 PUBS
OAP BATTERED IN STREET ATTACK
8 YOUTHS DENY EC1 GANG MURDER
'LOVE EMAILS LED TO MURDER
FLEEING TEEN DEATH PLUNGE VERDICT
A-LEVEL SCHOOLS RESULTS TABLE
AGNES GUN MURDER: TWO JAILED
SCHOOLBOY'S KILLERS JAILED FOR LIFE
COUNCIL CRUCIFIED OVER CHURCH SCHOOL
SCHOOLBOY'S MURDER INSPIRES STAGE PLAY
TEENAGERS ATTACK SCHOOLBOY WITH A HAMMER
TEEN STABBED IN STREET
'HOLLOWAY STRANGLER': I'LL APPEAL SAYS MUM
TEACHER DENIES MOLESTING PUPILS
MISSING WOMAN REMAINS FOUND
PUPILS JAILED FOR GANG STABBING
BIRTHDAY PARTY CLUBBER SHOT DEAD
FAMILY O £1460 WEEKLY BENEFIT

ROYAL COPYCAT COUPLE
ADDICT BANNED FROM SEEING PARENTS
MUSLIMS RISK LIVES FOR RAMADAN
ONE IN FIVE CHURCHES AT RISK
NAVY RESCUES STRANDED HACKNEY SCHOOLKIDS
TOM JONES SET FOR GIG IN N1 CHURCH
BOY'S
FAKE CONDOMS SPARK HEALTH SCARE
ROGUE DOC SPARKS HEATH ALERT
STOWAWAY ON ROYAL JET TO HEATHROW
ESSEX RD MAN'S BID TO TORCH HIMSELF
CITY DRUNKS SPARK 999 CRISIS
CABBIE
MAN DIES IN FLAT FIRE
PARADISE GARDENS PICTURE SPECIAL
SOLDIERS DROWN IN CANAL CRASH
FRESH APPEAL IN HOOKER'S MURDER
TEACHERS STRIKE OVER NEW SCHOOL BUILDING
WOMEN OVER 55
DAD DIES IN BIKE CRASH TRAGEDY
COUNCIL DESTROYS GRIEVING KIDS' KEEPSAKES
HALF OUR KIDS IN JOBLESS FAMILIES
MAN HURT OUTSIDE NIGHT CLUB
NAG'S HEAD SUICIDE BID BLAZE DRAMA
LOVE
SUSPECT PLUNGES FROM ROOFTOP
REVOLT OVER BAN ON STRIPPERS
SCHOOL FALL GIRL DIES
STRIPPERS IN COUNCIL BAN FILM PROTEST
FAMILY STRAIGHT
2011
A LONDON PICTURE
IT'S WRITTEN ALL OVER THEM

FAMILY STRAIGHT

2011

377 x 825 cm

GIRL FOUND HANGED IN WARDROBE
FOUND: TOURIST'S £2,000 LEFT ON TUBE
CANNABIS HAUL FOUND IN N1 GARAGE
FOUND
2011
A LONDON PICTURE
IT'S WRITTEN ALL OVER THEM

FOUND. 2011. 151 x 127 cm

FURY OVER DRUG CENTRE NEXT TO SCHOOL
FURY OVER FOX VIGILANTES
SPECIAL SCHOOL'S EXPANSION SPARKS FURY
FURY AS POLICE ESCAPE CHARGES
FURY OVER SCHOOL WALL COLLAPSE
HEAD'S FURY AT THEFTS OF SCHOOL COMPUTERS
FAMILY FURY AT 'GAY' SPY SMEARS
FURY OVER RAIL TANNOY DIN
FURY
2011
A LONDON PICTURE
IT'S WRITTEN ALL OVER THEM

FURY. 2011. 226 x 190 cm

MURDER BID GANG APPEAL AGAINST SENTENCES
WILD BIRD GANG FINED
HIGHBURY FIELDS KNIFE GANG IN BIKE SNATCH
HERO DA
TACKLES
RAZOR
GANG
GANG RAPE TRIAL LATEST
EAST END DRUGS GANG JAILED
HERO'S GANG KILLERS JAILED FOR LIFE
LONDON
FIELDS
MURDER
GANG
JAILED
NEW YEAR GONG GANG
PROTEST HALTS CHAINSAW GANG
GANG DUO GUILTY OF MURDER
CLAPTON LINK TO
COLUMBIA
COCAINE GANG
YOUTHS DENY GANG KILLING
PUPILS FACE GANG TERROR
PAIR JAILED FOR GANG MURDER
MP'S ALARM
OVER GANG RAPES

GANG STRAIGHT. 2011. 302 x 571 cm

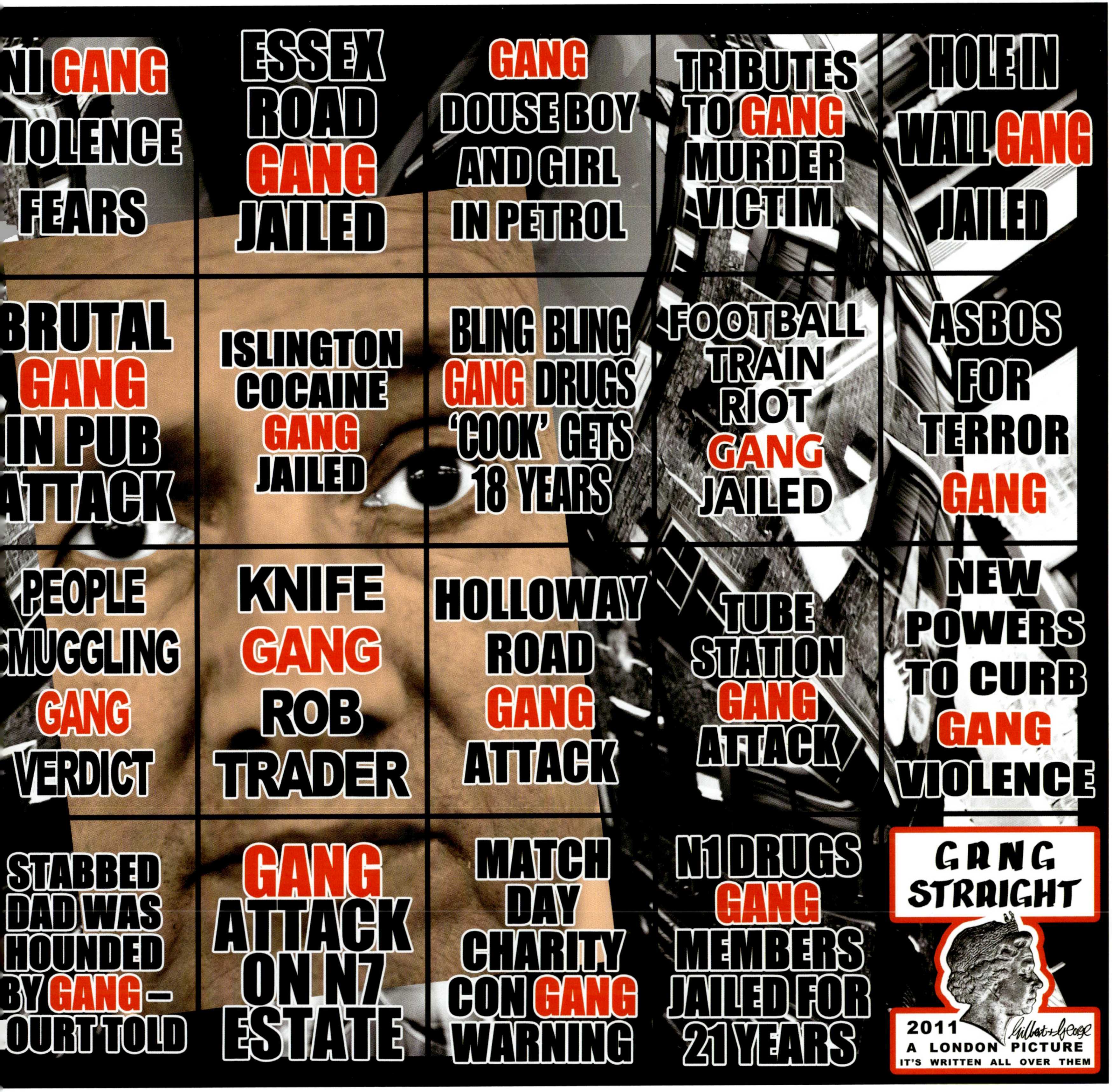

NI GANG VIOLENCE FEARS
ESSEX ROAD GANG JAILED
GANG DOUSE BOY AND GIRL IN PETROL
TRIBUTES TO GANG MURDER VICTIM
HOLE IN WALL GANG JAILED
BRUTAL GANG IN PUB ATTACK
ISLINGTON COCAINE GANG JAILED
BLING BLING GANG DRUGS 'COOK' GETS 18 YEARS
FOOTBALL TRAIN RIOT GANG JAILED
ASBOS FOR TERROR GANG
PEOPLE MUGGLING GANG VERDICT
KNIFE GANG ROB TRADER
HOLLOWAY ROAD GANG ATTACK
TUBE STATION GANG ATTACK
NEW POWERS TO CURB GANG VIOLENCE
STABBED DAD WAS HOUNDED BY GANG – OURT TOLD
GANG ATTACK ON N7 ESTATE
MATCH DAY CHARITY CON GANG WARNING
N1 DRUGS GANG MEMBERS JAILED FOR 21 YEARS
GANG STRAIGHT
2011 A LONDON PICTURE
IT'S WRITTEN ALL OVER THEM

GANG ARMOURER LINKED TO MURDERS
LUXURY CAR GANG CAUGHT
WOOD GREEN CRIME GANG EXPOSED
500 POLICE SMASH CHEQUE BOOK GANG
SMASH AND GRAB GANG TARGET WEST END
STRATFORD CAR GANG SMASHED -PICTURES
HUGE CAR GANG SMASHED -PICTURES
WANTED: WEST END SMASH AND GRAB GANG
GANG
2011
A LONDON PICTURE
IT'S WRITTEN ALL OVER THEM

GANG. 2011. 226 x 190 cm

GANGS. 2011. 151 x 127 cm

GRAFFITI
GANGS
£70,000
RAMPAGE
TURKISH
GANGS
TURF
WAR
FEAR
RADIOS
TO BEAT
EESEX RD
SHOP
GANGS
TURKISH
GANGS
ORGY OF
VIOLENCE
NEW
CRIMEBUSTER
VOWS TO
TACKLE GANGS
GANGS
STRAIGHT
2011
A LONDON PICTURE
IT'S WRITTEN ALL OVER THEM

GANGS STRAIGHT. 2011. 151 x 190 cm

GAY MURDER 'FILMED ON MOBILES'
FIRST GAY WEDDING - PICTURES
ROYAL GAY SEX BLACKMAIL PLOT
BP CHIEF LIES OVER GAY LOVER
DEATH FALL AT CHELSEA GAY ORGY
ROBBIE WILLIAMS: 'I'M NOT GAY'
SIMON HUGHES: MY GAY AFFAIRS
TORY HOPEFUL AND GAY SMEARS
ROYAL GAY SEX BLACKMAIL - NEW CLAIMS
BP CHIEF AND THE GAY ESCORT AGENCY
SIMON HUGHES: I AM GAY, TOO
GAY
2011
A LONDON PICTURE
IT'S WRITTEN ALL OVER THEM

GAY. 2011. 226 x 254 cm

GAY KNIFE VICTIM FIGHTS FOR LIFE
SEX TOYS FEAR AT GAY PARK GIG
YOUTH. 16, ADMITS 'GAY' STABBING
THUGS TARGET GAY MEN
ROBBER PREYED ON GAY MEN
POLICE TARGET GAY BASHERS
MAN LEFT IN COMA AFTER ANTI-GAY ATTACK
GAY SHOW FIRST FOR BUSINESS CENTRE
OUTRAGE OVER GAY WEDDINGS RULING
80 GAY 'WEDDINGS' SET FOR TOWN HALL
STRAIGHT COUPLE IN BATTLE FOR 'GAY WEDDING'
'CALLOUS' THIEF TARGETED GAY MEN
MYSTERY DEATH IN GAY SAUNA
CHEF IS GUILTY OF STABBING GAY LOVER TO DEATH
GAY LOVER STABBED TO DEATH IN DRUNKEN ROW
FOUR YEARS FOR CHEF WHO KILLED GAY LOVER
POOL IS GAY CRUISING HOTSPOT
£6,500 AWARD FOR GAY SQUASH CLUB
STORE TOILETS USED FOR GAY SEX
GAY STRAIGHT
2011
A LONDON PICTURE
IT'S WRITTEN ALL OVER THEM

GAY STRAIGHT. 2011. 302 x 317 cm

KIDNAP GIRL JAYCEE: FIRST PICTURE
HACKNEY: GIRL KILLED BY HEROIN
KIDNAP GIRL: I FEEL GUILTY
20 YEARS FOR GIRL KILLER
POLICE 'FAILINGS' IN STAB GIRL CASE
MURDERED A-LEVEL GIRL: LAST PICTURE
A-LEVEL GIRL MURDERED
FIRST PICTURE: MAJORCA PLUNGE GIRL
MISSING INTERNET GIRL: DRAMATIC PICTURE
GIRL FOOTBALL THUG LOCKED UP
TORTURE GIRL: DRAMATIC ARREST
GIRL
2011
A LONDON PICTURE
IT'S WRITTEN ALL OVER THEM

GIRL. 2011. 226 x 254 cm

GIRL, 15 RAPED AT PRINCE'S TRUST CONCERT
GIRL, 14 ON GANGSTER GUN CHARGES
KIDNAP ORDEAL OF GIRL, 3
BULLIED GIRL, 15 STABBED IN HEAD
GIRL, 5, ROBS PENSIONER
MURDERED GIRL, 15: FIRST PICTURE
GIRL, 3 DIES IN BEACH TRAGEDY
GIRL, 13, KNIFED AT SCHOOL
LONDON GIRL, 2, STABBED TO DEATH
GIRL, 16, GUILTY OF HONEY-TRAP MURDER
'GIRL, 6, SEARCHED BY TERROR POLICE'
GIRL, 13, ARRESTED WITH GUN IN BEDROOM
GIRL, 5 ABDUCTED FROM SHOPPING CENTRE
GIRL AGED 7 IN DIET ALERT
KIDNAP FEARS FOR HOLIDAY GIRL, 3
JAILED: GIRL, 14 WHO KILLED FOR KICKS
HACKNEY WITCH CASE: GIRL, 8 GIVES EVIDENCE
GIRL AGED
2011
A LONDON PICTURE
IT'S WRITTEN ALL OVER THEM

GIRL AGED. 2011. 226 x 381 cm

GIRL, 7, DIES IN SWIMMING POOL TRAGEDY
GIRL, 15 SURVIVES CANAL PLUNGE
GIRL, 8, SEX ORDEAL
GIRL, 5 IN PARK KIDNAP ATTEMPT
GIRL GANG LEADER, 17, GETS 3 YEARS
GIRL, 3, MAULED BY DOG
GIRL, 5, KILLED IN BUS TRAGEDY
PREGNANT GIRL OF 15 THROWN INTO CANAL
GIRL, 13, ESCAPES HIGHBURY SEX ATTACKER
FEARS FOR MISSING ESSEX GIRL, 14
SWINE FLU KILLS HEALTHY LONDON GIRL, 6
BULLY GANG ATTACKS GIRL, 13
SHOTGUN BLAST JUST MISSES GIRL, 4
WALWORTH YOUTH WORKER MOLESTED 6-YR-OLD GIRL
HUNT FOR SEX BEAST AFTER PARK ATTACK ON GIRL, 12
RESCUE GIRL, 7 SAVES HER MUM
TEENAGER JAILED FOR RAPING GIRL, 17
GIRL, 18, BIDS TO WIN TOWN HALL SEAT
GIRL, 6, WINS £5M PAYOUT
GIRL, 12, IN ATTEMPTED ABDUCTION
GIRL, 2, DIES IN ROAD HORROR
GIRL, 3, WINS CANCER BRAVERY AWARD
MUM KILLS GIRL, 4
GIRL AGED STRAIGHT
2011
A LONDON PICTURE
IT'S WRITTEN ALL OVER THEM
Gilbert & George

GIRL AGED STRAIGHT. 2011. 302 x 381 cm

HOLIDAY SWINE FLU GIRL 'CRITICAL'
SCHOOL GIRL BRIDE RAPE
FEARS FOR MISSING SCHOOL GIRL
DONOR GIRL SAVES 7 HER AFTER DEATH
WOMAN'S HAIR SET ALIGHT BY GIRL GANG
BOSS'S HORROR ATTACK ON SALES GIRL
GIRL SCARRED IN BOTTLE ATTACK
FATHER OF MURDERED GIRL SPEAKS
GIRL TRIO FACING JAIL
CLUBBER WHO PARALYSED GIRL WAS HIGH ON ECSTASY
FIVE YEAR OLD GIRL KILLED IN HIT AND RUN
CALL GIRL KILLER IN BID FOR FREEDOM
GIRL IN 15 FLOOR DEATH FALL
GIRL BOTTOM-BOOSTER PILL PERIL
TEENAGE GIRL IN 3AM SEX ASSAULT
GIRL DIED SLIDING DOWN BANISTER
ARTISTS SUPPORT SICK GIRL
BLIND GIRL WINS PAYOUT
SWINE FLU GIRL DIES IN CRASH
GIRL STRAIGHT
2011
A LONDON PICTURE
IT'S WRITTEN ALL OVER THEM

GIRL STRAIGHT. 2011. 302 x 317 cm

GRANDAD
WINS
£25,000
JACKPOT
GRANDAD
KILLED BY
SPEEDING
COP CAR
GRANDAD
KILLED
BY
HIT & RUN
MOTORBIKE
GRANDAD
2011
A LONDON PICTURE
IT'S WRITTEN ALL OVER THEM

GRANDAD. 2011. 151 x 127 cm

TUBE GUN MANIAC LOCKED UP
HACKNEY GUN SIEGE -PICTURE
NORTH LONDON GUN HORROR
LONDON RUSH HOUR GUN HORROR
CHELSEA GUN SIEGE POLICE CLEARED
POLICE BLUNDER OVER MAN WHO FOUND LOADED GUN
LAST MOMENTS OF GUN MURDER. SCHOOLBOY
MINISTER CAUGHT IN GUN HORROR
GUN
2011
A LONDON PICTURE
IT'S WRITTEN ALL OVER THEM

GUN. 2011. 226 x 190 cm

TORCHED CAR GUN LINK
DEADLY MINIATURE KEYRING GUN SEIZED
END BLOODBATH PLEA TO GUN GANGS
COPS FOIL GUN GANG
DRUG CHARGE MOTHER 'KEPT GUN'
VERDICT IN GUN TERROR TRIAL
MACHINE GUN COPS RAID FLAT
SECRET GUN : STREET DANGER
EVIL GUN GANG JAILED
FAKE GUN SCANDAL
HUNT FOR ESSEX RD GUN RAIDERS
GUN CRIME DOUBLES IN A YEAR
EAST END'S HIDDEN GUN CULTURE
SECURITY GUARD ROBBED BY GUN GANG
GARAGE GUN RAIDERS SNATCH £20,000
HOLLOWAY GANGS IN GUN BATTLE
GUN VICTIM'S FUNERAL DRAWS CROWDS
GUN SIEGE INQUEST VERDICT
GUN VIOLENCE ESCALATES 3 - MORE SHOOTINGS
GUN FOUND IN MAN'S BUM
GUN TRADE TRIAL : LATEST
"GANGBUSTERS" SEIZE DEADLY MACHINE GUN
COPS SEIZE GUN HAUL
GUN THREAT NURSE JAILED
DRAMATIC TAPE OF GUN SIEGE POLICE
GUN AND AMMO FOUND BY BINS
PLAYGROUND GUN SHOCK - REACTIONS
GUN STRAIGHT
2011
A LONDON PICTURE
IT'S WRITTEN ALL OVER THEM

GUN STRAIGHT. 2011. 302 x 444 cm

GUNMAN EXECUTES LONDON CLUBBER
POLICE SHOOT GUNMAN DEAD
'GUNMAN KILLED PC IN COLD BLOOD'
GUNMAN
2011
Gilbert & George
A LONDON PICTURE
IT'S WRITTEN ALL OVER THEM

GUNMAN. 2011. 151 x 127 cm

N1 MACHINE GUN MAN 'COULD HAVE CAUSED MAYHEM'
GUNMAN RAIDS ST JOHN STREET BETS SHOP
GUNMAN IN ESSEX ROAD RAID
GUNMAN RAIDS N1 BETS SHOP
FIVE LIFE TERMS FOR RUSH HOUR GUNMAN
GUNMAN FIRED AT POLICE IN CAR CHASE
GUNMAN OPENS FIRE IN MARKET
DRIVE-BY GUNMAN TARGETS TAKEAWAY DINERS
GUNMAN WHO FIRED INTO PARTY CROWD FACES JAIL
DRUG DEALER GUNMAN JAILED
GUNMAN JAILED FOR CLUB ATTACK
GUNMAN IN GYM ROBBERY
MET SNIPERS SENT TO HUNT GUNMAN
GUNMAN CAUGHT ON CCTV
FOUR KILLED IN GUNMAN RAMPAGE
GUNMAN OPENS FIRE ON CLUB
GUNMAN WAS KNOWN 'FACE'
GUNMAN STRAIGHT
2011 A LONDON PICTURE
IT'S WRITTEN ALL OVER THEM

GUNMAN STRAIGHT. 2011. 226 x 381 cm

PUSHBIKE
GUNMEN
SHOOT
TEEN
TERROR
GUNMEN
BLAST
CRICKET
STARS
GUMEN
SHOOT
FATHER
AND SON
GUNMEN
2011
A LONDON PICTURE
IT'S WRITTEN ALL OVER THEM

GUNMEN. 2011. 151 x 127 cm

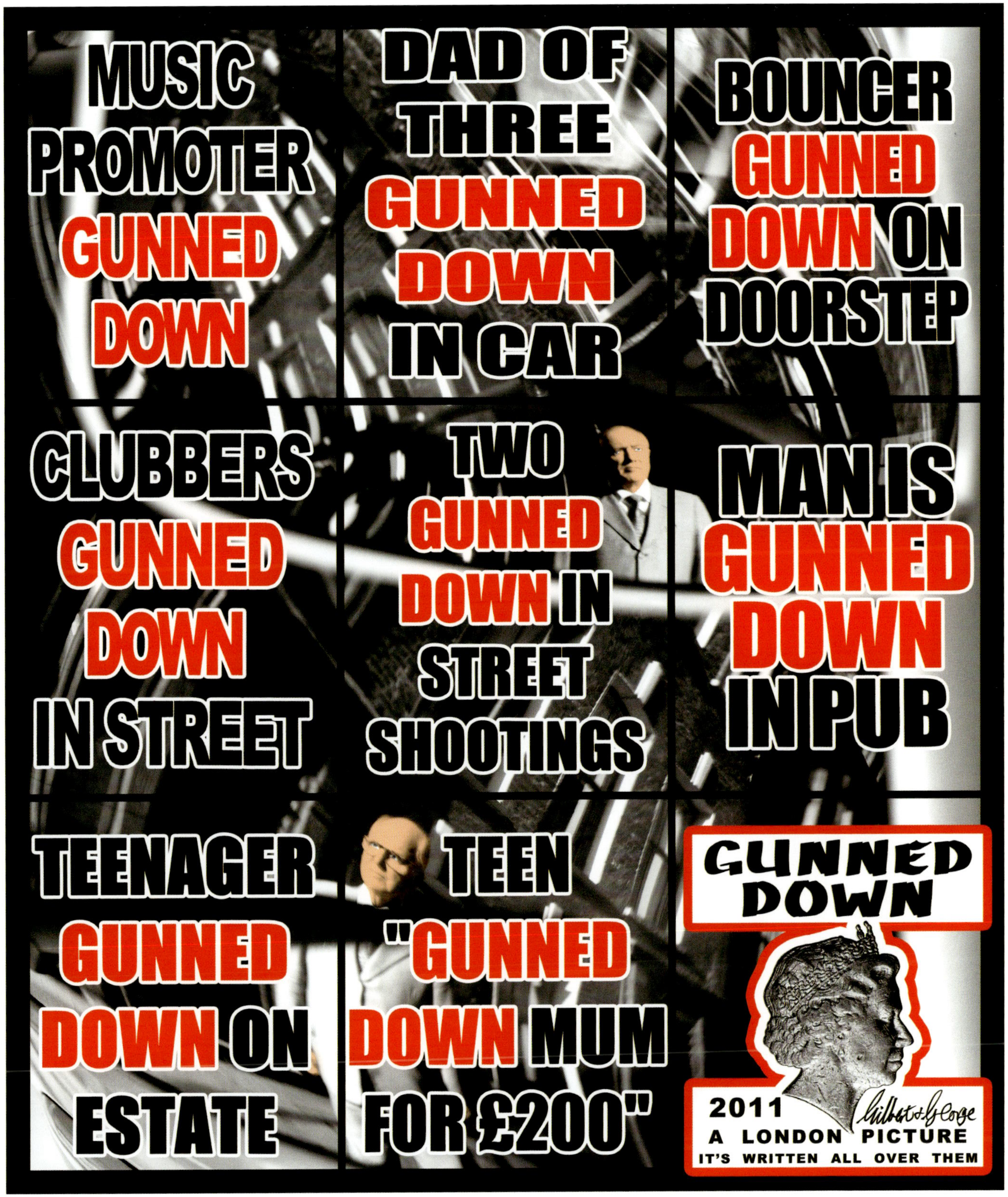
MUSIC PROMOTER GUNNED DOWN
DAD OF THREE GUNNED DOWN IN CAR
BOUNCER GUNNED DOWN ON DOORSTEP
CLUBBERS GUNNED DOWN IN STREET
TWO GUNNED DOWN IN STREET SHOOTINGS
MAN IS GUNNED DOWN IN PUB
TEENAGER GUNNED DOWN ON ESTATE
TEEN "GUNNED DOWN MUM FOR £200"
GUNNED DOWN
2011
A LONDON PICTURE
IT'S WRITTEN ALL OVER THEM

GUNNED DOWN. 2011. 226 x 190 cm

HACKNEY
GUNPOINT
MUGGINGS
SOAR
DOG
STOLEN
AT
GUNPOINT
CITY
SUPERWOMAN
MUGGED
AT
GUNPOINT
GUNPOINT
2011
Gilbert & George
A LONDON PICTURE
IT'S WRITTEN ALL OVER THEM

GUNPOINT. 2011. 151 x 127 cm

YOUNG GUNS BID FOR CUP GLORY
GUNS FOR SALE' TRIAL LATEST
ASSASSIN GUNS DOWN MOTORIST
GUNS
2011
Gilbert & George
A LONDON PICTURE
IT'S WRITTEN ALL OVER THEM

GUNS. 2011. 151 x 127 cm

MENTAL PATIENT FOUND HANGED
MAN IS FOUND HANGED IN FLAT
GAMBLING FATHER HANGED HIMSELF FROM TREE
CABBIE'S KILLER FOUND HANGED IN HIS CELL
TRAGEDY OF SON FOUND HANGED
SOCIAL WORKER FOUND HANGED
GIRL, 18, FOUND HANGED IN BEDROOM
MAN IS FOUND HANGED AT HIGHBURY HOME
BIZARRE DEATH OF FATHER HANGED FROM TREE
MUM'S FURY OVER STUDENT FOUND HANGED
DRIVING BAN DAD HANGED HIMSELF
MISSING WOMAN FOUND HANGED
TRAGEDY OF JOBLESS MAN FOUND HNAGED
ESSEX RD WOMAN FOUND HANGED
MYSTERY OF BOY, 10, FOUND HANGED
HANGED
2011
A LONDON PICTURE
IT'S WRITTEN ALL OVER THEM

HANGED

2011

302 x 254 cm

PAL DIES IN COPYCAT HANGING
FRESH INQUEST ON CELL HANGING
MAN FOUND HANGING IN GRAVEYARD
WOMAN FOUND HANGING IN CELL
HANGING TRAGEDY OF BOY AGED 10
BOY, 9, IN HANGING TRAGEDY
HANGING BOY'S "WARNINGS" WENT UNHEEDED
FATHER FOUND HANGING FROM TREE
HANGING
2011
A LONDON PICTURE
IT'S WRITTEN ALL OVER THEM

HANGING. 2011. 226 x 190 cm

BRITONS FLEE HOLIDAY BLAZE: PICTURES
HOLIDAY POISON FATHER: FIRST PICTURE
CITY BANKER HOLIDAY MURDER PROBE
HOLIDAY
2011
A LONDON PICTURE
IT'S WRITTEN ALL OVER THEM

HOLIDAY. 2011. 151 x 127 cm

OAP ROUTS HOODIES: DRAMATIC PICTURE
HOODIES THROW MAN FROM TRAIN
ISLINGTON: TORY MP CONFRONTS ESTATE HOODIES
HOODIES
2011
A LONDON PICTURE
IT'S WRITTEN ALL OVER THEM

HOODIES. 2011. 151 x 127 cm

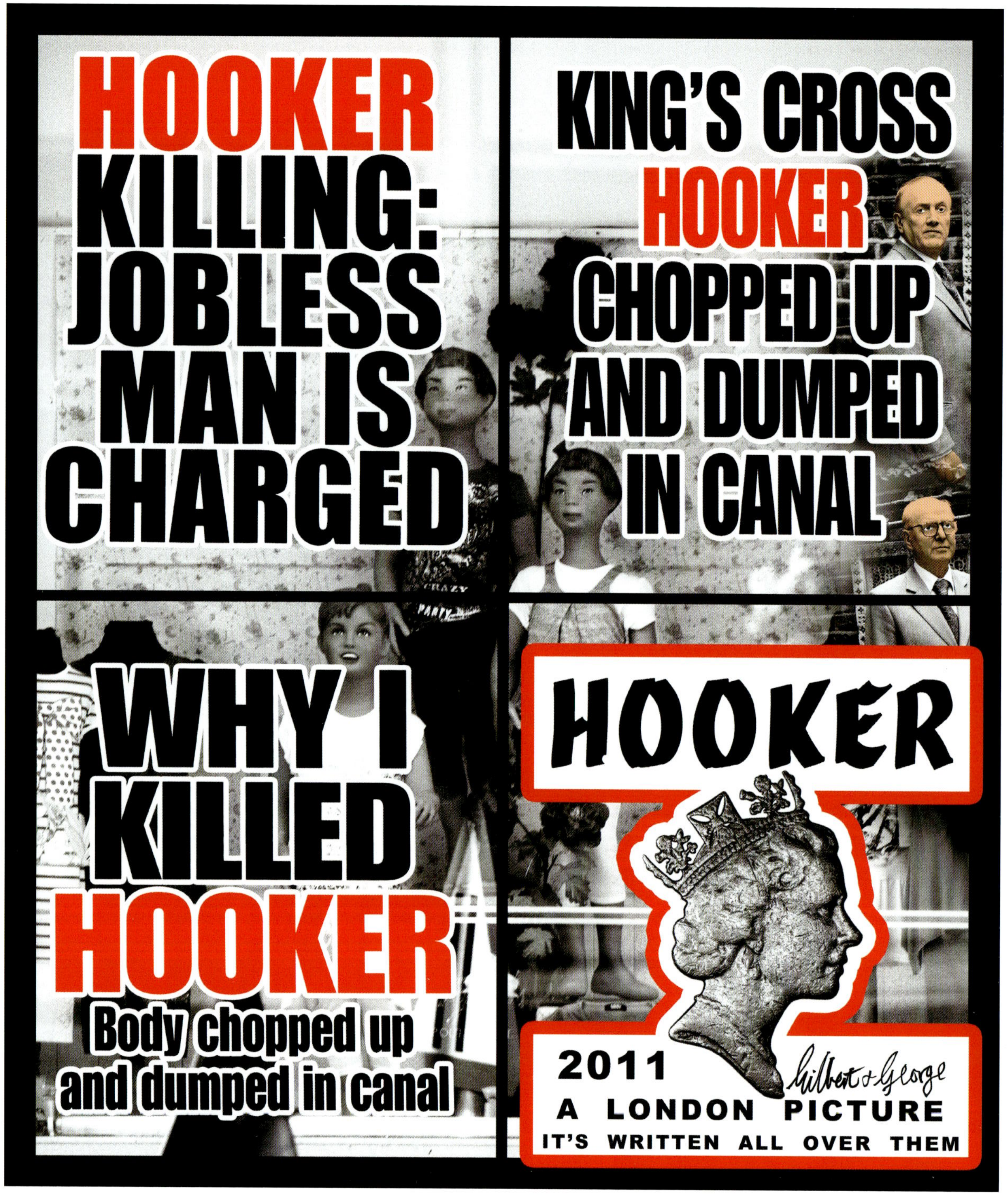
HOOKER
KILLING:
JOBLESS
MAN IS
CHARGED
KING'S CROSS
HOOKER
CHOPPED UP
AND DUMPED
IN CANAL
WHY I
KILLED
HOOKER
Body chopped up
and dumped in canal
HOOKER
2011
A LONDON PICTURE
IT'S WRITTEN ALL OVER THEM
Gilbert & George

HOOKER. 2011. 151 x 127 cm

ISLINGTON: PARTY SHOOTINGS
HORROR
HALF-TERM FAMILIES IN ALGARVE DROWNING
HORROR
BRITONS DROWN IN CRUISE
HORROR
HORROR
2011
A LONDON PICTURE
IT'S WRITTEN ALL OVER THEM

HORROR. 2011. 151 x 127 cm

HUNT FOR JAIL BREAK PRISONER
HUNT FOR SEX ATTACK GANG
COPS HUNT KILLER GANG SUSPECTS
HUNT FOR CLUES TO STREET FIGHT DEATH
HUNT FOR DRIVER'S RIDE-BY KILLER
MURDER HUNT AFTER PARK ASSAULT
£20,000 REWARD OFFERED IN MURDER HUNT
MURDER HUNT AFTER MYSTERY BEATING
HUNT FOR RAPE THREAT CONMAN
HUNT FOR N1 'SEX SNATCH' ATTACKERS
WHITECHAPEL POLICE HUNT RAPE GANG
SPY IN BAG: HUNT FOR MYSTERY COUPLE
GHOST HUNT AT SPOOKY NIGHTSPOT
"POO DUNNIT" HUNT FOR LOUT
HUNT FOR HIT MEN AFTER 2 ARE SHOT
HUNT
2011
A LONDON PICTURE
IT'S WRITTEN ALL OVER THEM

HUNT

2011

302 x 254 cm

ALLEY RAPE GANG HUNTED
999 CALLER HUNTED IN WOMAN'S KILLING
HOODIE GANG HUNTED AFTER ATTACKS
SEX ATTACKER HUNTED
BEDROOM SEX PROWLER HUNTED
HUNTED
2011
A LONDON PICTURE
IT'S WRITTEN ALL OVER THEM

HUNTED. 2011. 151 x 190 cm

SHOP
WORKER
IS HURT IN
GANG RACE
ATTACK
THREE
HURT
IN MOB
ATTACK
MAN IS
SERIOUSLY
HURT IN
UPPER ST
ATTACK
CAR WASH
WORKER
HURT IN
STABBING
COPS
HURT IN
SALES
FRENZY
HURT
2011
A LONDON PICTURE
IT'S WRITTEN ALL OVER THEM

HURT. 2011. 151 x 190 cm

LONDON ISLAM SCHOOL 'TEACHES HATE'
ISLAM 'INSULT' BRITON FACES LASH
BBC IN ISLAM CARTOON WAR
ISLAM
2011
A LONDON PICTURE
IT'S WRITTEN ALL OVER THEM

ISLAM. 2011. 151 x 127 cm

EXTREMIST
ISLAM
STRATEGY
ATTACKED
LONDON
ISLAM
SCHOOL
'TEACHES
HATE'
ISLAM
GROUP'S
LAST
MEETING
ISLAM
STRAIGHT
2011
Gilbert & George
A LONDON PICTURE
IT'S WRITTEN ALL OVER THEM

ISLAM STRAIGHT. 2011. 151 x 127 cm

WORLD'S TOP CONMAN ESCAPES JAIL
SOHAM KILLER'S JAIL SENTENCE
PHONE MUGGERS CAN ESCAPE JAIL
ARSENAL STAR'S JAIL PAY ROW
POP MOGUL OUT OF JAIL: PICTURE
DOHERTY IN JAIL OVER HEROIN
ROCK STAR'S JAIL WARNING
JAIL
2011
A LONDON PICTURE
IT'S WRITTEN ALL OVER THEM

JAIL. 2011. 151 x 254 cm

'COCKNEY CANNIBAL' FACING JAIL
TV EXEC FACES YEARS IN MIDDLE EAST JAIL
KILLER TO SPEND REST OF LIFE IN JAIL
JAIL BLOW FOR VIOLENT HIJACK RAIDER
JAIL FOR BARRISTER WHO TOOK PICTURES UP SKIRTS
ARSENAL STAR'S BROTHER FACES JAIL
BIN LADEN FANATIC FACES JAIL
EX-SPY FACES JAIL
SEX FIEND EX-COP FACES LIFE IN JAIL
SEX BEAST FACES JAIL
ANIMAL ACTIVISTS FACE JAIL FOR BLACKMAIL
LAW GRADUATES' BRAZIL JAIL ORDEAL
FURY AT BABY P MOTHER'S JAIL SENTENCE
GOOGLE BOSSES IN JAIL SHOCK
FATHER FACES JAIL FOR CRUELTY
JAIL STRAIGHT
2011
A LONDON PICTURE
IT'S WRITTEN ALL OVER THEM

JAIL STRAIGHT

2011

302 x 254 cm

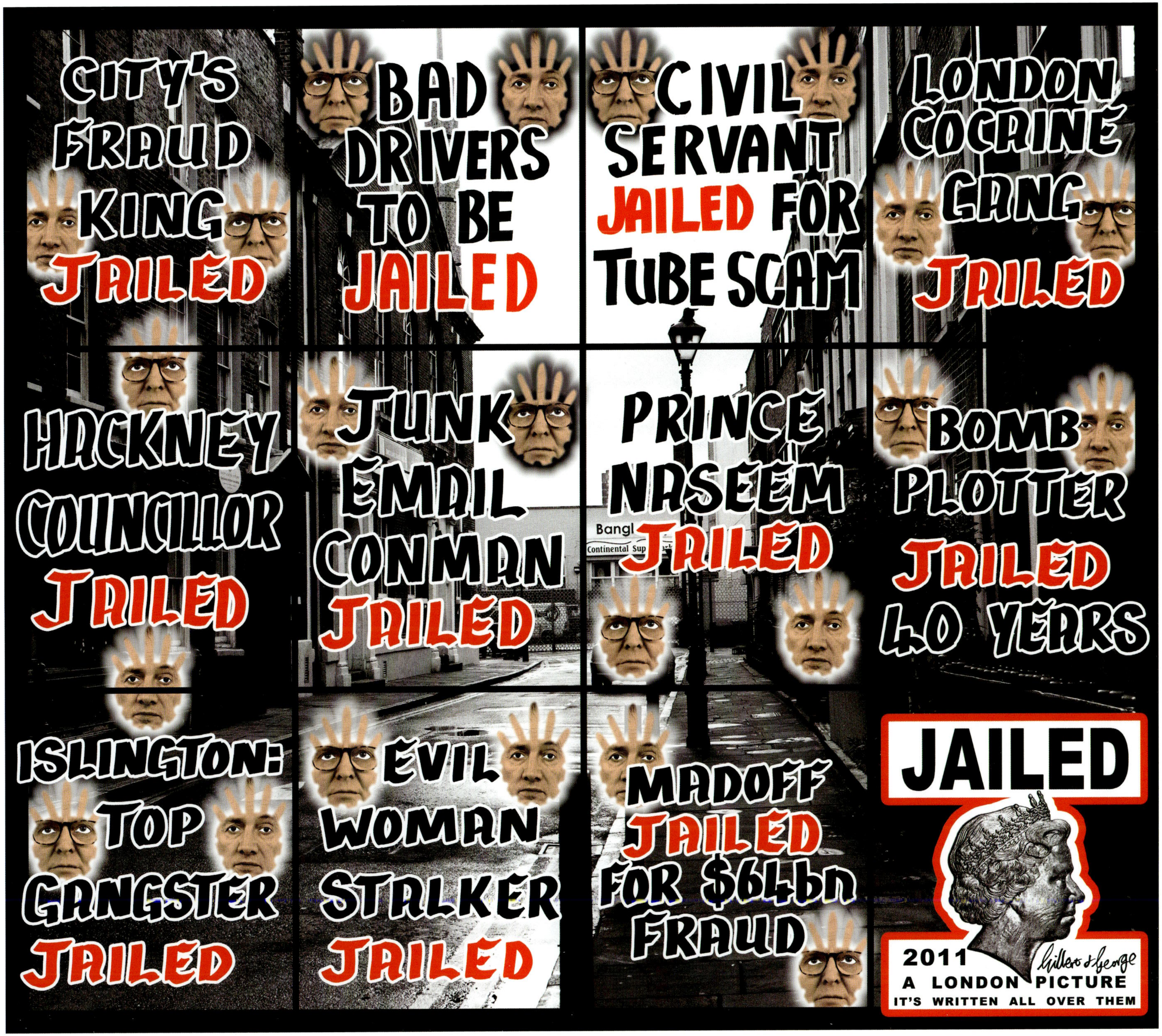
CITY'S FRAUD KING JAILED
BAD DRIVERS TO BE JAILED
CIVIL SERVANT JAILED FOR TUBE SCAM
LONDON COCAINE GANG JAILED
HACKNEY COUNCILLOR JAILED
JUNK EMAIL CONMAN JAILED
PRINCE NASEEM JAILED
Bangl
Continental Sup
BOMB PLOTTER JAILED 40 YEARS
ISLINGTON: TOP GANGSTER JAILED
EVIL WOMAN STALKER JAILED
MADOFF JAILED FOR $64bn FRAUD
JAILED
2011
A LONDON PICTURE
IT'S WRITTEN ALL OVER THEM

JAILED. 2011. 226 x 254 cm

SAUNA BROTHELS GANG JAILED
14-YEAR-OLD KILLER JAILED FOR SIX YEARS
BEGGAR JAILED FOR ASBO BREACH
DEPRAVED FORMER COUNCILLO JAILED AGAIN
CHARITY BOSS JAILED FOR FRAUD
MUM-BASH BLACKMAILER JAILED
TRAFFIC WARDEN JAILED FOR KILLING BEGGAR
LANDLORD JAILED FOR STEALING ELECTRICIT
LONDON'S TOP GANGSTER JAILED
MATALAN MURDER TRIAL 7 JAILED
JEALOUS GARDENER JAILED FOR PUB ATTACK
ESTATE RAPISTS JAILED FOR 23 YEARS
BLOOD FEUD' BROTHERS JAILED FOR PC ATTACK
ADAMS FAMILY CRIME BOSS JAILED
LUXURY STOLEN CAR RING: 2 JAILED
TOP TOTS - SEE INSIDE PAPER FOR DETAILS
JAILED GROOM WELCOME HOME

JAILED STRAIGHT. 2011. 302 x 571 cm

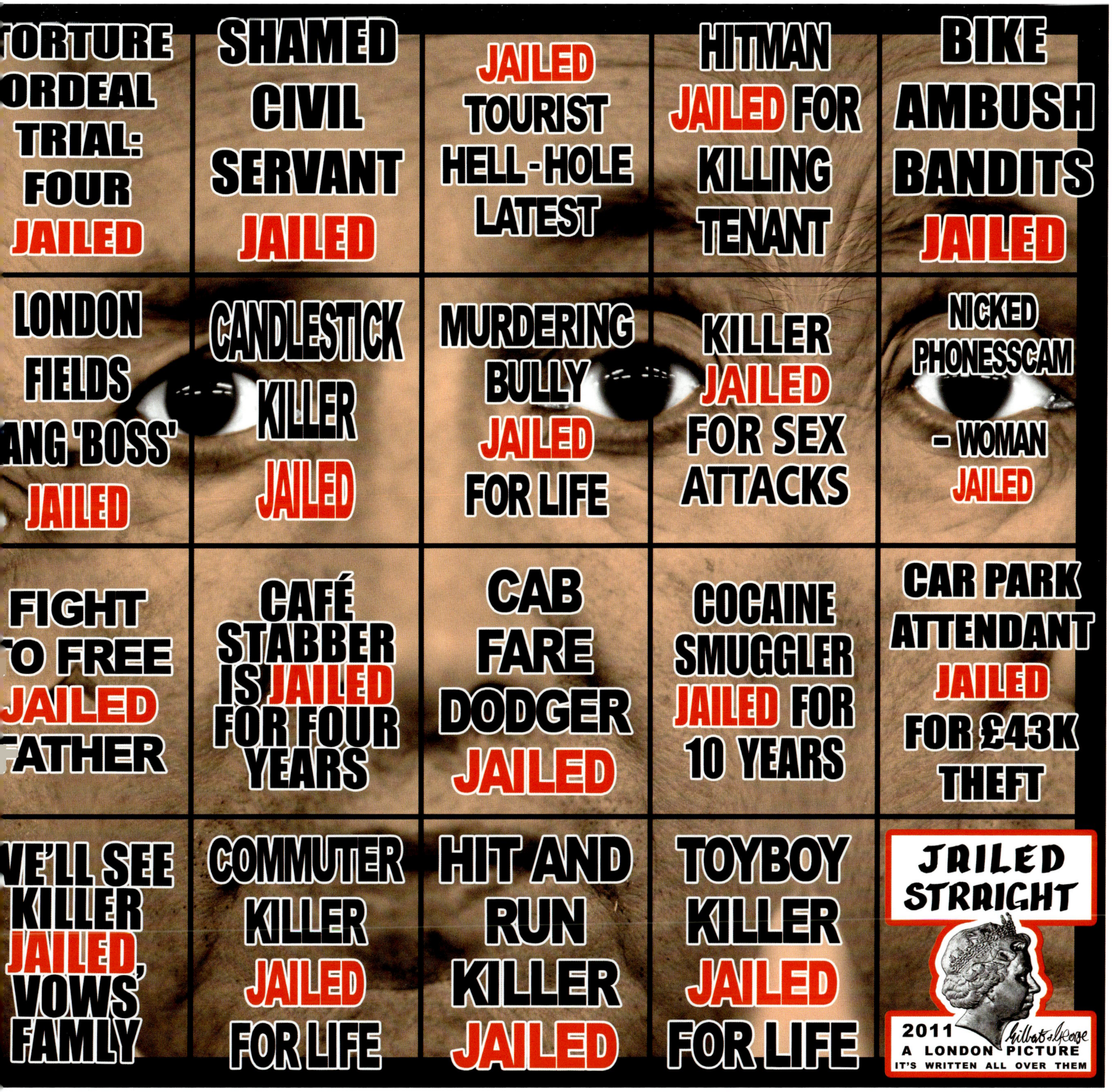
ORTURE
ORDEAL
TRIAL:
FOUR
JAILED
SHAMED
CIVIL
SERVANT
JAILED
JAILED
TOURIST
HELL-HOLE
LATEST
HITMAN
JAILED FOR
KILLING
TENANT
BIKE
AMBUSH
BANDITS
JAILED
LONDON
FIELDS
ANG 'BOSS'
JAILED
CANDLESTICK
KILLER
JAILED
MURDERING
BULLY
JAILED
FOR LIFE
KILLER
JAILED
FOR SEX
ATTACKS
NICKED
PHONESSCAM
- WOMAN
JAILED
FIGHT
O FREE
JAILED
ATHER
CAFÉ
STABBER
IS JAILED
FOR FOUR
YEARS
CAB
FARE
DODGER
JAILED
COCAINE
SMUGGLER
JAILED FOR
10 YEARS
CAR PARK
ATTENDANT
JAILED
FOR £43K
THEFT
E'LL SEE
KILLER
JAILED,
VOWS
FAMLY
COMMUTER
KILLER
JAILED
FOR LIFE
HIT AND
RUN
KILLER
JAILED
TOYBOY
KILLER
JAILED
FOR LIFE
JAILED
STRAIGHT
2011
A LONDON PICTURE
IT'S WRITTEN ALL OVER THEM

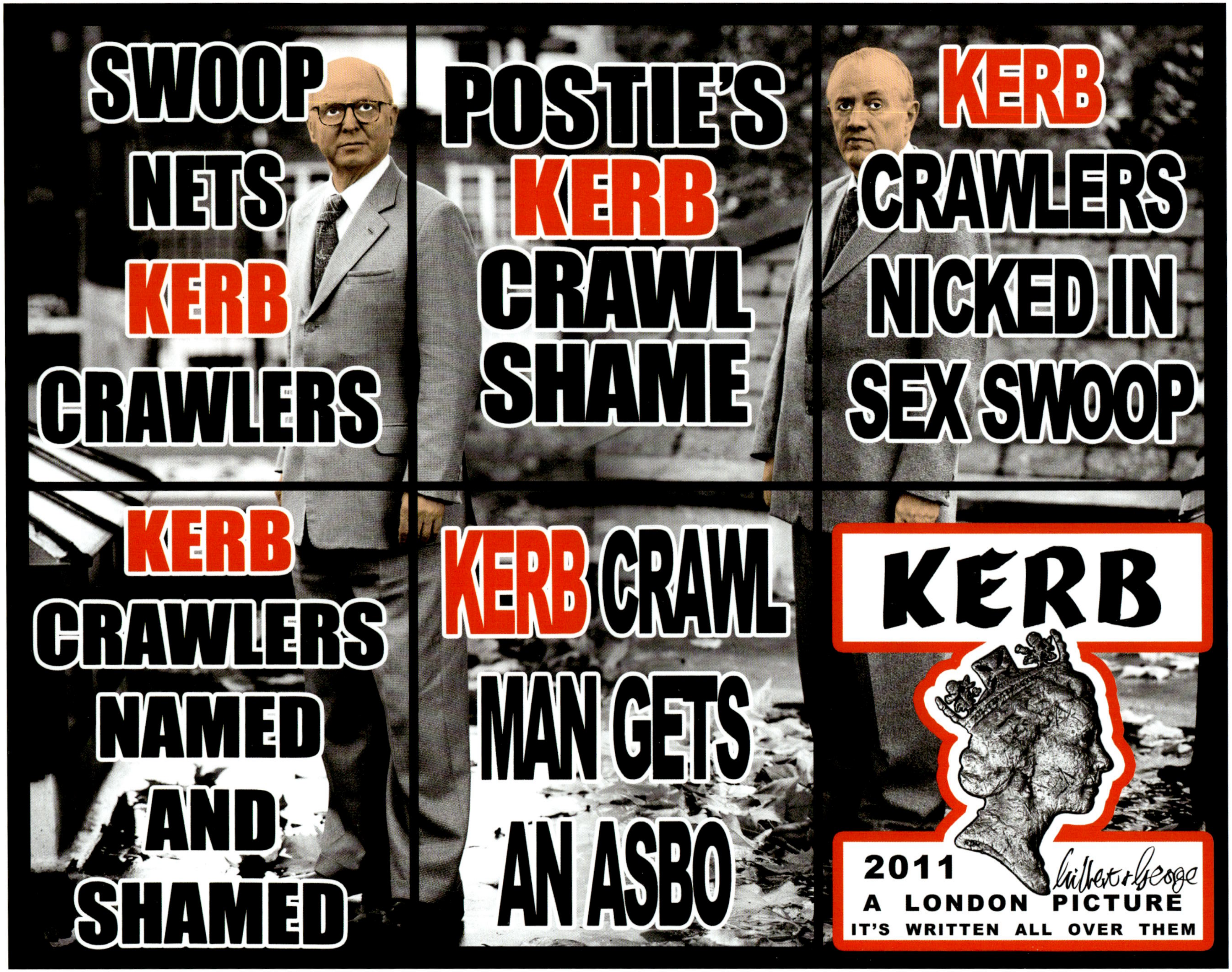
SWOOP
NETS
KERB
CRAWLERS
POSTIE'S
KERB
CRAWL
SHAME
KERB
CRAWLERS
NICKED IN
SEX SWOOP
KERB
CRAWLERS
NAMED
AND
SHAMED
KERB CRAWL
MAN GETS
AN ASBO
KERB
2011
A LONDON PICTURE
IT'S WRITTEN ALL OVER THEM

KERB. 2011. 151 x 190 cm

SCHOOLS' WARN OF KIDNAP BIDS
ESTATE AGENT JAILED OVER KIDNAP
'KIDNAP WAITER' MURDER CHARGES
KIDNAP
2011
Gilbert+George
A LONDON PICTURE
IT'S WRITTEN ALL OVER THEM

KIDNAP. 2011. 151 x 127 cm

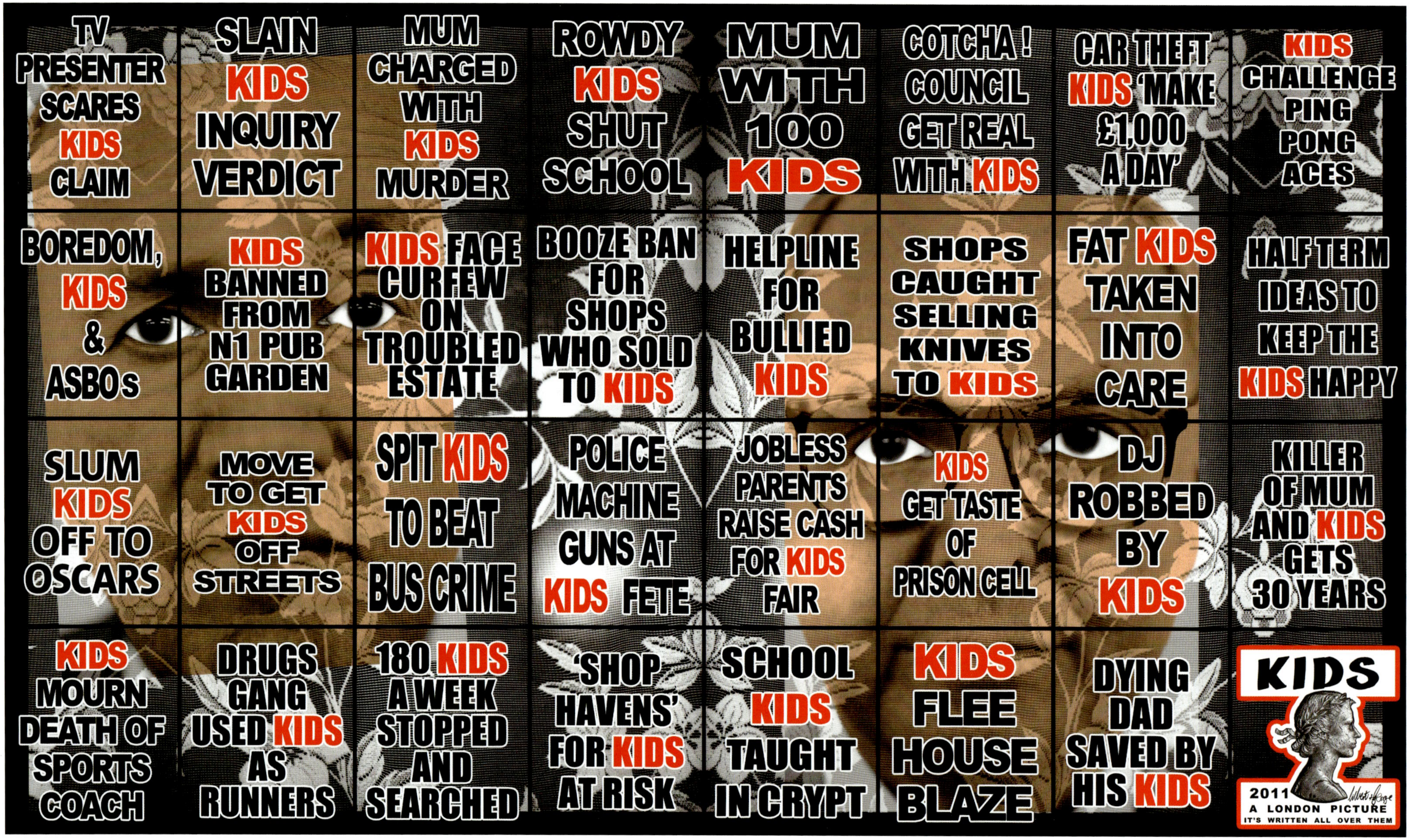
TV PRESENTER SCARES KIDS CLAIM
SLAIN KIDS INQUIRY VERDICT
MUM CHARGED WITH KIDS MURDER
ROWDY KIDS SHUT SCHOOL
MUM WITH 100 KIDS
COTCHA! COUNCIL GET REAL WITH KIDS
CAR THEFT KIDS 'MAKE £1,000 A DAY'
KIDS CHALLENGE PING PONG ACES
BOREDOM, KIDS & ASBOs
KIDS BANNED FROM N1 PUB GARDEN
KIDS FACE CURFEW ON TROUBLED ESTATE
BOOZE BAN FOR SHOPS WHO SOLD TO KIDS
HELPLINE FOR BULLIED KIDS
SHOPS CAUGHT SELLING KNIVES TO KIDS
FAT KIDS TAKEN INTO CARE
HALF TERM IDEAS TO KEEP THE KIDS HAPPY
SLUM KIDS OFF TO OSCARS
MOVE TO GET KIDS OFF STREETS
SPIT KIDS TO BEAT BUS CRIME
POLICE MACHINE GUNS AT KIDS FETE
JOBLESS PARENTS RAISE CASH FOR KIDS FAIR
KIDS GET TASTE OF PRISON CELL
DJ ROBBED BY KIDS
KILLER OF MUM AND KIDS GETS 30 YEARS
KIDS MOURN DEATH OF SPORTS COACH
DRUGS GANG USED KIDS AS RUNNERS
180 KIDS A WEEK STOPPED AND SEARCHED
'SHOP HAVENS' FOR KIDS AT RISK
SCHOOL KIDS TAUGHT IN CRYPT
KIDS FLEE HOUSE BLAZE
DYING DAD SAVED BY HIS KIDS
KIDS
2011
A LONDON PICTURE
IT'S WRITTEN ALL OVER THEM

KIDS. 2011. 302 x 508 cm

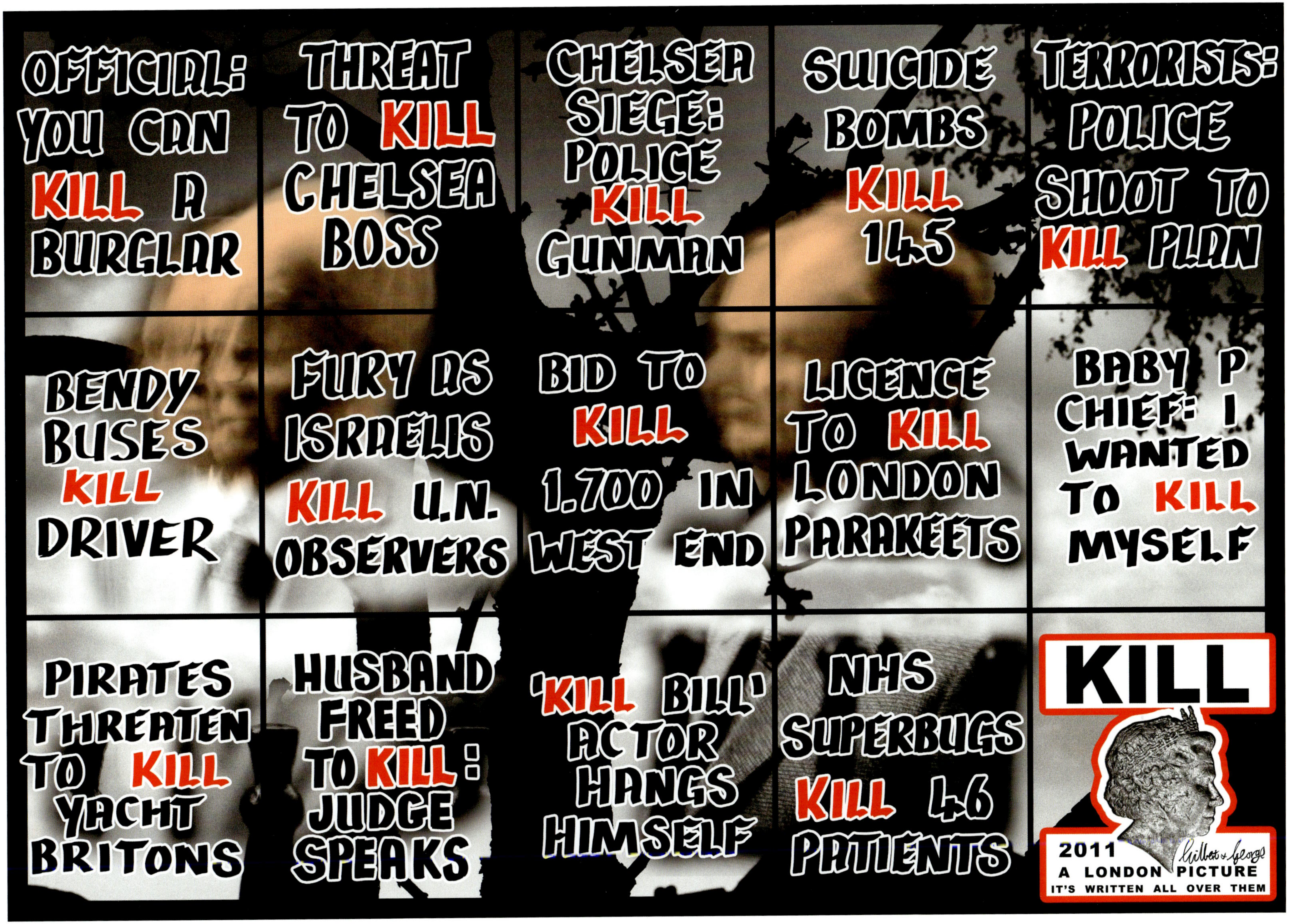
OFFICIAL: YOU CAN KILL A BURGLAR
THREAT TO KILL CHELSEA BOSS
CHELSEA SIEGE: POLICE KILL GUNMAN
SUICIDE BOMBS KILL 145
TERRORISTS: POLICE SHOOT TO KILL PLAN
BENDY BUSES KILL DRIVER
FURY AS ISRAELIS KILL U.N. OBSERVERS
BID TO KILL 1,700 IN WEST END
LICENCE TO KILL LONDON PARAKEETS
BABY P CHIEF: I WANTED TO KILL MYSELF
PIRATES THREATEN TO KILL YACHT BRITONS
HUSBAND FREED TO KILL: JUDGE SPEAKS
'KILL BILL' ACTOR HANGS HIMSELF
NHS SUPERBUGS KILL 46 PATIENTS
KILL
2011
A LONDON PICTURE
IT'S WRITTEN ALL OVER THEM
Gilbert & George

KILL. 2011. 226 x 317 cm

ROBBERS KILL SHOP BOSS: LATEST
SIX VICTIMS OF SLASHER'S MISSION TO KILL
WHY WAS MANIAC FREE TO KILL OUR MUM?
ASBO FOR MAN OVER KILL THREATS
DRUG DEALER: 'I DIDN'T KILL BETHNAL GREEN ARCHITECT'
MURDER COPS KILL RUMOURS
RAPPER'S PLOT TO KILL PREGNANT "EX"
BLUNDERS FREED SADIST TO KILL STUDENTS
KILL STRAIGHT
2011
A LONDON PICTURE
IT'S WRITTEN ALL OVER THEM

KILL STRAIGHT. 2011. 226 x 190 cm

BRITONS KILLED IN FERRY HORROR
LONDON BOYS KILLED BY TRAIN -PICTURES
COUPLE KILLED BY BURGLAR
BOMB HERO KILLED: DRAMATIC PICTURES
MANIAC WHO KILLED FOUR TIMES
100th BRITISH SOLDIER KILLED IN IRAQ
'1000 KILLED' IN STAMPEDE
TV CROCODILE HUNTER KILLED
NURSE KILLED PATIENTS FOR KICKS
SHOPKEEPER KILLED IN ARSON -PICTURE
LONDON SOLDIER KILLED IN IRAQ -PICTURE
BANKER KILLED BY 'POWER DRINKERS'
MOTORIST KILLED BY CAR THIEVES
CHILD MINDER KILLED BABY
DOME CASINO TYCOON KILLED
TRIBUTES TO SOLDIERS KILLED BY POLICEMAN
'INSANE' CITY BOSS KILLED BABY
AT RISK BABY 'KILLED BY MOTHER'
ESSEX: COUPLE KILLED ON RAIL TRACKS
INNOCENT SHOPPER KILLED AT CHECKOUT
BRITISH TROOPS KILLED IN AMBUSH
LONDON GIRL KILLED WITH PENKNIFE
NURSE KILLED IN GANG SHOOTOUT
KILLED
2011
A LONDON PICTURE
IT'S WRITTEN ALL OVER THEM

KILLED. 2011. 302 x 381 cm

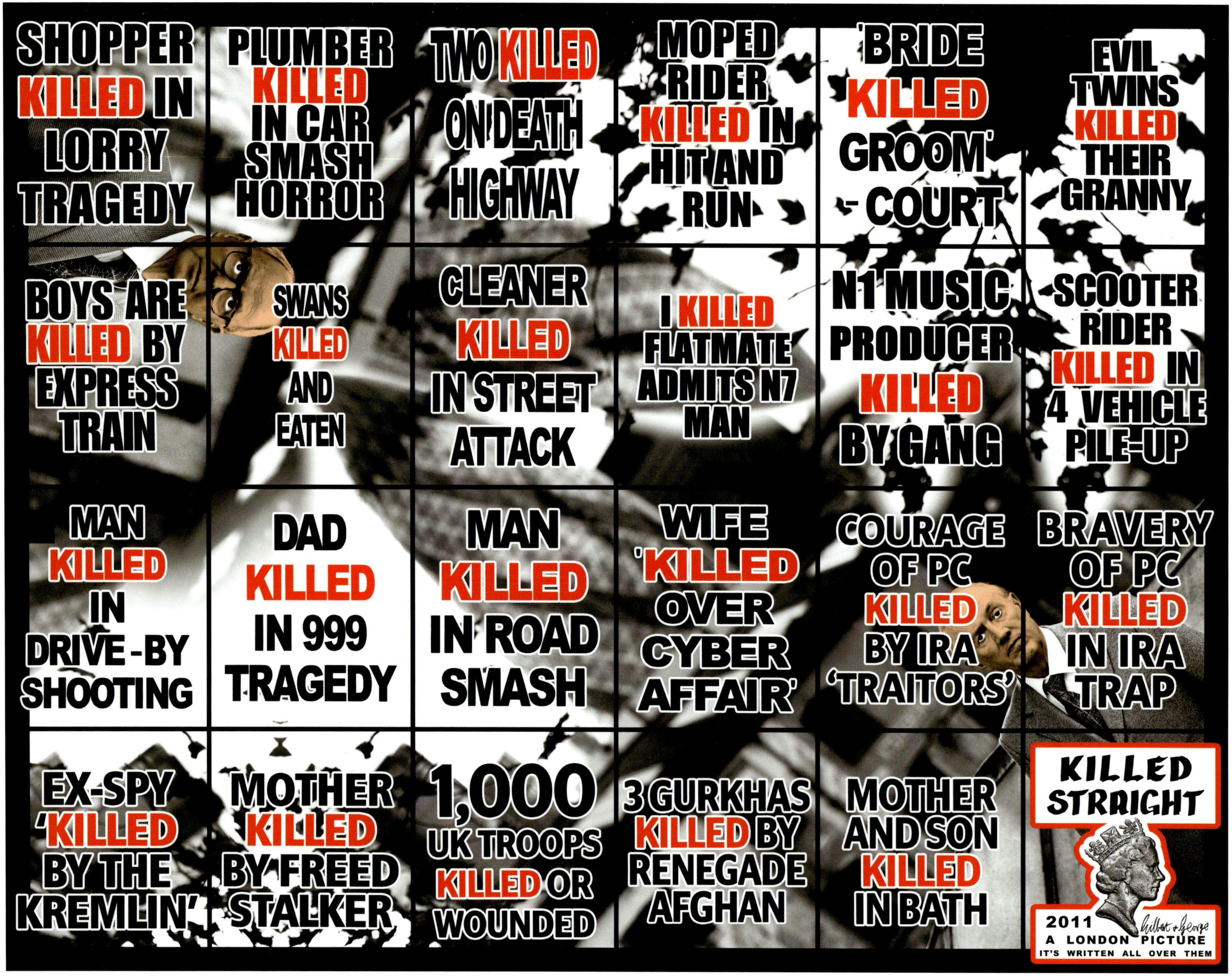
SHOPPER KILLED IN LORRY TRAGEDY
PLUMBER KILLED IN CAR SMASH HORROR
TWO KILLED ON DEATH HIGHWAY
MOPED RIDER KILLED IN HIT AND RUN
'BRIDE KILLED GROOM' - COURT
EVIL TWINS KILLED THEIR GRANNY
BOYS ARE KILLED BY EXPRESS TRAIN
SWANS KILLED AND EATEN
CLEANER KILLED IN STREET ATTACK
I KILLED FLATMATE ADMITS N7 MAN
N1 MUSIC PRODUCER KILLED BY GANG
SCOOTER RIDER KILLED IN 4 VEHICLE PILE-UP
MAN KILLED IN DRIVE-BY SHOOTING
DAD KILLED IN 999 TRAGEDY
MAN KILLED IN ROAD SMASH
WIFE 'KILLED OVER CYBER AFFAIR'
COURAGE OF PC KILLED BY IRA 'TRAITORS'
BRAVERY OF PC KILLED IN IRA TRAP
EX-SPY 'KILLED BY THE KREMLIN'
MOTHER KILLED BY FREED STALKER
1,000 UK TROOPS KILLED OR WOUNDED
3 GURKHAS KILLED BY RENEGADE AFGHAN
MOTHER AND SON KILLED IN BATH
KILLED STRAIGHT
2011
A LONDON PICTURE
IT'S WRITTEN ALL OVER THEM

KILLED STRAIGHT. 2011. 302 x 381 cm

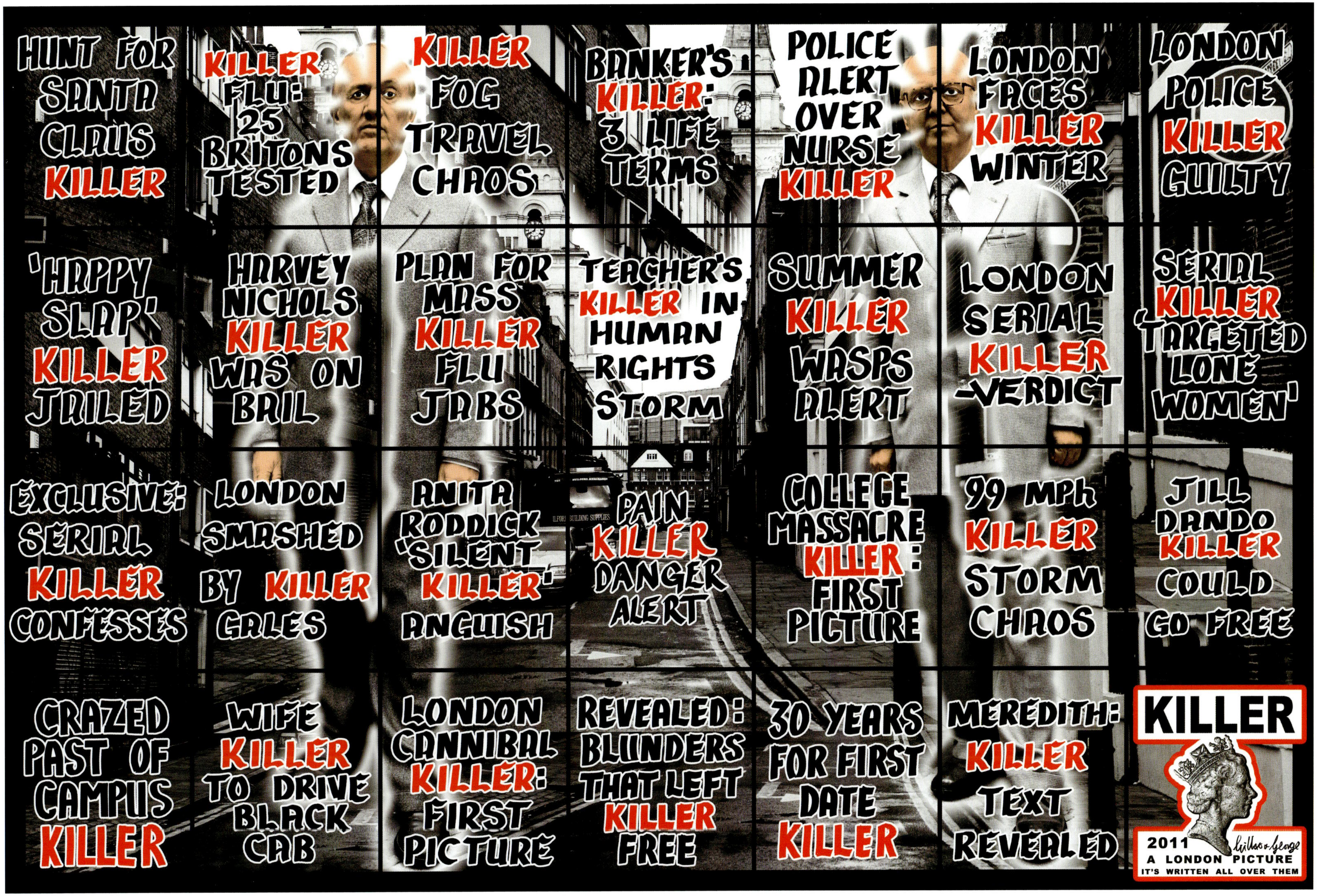
HUNT FOR SANTA CLAUS KILLER
KILLER FLU: 25 BRITONS TESTED
KILLER FOG TRAVEL CHAOS
BANKER'S KILLER: 3 LIFE TERMS
POLICE ALERT OVER NURSE KILLER
LONDON FACES KILLER WINTER
LONDON POLICE KILLER GUILTY
'HAPPY SLAP' KILLER JAILED
HARVEY NICHOLS KILLER WAS ON BAIL
PLAN FOR MASS KILLER FLU JABS
TEACHER'S KILLER IN HUMAN RIGHTS STORM
SUMMER KILLER WASPS ALERT
LONDON SERIAL KILLER -VERDICT
SERIAL KILLER 'TARGETED LONE WOMEN'
EXCLUSIVE: SERIAL KILLER CONFESSES
LONDON SMASHED BY KILLER GALES
ANITA RODDICK 'SILENT KILLER' ANGUISH
PAIN KILLER DANGER ALERT
COLLEGE MASSACRE KILLER: FIRST PICTURE
99 MPH KILLER STORM CHAOS
JILL DANDO KILLER COULD GO FREE
CRAZED PAST OF CAMPUS KILLER
WIFE KILLER TO DRIVE BLACK CAB
LONDON CANNIBAL KILLER: FIRST PICTURE
REVEALED: BLUNDERS THAT LEFT KILLER FREE
30 YEARS FOR FIRST DATE KILLER
MEREDITH: KILLER TEXT REVEALED
KILLER
2011
A LONDON PICTURE
IT'S WRITTEN ALL OVER THEM

KILLER. 2011. 302 x 444 cm

LOVE KILLER FOR HIRE CONVICTED
TOYNBEE HALL KILLER BID FOR FREEDOM
MATALAN KILLER WAS OUT ON BAIL
PLEA TO FIND BOXER'S KILLER
KILLER GUNS FOR HIRE
MY SON'S KILLER SHOULD NOT HAVE BEEN FREE
EMINEM KILLER QUIZZED OVER MULLER MURDER
NINE OVERCOM
BY KILLER
FUMES
KILLER KNIVES HAUL IS SEIZED
HIT & RUN TWIN KILLER JAILED
FERGIE'S KILLER AIDE CAUGHT
HEAD'S KILLER: CRUCIAL EVIDENC
DAMILOLA KILLER FREE AFTER JUST FOUR YEARS
MOTHER'S APPEAL TO FIND HER SON'S KILLER
KILLER OF TRANSEX PROSTITUTE FACES LIFE IN JAIL
WIFE KILLER GETS 8
YEARS

KILLER STRAIGHT. 2011. 302 x 635 cm

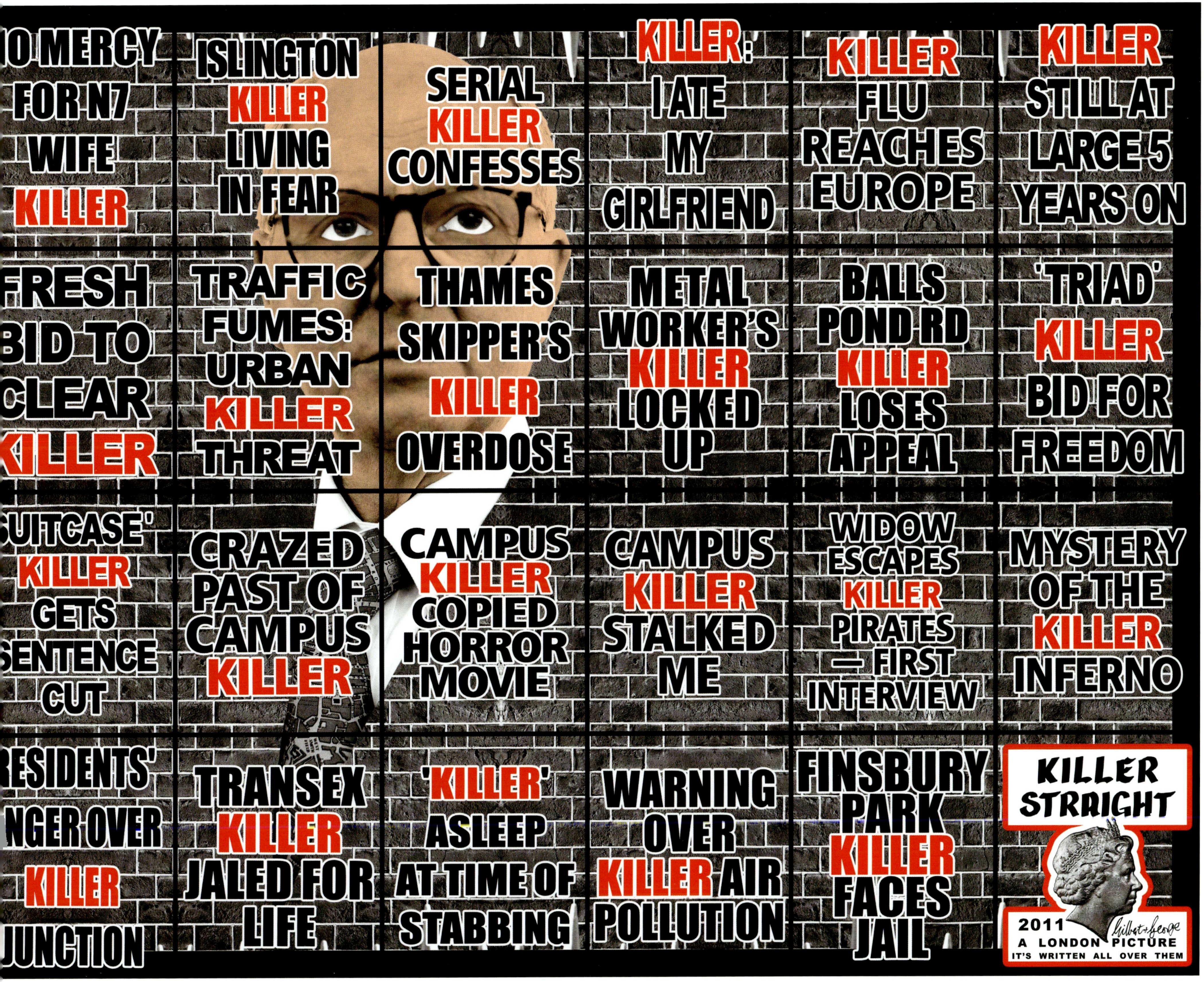
FOR N7
WIFE
KILLER
ISLINGTON
KILLER
LIVING
IN FEAR
SERIAL
KILLER
CONFESSES
KILLER:
I ATE
MY
GIRLFRIEND
KILLER
FLU
REACHES
EUROPE
KILLER
STILL AT
LARGE 5
YEARS ON
FRESH
BID TO
TRAFFIC
FUMES:
URBAN
KILLER
THREAT
THAMES
SKIPPER'S
KILLER
OVERDOSE
METAL
WORKER'S
KILLER
LOCKED
UP
BALLS
POND RD
KILLER
LOSES
APPEAL
'TRIAD'
KILLER
BID FOR
FREEDOM
KILLER
GETS
CUT
CRAZED
PAST OF
CAMPUS
KILLER
CAMPUS
KILLER
COPIED
HORROR
MOVIE
CAMPUS
KILLER
STALKED
ME
WIDOW
ESCAPES
KILLER
PIRATES
— FIRST
INTERVIEW
MYSTERY
OF THE
KILLER
INFERNO
KILLER
TRANSEX
KILLER
JAILED FOR
LIFE
'KILLER'
ASLEEP
AT TIME OF
STABBING
WARNING
OVER
KILLER AIR
POLLUTION
FINSBURY
PARK
KILLER
FACES
JAIL
KILLER
STRAIGHT
2011
A LONDON PICTURE
IT'S WRITTEN ALL OVER THEM

DAMILOLA KILLERS JAILED
KINSELLA KILLERS 'ANIMALS' SAYS DAD
MARY-ANN: LONDON KILLERS GET 27 YEARS
DAMILOLA KILLERS 'FREE IN 3 YEARS'
KILLERS FREED BY MISTAKE
MARY-ANN SHOCK: KILLERS WERE ON PROBATION
LAWYER'S KILLERS CAUGHT ON CCTV -PICTURE
KILLERS
2011
A LONDON PICTURE
IT'S WRITTEN ALL OVER THEM

KILLERS. 2011. 151 x 254 cm

HOLLOWAY: CCTV CLUE TO MOTORBIKE KILLERS
MUM'S PLEA TO CATCH SON'S KILLERS
THE STORY OF BEN KINSELLA'S EVIL KILLERS
NEWINGTON GREEN KILLERS JAILED FOR LIFE
BROTHER & SISTER TURNED KILLERS
VICTIM'S PARENTS FEAR KILLERS RELEASE
EC1 CANNABIS KILLERS JAILED FOR 19 YEARS
KILLERS STRAIGHT
2011
A LONDON PICTURE
IT'S WRITTEN ALL OVER THEM

KILLERS STRAIGHT. 2011. 151 x 254 cm

POLICE TERROR KILLING: LABOUR APOLOGY
'HAPPY SLAPPING' KILLING — VERDICT
EXCLUSIVE: MET CHIEF'S ANGER OVER TUBE KILLING
CAMDEN FOSTER MOTHER KILLING: MAN HELD
TESCO 'KILLING HACKNEY, HACKNEY MARKET'
SWINE FLU KILLING HEALTHY PEOPLE
RIOT OFFICER QUIZZED ON 'KILLING'
HACKNEY BOY'S KILLING: FIRST ARREST
HACKNEY MATALAN KILLING - PICTURES
CITY LAWYER KNIFE KILLING: VERDICT
HARROW MANIAC'S SEX KILLING
KILLING
2011
A LONDON PICTURE
IT'S WRITTEN ALL OVER THEM

KILLING. 2011. 226 x 254 cm

RAHMAN KILLING: 'TWO IN COURT
CLERKENWELL KILLING: 'LIFER' BIDS TO CLEAR HIS NAME
'V-SIGN LED TO UPPER STREET KILLING'
ESTATE'S SHOCK AT FIFTH KILLING
HOSPICE SLAMS MERCY KILLING
BUS KILLING: FAMILY'S FURY
PLEASURE BOAT KILLING: VERDICT
HORROR OF HIGHBURY STATION KILLING
CAR CLUE TO SHOP BOSS KILLING
SECOND CHARGE OVER ETEM KILLING
NEW CLUES IN SHOP BOSS' KILLING
'KILLING' FURY OVER KUNG-FU TRAINER'S CLASSES
FAMILY'S GRIEF AT SON'S KILLING
TWO MEN CHARGED IN BAR KILLING
FIVE CHARGED WITH KILLING SHAQUILLE
SIX CHARGED OVER SHOP BOSS KILLING
FOUR GUILTY OF MATALAN KILLING
MADDY: PARENTS SUE OVER KILLING CLAIM
RACHEL NICKELL KILLING - VERDICT
CCTV CLUE OVER UNSOLVED KILLING
MAN CHARGED WITH SCHOOLGIRL'S KILLING
POLICE PROBE HOSPITAL KILLING
TWO MORE ARRESTS OVER PC BLAKELOCK KILLING
FACEBOOK KILLING VERDICT
BUNGLED HONOUR KILLING TRIAL
HAPPY-SLAP KILLING: DRAMATIC PICTURES
FOOTBALL PLAYER KILLING: MAN IS CLEARED
KILLING STRAIGHT
2011
A LONDON PICTURE
IT'S WRITTEN ALL OVER THEM

KILLING STRAIGHT. 2011. 302 x 444 cm

BRUTAL KILLINGS HAUNT FAMILY
CALLS GROW TO SHUT CLUB AND END KILLINGS
KILLINGS SPARK MENTAL HEALTH REVIEW
MAN ON TRIAL FOR HIGHGATE KILLINGS
DASH TO ULSTER AFTER KILLINGS
KILLINGS
2011
Gilbert+George
A LONDON PICTURE
IT'S WRITTEN ALL OVER THEM

KILLINGS. 2011. 151 x 190 cm

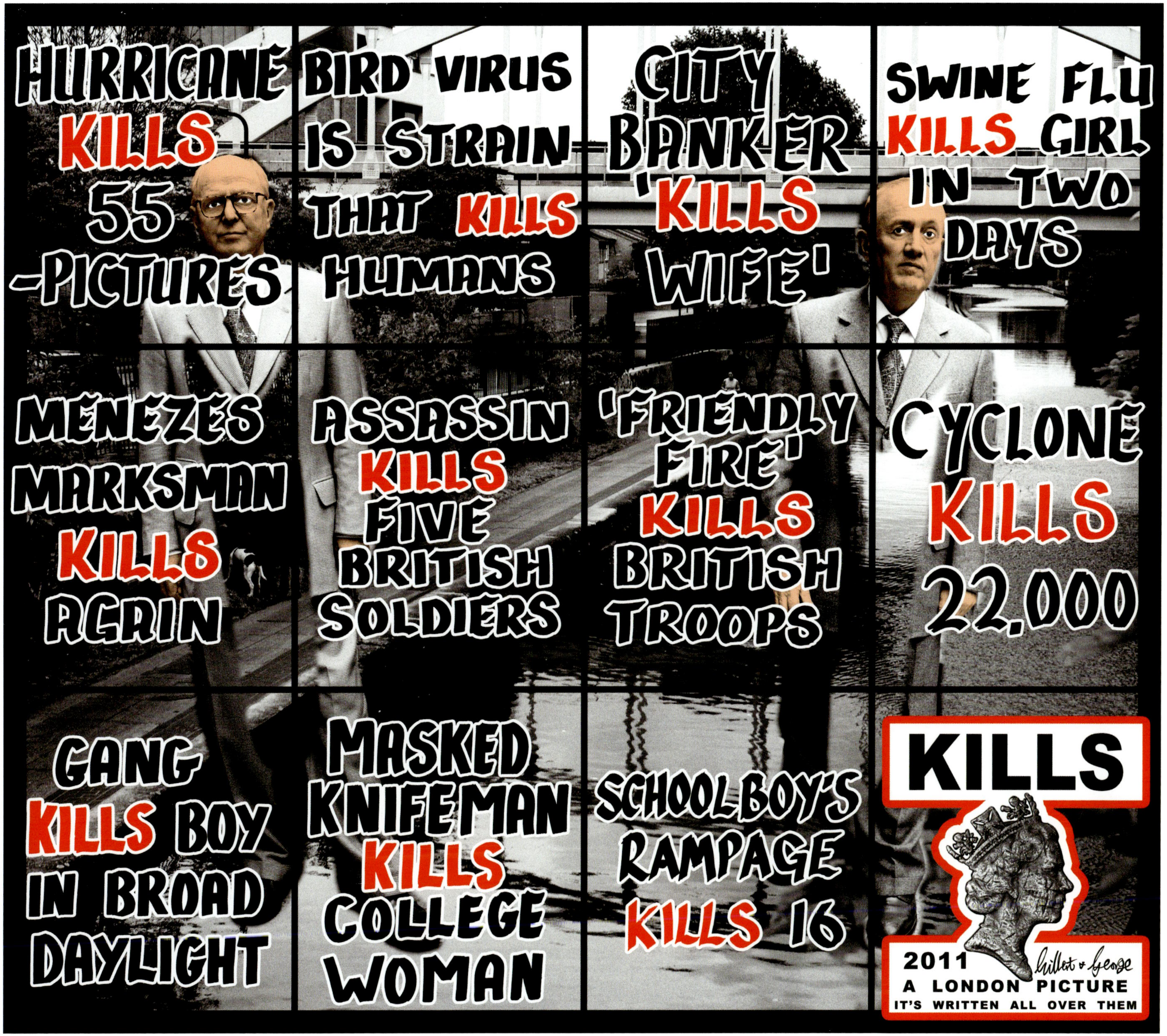
HURRICANE KILLS 55 -PICTURES
BIRD VIRUS IS STRAIN THAT KILLS HUMANS
CITY BANKER 'KILLS WIFE'
SWINE FLU KILLS GIRL IN TWO DAYS
MENEZES MARKSMAN KILLS AGAIN
ASSASSIN KILLS FIVE BRITISH SOLDIERS
'FRIENDLY FIRE' KILLS BRITISH TROOPS
CYCLONE KILLS 22,000
GANG KILLS BOY IN BROAD DAYLIGHT
MASKED KNIFEMAN KILLS COLLEGE WOMAN
SCHOOLBOY'S RAMPAGE KILLS 16
KILLS
2011
A LONDON PICTURE
IT'S WRITTEN ALL OVER THEM

KILLS. 2011. 226 x 254 cm

MENEZES MARKSMAN KILLS AGAIN
DODGY HEROIN KILLS THREE
BLAST KILLS THREE BRITISH SOLDIERS
KNIFE MANIAC KILLS 3 AT CRECHE
MURDER INQUIRY AS FIRE KILLS TWO
KILLS STRAIGHT
2011
A LONDON PICTURE
IT'S WRITTEN ALL OVER THEM
Gilbert & George

KILLS STRAIGHT. 2011. 151 x 190 cm

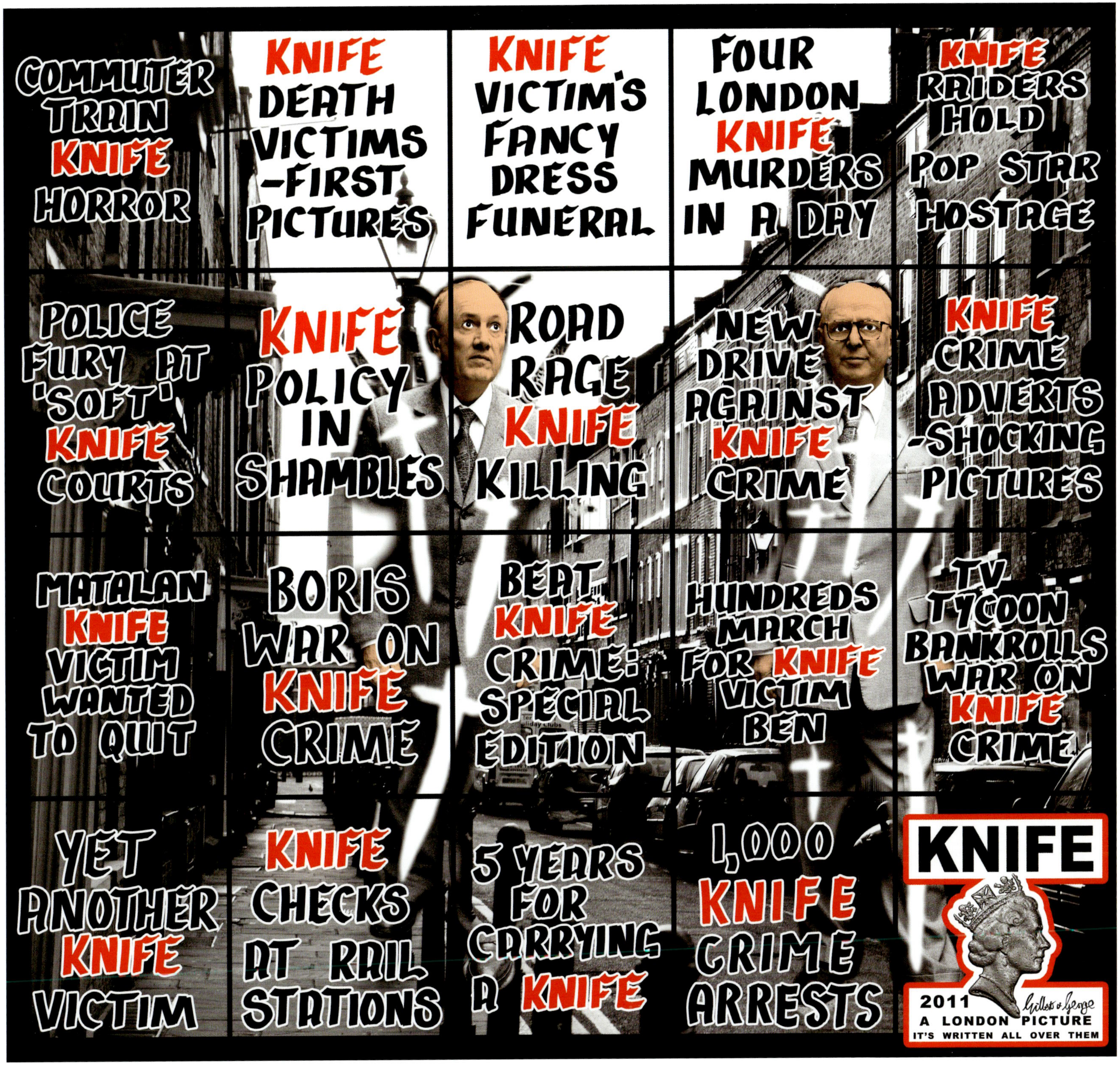
COMMUTER TRAIN KNIFE HORROR
KNIFE DEATH VICTIMS -FIRST PICTURES
KNIFE VICTIM'S FANCY DRESS FUNERAL
FOUR LONDON KNIFE MURDERS IN A DAY
KNIFE RAIDERS HOLD POP STAR HOSTAGE
POLICE FURY AT 'SOFT' KNIFE COURTS
KNIFE POLICY IN SHAMBLES
ROAD RAGE KNIFE KILLING
NEW DRIVE AGAINST KNIFE CRIME
KNIFE CRIME ADVERTS -SHOCKING PICTURES
MATALAN KNIFE VICTIM WANTED TO QUIT
BORIS WAR ON KNIFE CRIME
BEAT KNIFE CRIME: SPECIAL EDITION
HUNDREDS MARCH FOR KNIFE VICTIM BEN
TV TYCOON BANKROLLS WAR ON KNIFE CRIME
YET ANOTHER KNIFE VICTIM
KNIFE CHECKS AT RAIL STATIONS
5 YEARS FOR CARRYING A KNIFE
1,000 KNIFE CRIME ARRESTS
KNIFE
2011
A LONDON PICTURE
IT'S WRITTEN ALL OVER THEM

KNIFE. 2011. 302 x 317 cm

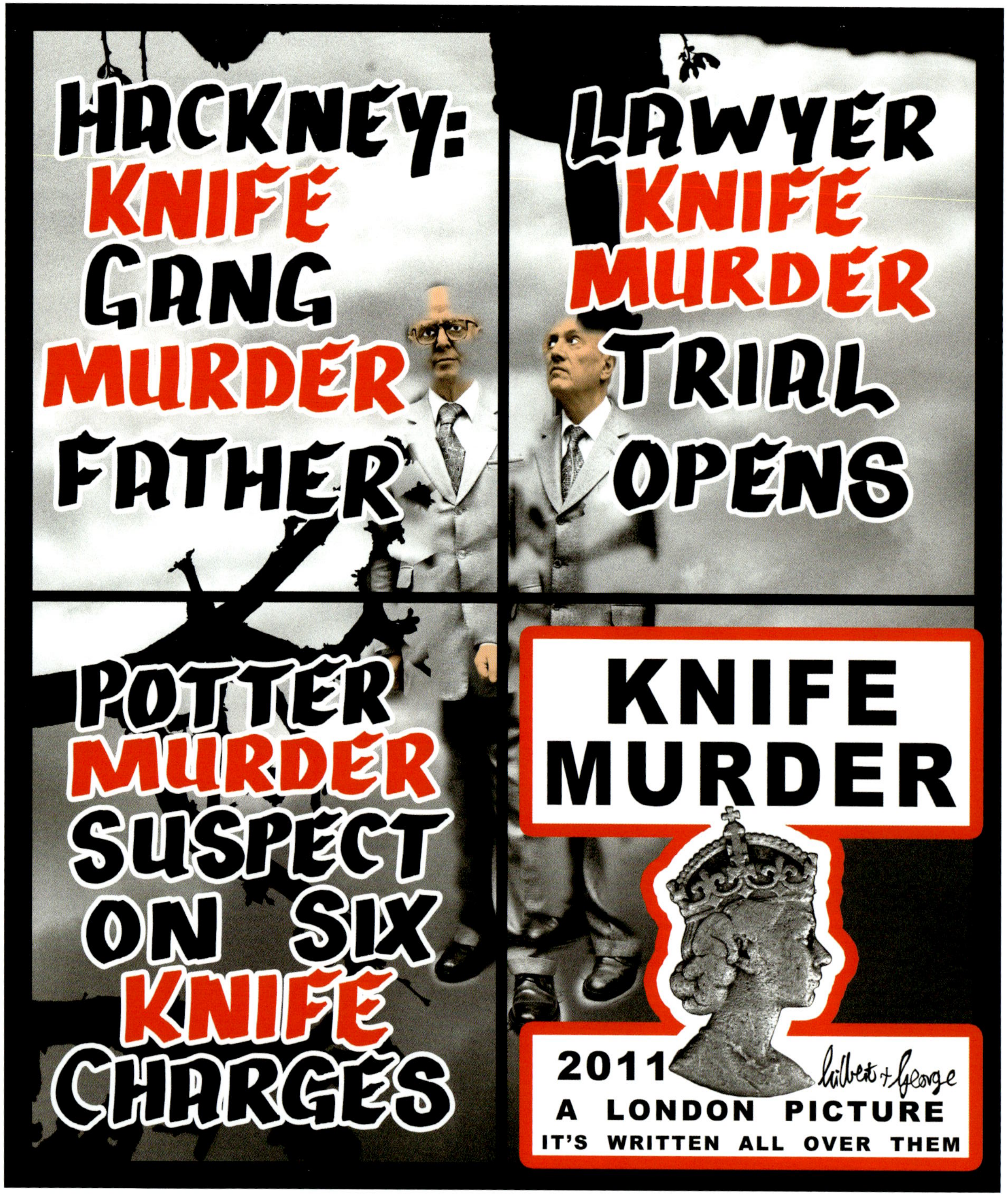
HACKNEY:
KNIFE
GANG
MURDER
FATHER
LAWYER
KNIFE
MURDER
TRIAL
OPENS
POTTER
MURDER
SUSPECT
ON SIX
KNIFE
CHARGES
KNIFE
MURDER
2011
Gilbert & George
A LONDON PICTURE
IT'S WRITTEN ALL OVER THEM

KNIFE MURDER. 2011. 151 x 127 cm

WOMAN'S DOORSTEP KNIFE TERROR
KNIFE GIRL'S THREAT TO KILL VICTIM
MP'S KNIFE CRIME HORROR
HOSPITAL CALL TO FIGHT KNIFE CRIME
PARKING WARDEN'S KNIFE TERROR
TERROR AT HANDS OF KNIFE KILLER
KNIFE CRIME: IS IT OUT OF CONTROL?
COUNCIL FLAT KNIFE KILLER ON THE RUN
N1 SHOP WORKER'S KNIFE ORDEAL
KNIFE SALES WARNING TO STORES
WINDOW CLEANER CHASED PARTNER WITH KNIFE
KNIFE FIEND DETAINED IN MENTAL HOSPITAL
POLICE LAUNCH KNIFE AMNESTY
MAN SURVIVES FRENZIED KNIFE ATTACK
CLUB DJ INJURED IN KNIFE ATTACK
TEEN'S FACE SLASHED BY KNIFE FIEND
FATHER'S KNIFE DEATH: MAN CHARGED
VICAR'S CRUSADE AGAINST KNIFE CMIME
COPS LAUNCH KNIFE AMNESTY
TEXT TIP-OFF SCHEME TO COMBAT KNIFE CRIME
OUTRAGE AT KNIFE SHOW LEAFLET STUNT
DRAMATIC FALL IN KNIFE CRIME
CAR-PARK KNIFE RAPIST IN COURT
ISSCHAN'S PARENTS' KNIFE CAMPAIGN
JUDGE STICKS KNIFE IN HACKNEY
BAKERY WORKER WENT HOME WITH KNIFE IN HEAD
OONA LAUNCHES KNIFE CRIME SCHEME
KNIFE STRAIGHT
2011
Gilbert & George
A LONDON PICTURE
IT'S WRITTEN ALL OVER THEM

KNIFE STRAIGHT. 2011. 302 x 444 cm

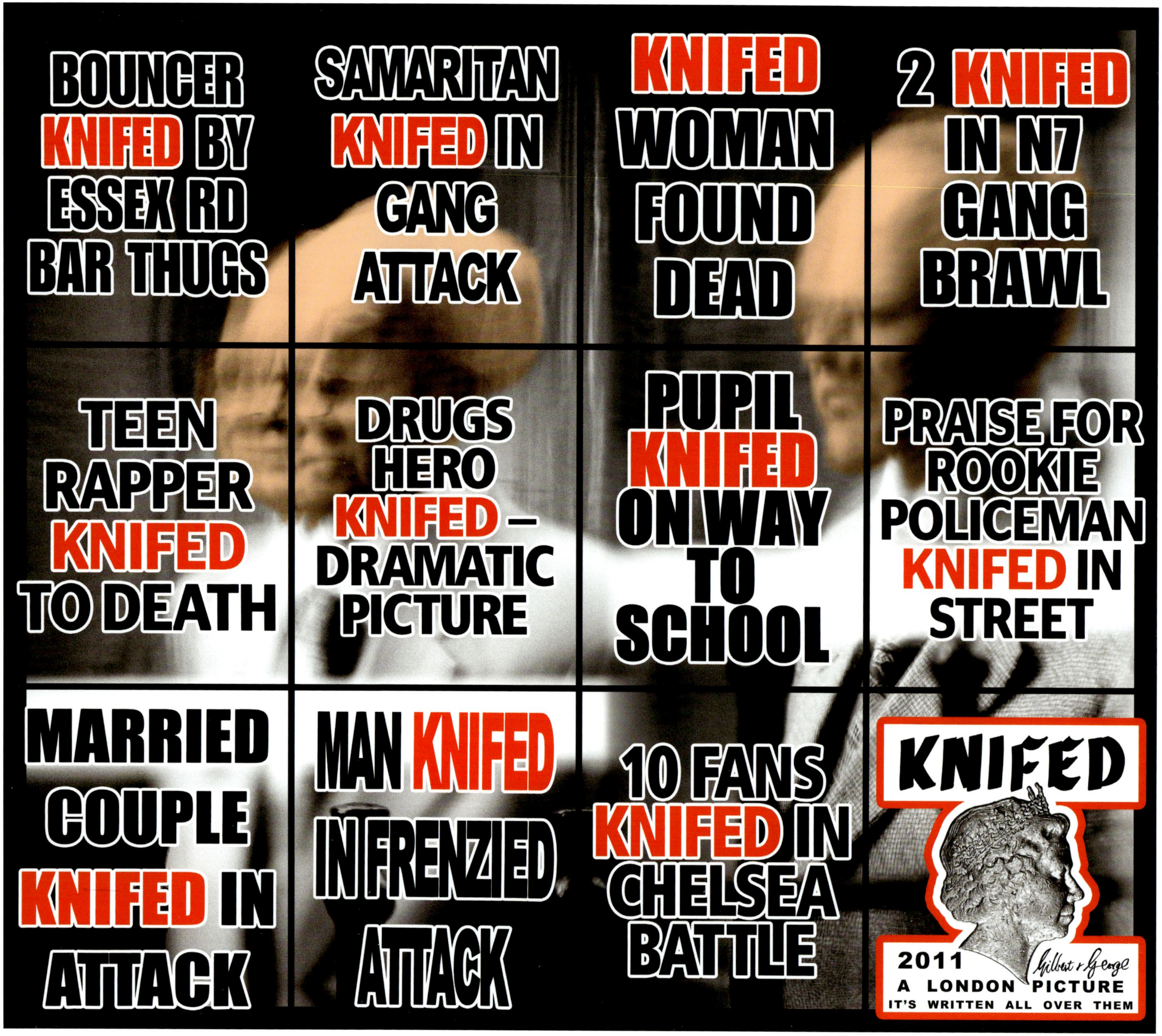
BOUNCER KNIFED BY ESSEX RD BAR THUGS
SAMARITAN KNIFED IN GANG ATTACK
KNIFED WOMAN FOUND DEAD
2 KNIFED IN N7 GANG BRAWL
TEEN RAPPER KNIFED TO DEATH
DRUGS HERO KNIFED – DRAMATIC PICTURE
PUPIL KNIFED ON WAY TO SCHOOL
PRAISE FOR ROOKIE POLICEMAN KNIFED IN STREET
MARRIED COUPLE KNIFED IN ATTACK
MAN KNIFED IN FRENZIED ATTACK
10 FANS KNIFED IN CHELSEA BATTLE
KNIFED
2011
A LONDON PICTURE
IT'S WRITTEN ALL OVER THEM

KNIFED. 2011. 226 x 254 cm

HAIRCUT
ROW DAD
KNIFED TO
DEATH
FATHER
KNIFED
TO DEATH
IN
STREET
BUTCHER
KNIFED
TO DEATH
KNIFED
TO
DEATH
2011
A LONDON PICTURE
IT'S WRITTEN ALL OVER THEM

KNIFED TO DEATH. 2011. 151 x 127 cm

CANAL KNIFEMAN HUNTED
TERROR OF NIGHT CLUB KNIFEMAN
KNIFEMAN HUNTED AFTER N1 RAMPAGE
MASKED KNIFEMAN ATTACKS PUPIL
SHOPPERS FLEE FROM KNIFEMAN IN CHASE
MY ESCAPE FROM CRAZED KNIFEMAN
CRAZED KNIFEMAN HORROR ATTACK
TEENAGE KNIFEMAN ESCAPES JAIL
'MURDER ATTACK' HUNT FOR KNIFEMAN
HUNT FOR ROAD RAGE KNIFEMAN
TRAIL OF CRAZED TERROR KNIFEMAN
KNIFEMAN
2011
A LONDON PICTURE
IT'S WRITTEN ALL OVER THEM

KNIFEMAN. 2011. 226 x 254 cm

LAD, 11, KNIFED MUM'S ATTACKER
TEENAGER JAILED FOR ATTACK ON SCHOOL MATE
EX - SOLDIER BEAT PAL INTO COMA
MY MATE TRIED TO MURDER ME
OSCAR GLORY FOR LOCAL LAD
LADPALMATE
2011
Gilbert & George
A LONDON PICTURE
IT'S WRITTEN ALL OVER THEM

LADPALMATE. 2011. 151 x 190 cm

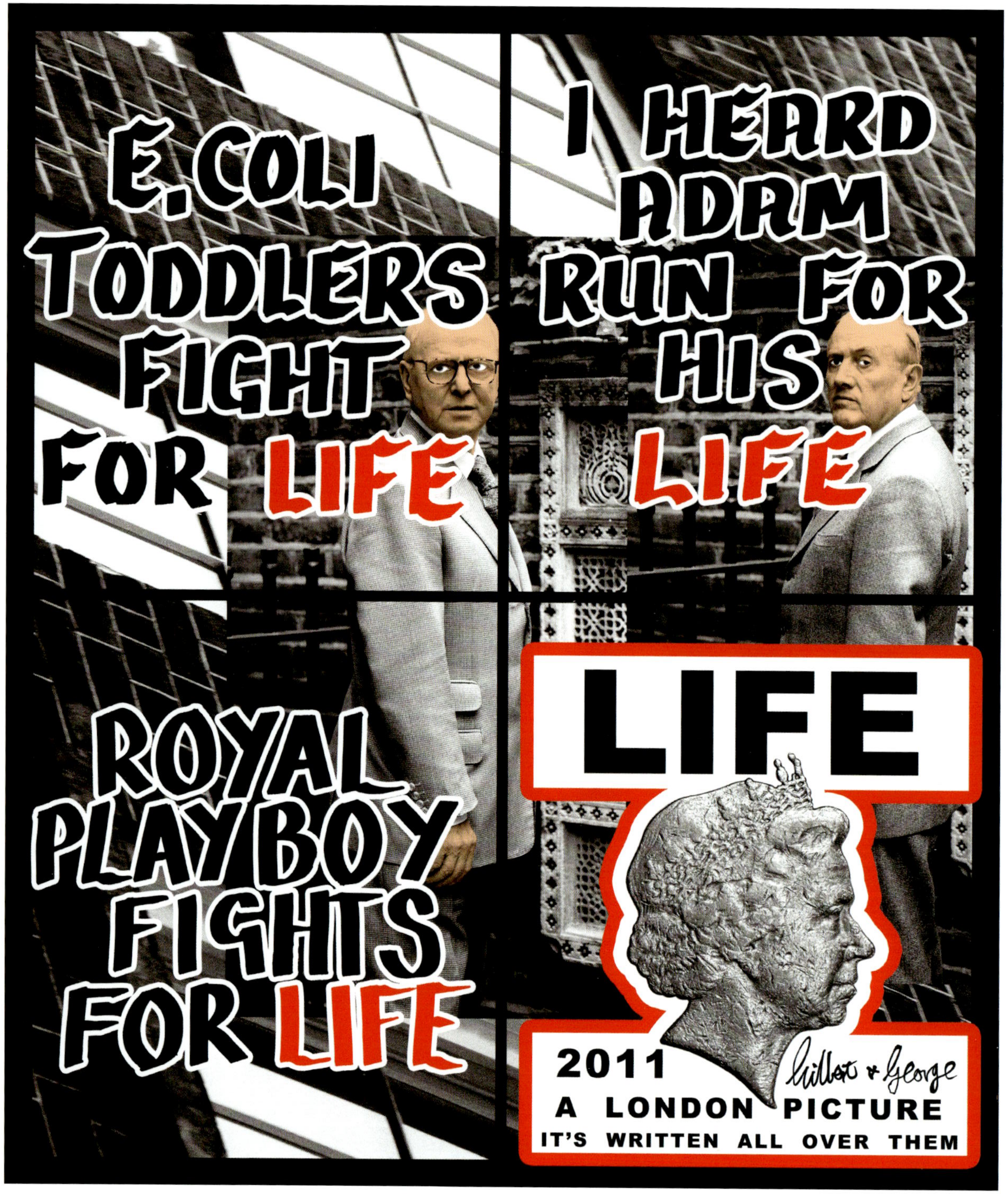
E.COLI TODDLERS FIGHT FOR LIFE
I HEARD ADAM RUN FOR HIS LIFE
ROYAL PLAYBOY FIGHTS FOR LIFE
LIFE
2011
Gilbert & George
A LONDON PICTURE
IT'S WRITTEN ALL OVER THEM

LIFE. 2011. 151 x 127 cm

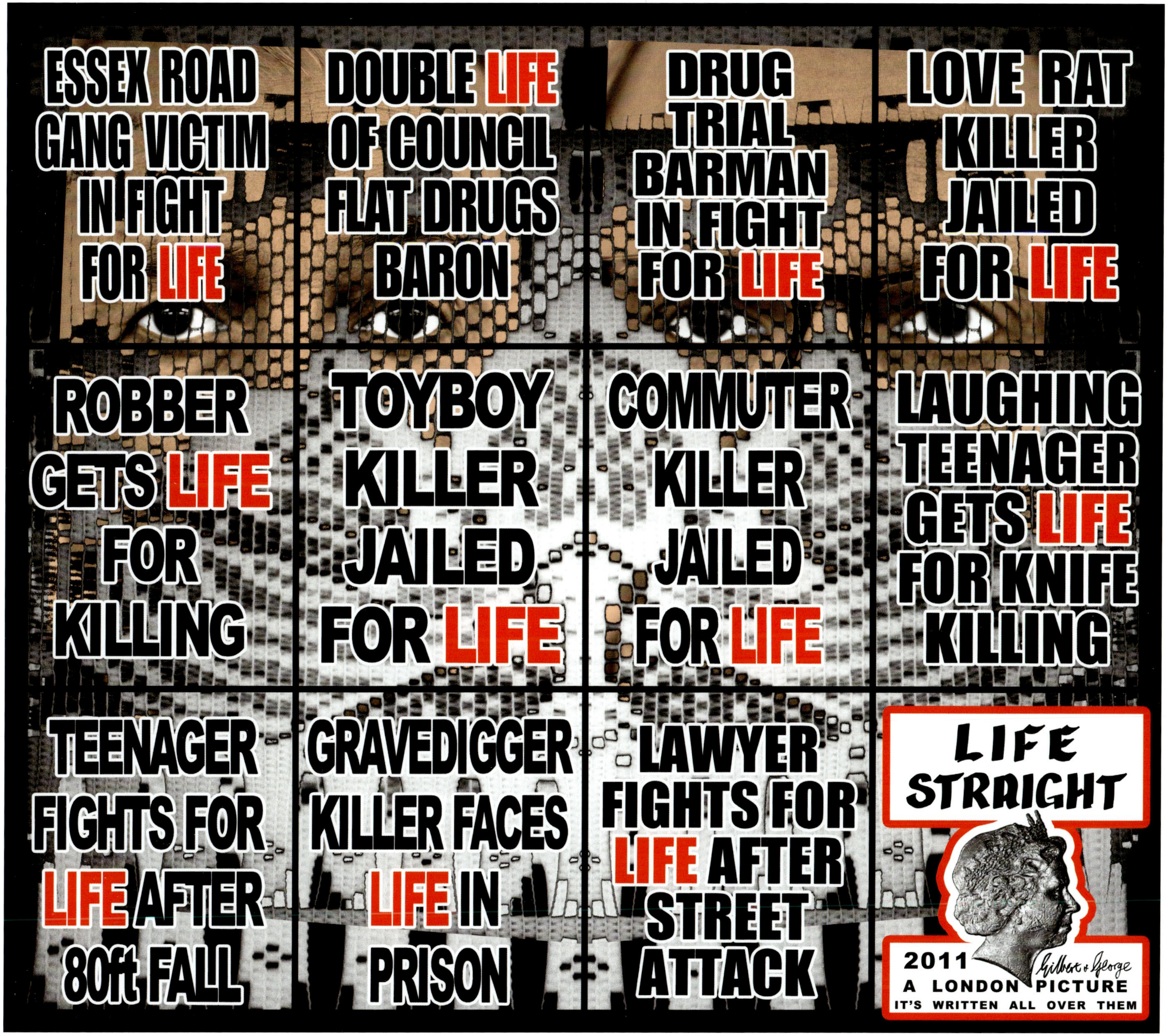
ESSEX ROAD GANG VICTIM IN FIGHT FOR LIFE
DOUBLE LIFE OF COUNCIL FLAT DRUGS BARON
DRUG TRIAL BARMAN IN FIGHT FOR LIFE
LOVE RAT KILLER JAILED FOR LIFE
ROBBER GETS LIFE FOR KILLING
TOYBOY KILLER JAILED FOR LIFE
COMMUTER KILLER JAILED FOR LIFE
LAUGHING TEENAGER GETS LIFE FOR KNIFE KILLING
TEENAGER FIGHTS FOR LIFE AFTER 80ft FALL
GRAVEDIGGER KILLER FACES LIFE IN PRISON
LAWYER FIGHTS FOR LIFE AFTER STREET ATTACK
LIFE STRAIGHT
2011
Gilbert & George
A LONDON PICTURE
IT'S WRITTEN ALL OVER THEM

LIFE STRAIGHT. 2011. 226 x 254 cm

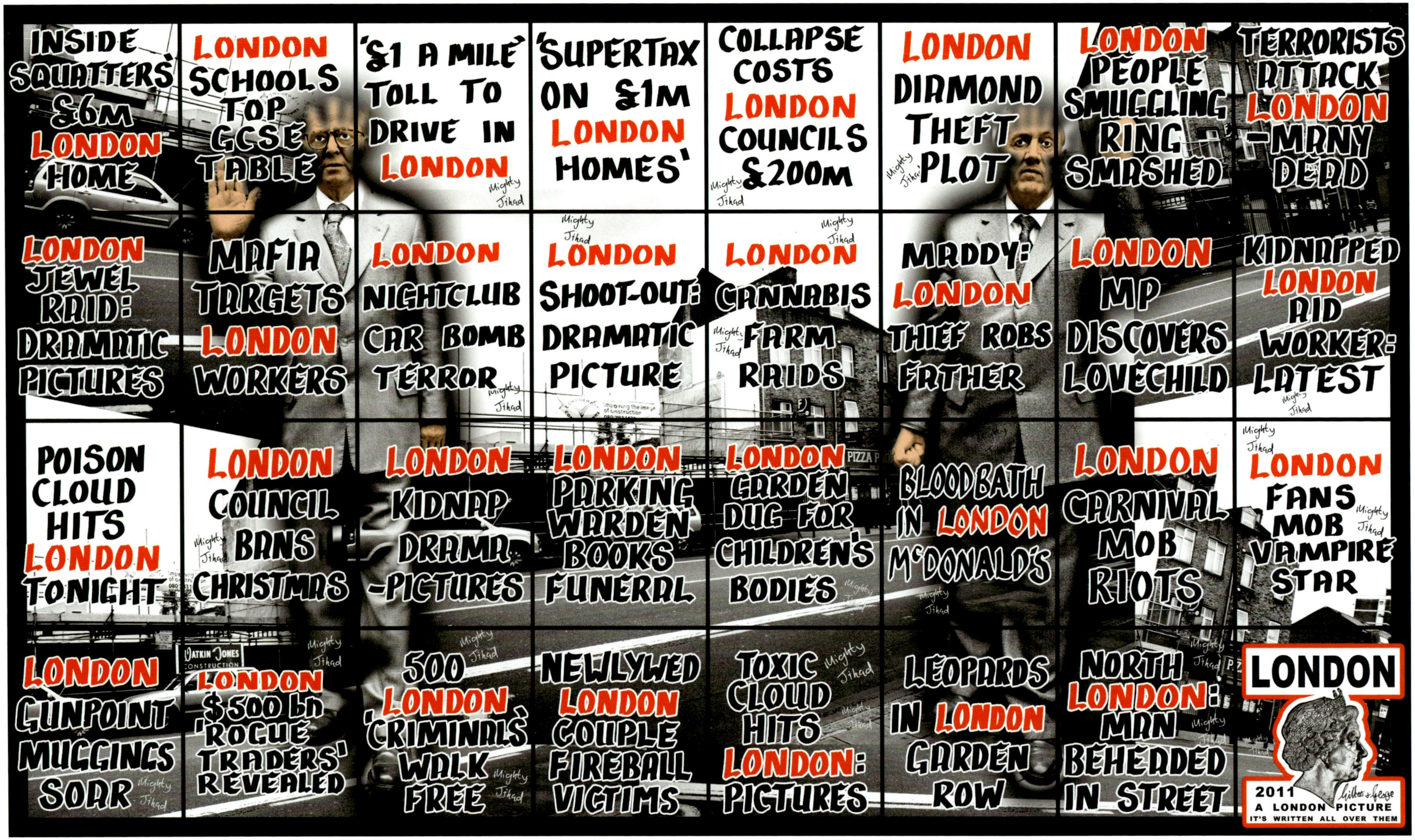
INSIDE SQUATTERS' £6M LONDON HOME
LONDON SCHOOLS TOP GCSE TABLE
'£1 A MILE' TOLL TO DRIVE IN LONDON
'SUPERTAX ON £1M LONDON HOMES'
COLLAPSE COSTS LONDON COUNCILS £200M
LONDON DIAMOND THEFT PLOT
LONDON PEOPLE SMUGGLING RING SMASHED
TERRORISTS ATTACK LONDON - MANY DEAD
LONDON JEWEL RAID: DRAMATIC PICTURES
MAFIA TARGETS LONDON WORKERS
LONDON NIGHTCLUB CAR BOMB TERROR
LONDON SHOOT-OUT: DRAMATIC PICTURE
LONDON CANNABIS FARM RAIDS
MADDY: LONDON THIEF ROBS FATHER
LONDON MP DISCOVERS LOVECHILD
KIDNAPPED LONDON AID WORKER: LATEST
POISON CLOUD HITS LONDON TONIGHT
LONDON COUNCIL BANS CHRISTMAS
LONDON KIDNAP DRAMA -PICTURES
LONDON PARKING WARDEN BOOKS FUNERAL
LONDON GARDEN DUG FOR CHILDREN'S BODIES
BLOODBATH IN LONDON McDONALD'S
LONDON CARNIVAL MOB RIOTS
LONDON FANS MOB VAMPIRE STAR
LONDON GUNPOINT MUGGINGS SOAR
LONDON $500 bn 'ROGUE TRADERS' REVEALED
500 LONDON 'CRIMINALS' WALK FREE
NEWLYWED LONDON COUPLE FIREBALL VICTIMS
TOXIC CLOUD HITS LONDON: PICTURES
LEOPARDS IN LONDON GARDEN ROW
NORTH LONDON: MAN BEHEADED IN STREET
LONDON
2011
A LONDON PICTURE
IT'S WRITTEN ALL OVER THEM

LONDON. 2011. 302 x 508 cm

LONDON LETTER BOMB BLAST
LONDON CLUBBERS' BOMB CARNAGE ESCAPE
BLITZ BOMB THREATENS EAST LONDON
LONDON 'DIRTY BOMB' PLOTTERS JAILED
LONDON TERROR BOMB TARGETS
BOMB SCARES ACROSS LONDON
LONDON CLUB BOMB: DOCTOR CHARGED
LONDON MEASLES 'TIME BOMB' FEARS
LONDON BOMB
2011
Gilbert & George
A LONDON PICTURE
IT'S WRITTEN ALL OVER THEM

LONDON BOMB. 2011. 226 x 190 cm

MAN SHOT OUTSIDE NEW YEAR PARTY
RAMPAGE GUNMAN'S HITLIST OF VICTIMS
PARTY GOERS SHOT BY SNIPER
REVEALED MISSED CHANCES T
CATCH 21/
BOMBERS
MUSLIMS ON TERROR HIT LIST
UK FREEZES £1BN GADDAFI ASSETS
PREGNANT WOMAN STABBED TO DEATH
ISLINGTON KINSELLA KILLERS JAILED
CEMETERY ATTACK TERROR
THIEVES TARGET CAR NUMBER PLATES
MAN'S SHOOTING SPARKS RENEWED FEARS
VIOLENT LONDON 4 DIE IN ATTACK
MAN SHOT BY MASKED GUNMAN
TUFNELL PARK ARMED RAID HORROR
BANKER JAILED FOR SWINDLING CUSTOMERS
HAMME
ATTACK IN STREET

LONDON CRIME STRAIGHT. 2011. 302 x 571 cm

EW YEAR HAMMER ATTACK HORROR
25 IN COURT AFTER DRUGS RAIDS
VERDICTS ON 21/7 TERROR GANG
KEPT IN THE DARK OVER DRUG DEATH
PREACHER OF HATE WINS 'RIGHTS' PAYOUT
KNIFE KILLER JAILED OR LIFE
DLR IN DOCK OVER RAIL DEATH
GUNPOINT STREET HOLD-UP HORROR
CITY STAR LEAPS TO DEATH
TWO ARRESTED OVER OAP DEATH
MORE TABBINGS AS KNIFE CRIME SPIRALS
AL-QAEDA BEHEAD BRITISH TOURIST
POLICE PROBE STUDENT'S DEATH
TEACHERS SUSPENDED IN £1m BONUS PROBE
POLICE HUNT KNIFE FIEND
ARMED POLICE WOOP IN UN SCARE
CALLY KILLER 'MAY HAVE ATTACKED DOZENS'
ASDA CAR PARK ATTACKERS JAILED
LONDON BIKE THEFTS SOARING
LONDON CRIME STRAIGHT
2011
A LONDON PICTURE
IT'S WRITTEN ALL OVER THEM

BRITISH TOURIST GUNNED DOWN
LONDON BOMBINGS MEMORIAL - FIRST PICTURE
KIDNAP EMBASSY BRITONS FREED
SVEN DEATH THREAT
TERROR LEADER KILLED
GUNMEN STORM BRITISH CENTRE
CITY BANK WORKER MURDER - PICTURES
£30m ANTIQUES GANG SMASHED
500 POLICE IN RAID
BRITONS AMONG 228 KILLED IN JET DISASTER
WATER CHIEFS £660,000 BONUS
HOUSE PRICES DROP £100,000
RYANAIR MAKES £500m ON 'EXTRAS'
£45bn HOLE IN BUDGET
BRITONS DROWN IN CRUISE HORROR
POISONED RUSSIAN'S SECRET TAPE
TERROR CRACKDOWN - FULL DETAILS
MUMBAI GUNMEN ARE BRITISH
POISONED SPY'S DEADLY COCKTAIL
LONDON CRIME
2011
A LONDON PICTURE
IT'S WRITTEN ALL OVER THEM
Gilbert + George

LONDON CRIME. 2011. 302 x 317 cm

HOW £50 WON A £400,000 LONDON HOME
RETURN OF THE £100,000 LONDON HOME
GRIDLOCK LONDON HIT BY 370,000 ROADWORKS IN A YEAR
£100M SHOPPERS BOOST LONDON
LONDON BANKER'S £50,000 SPACE TRIP
LONDON TYCOON: I LOST £1BILLION
LONDON $500 BN 'ROGUE TRADERS' REVEALED
LONDON COUPLE'S 1p A MONTH MORTGAGE
JACKO'S £100m LONDON CONCERTS DEAL
MEN'S LIFE SPAN WORST IN LONDON
MI5 PROBE FEMME FATALE'S LIFE IN LONDON
LONDON STRAIGHT
2011
Gilbert + George
A LONDON PICTURE
IT'S WRITTEN ALL OVER THEM

LONDON STRAIGHT. 2011. 226 x 254 cm

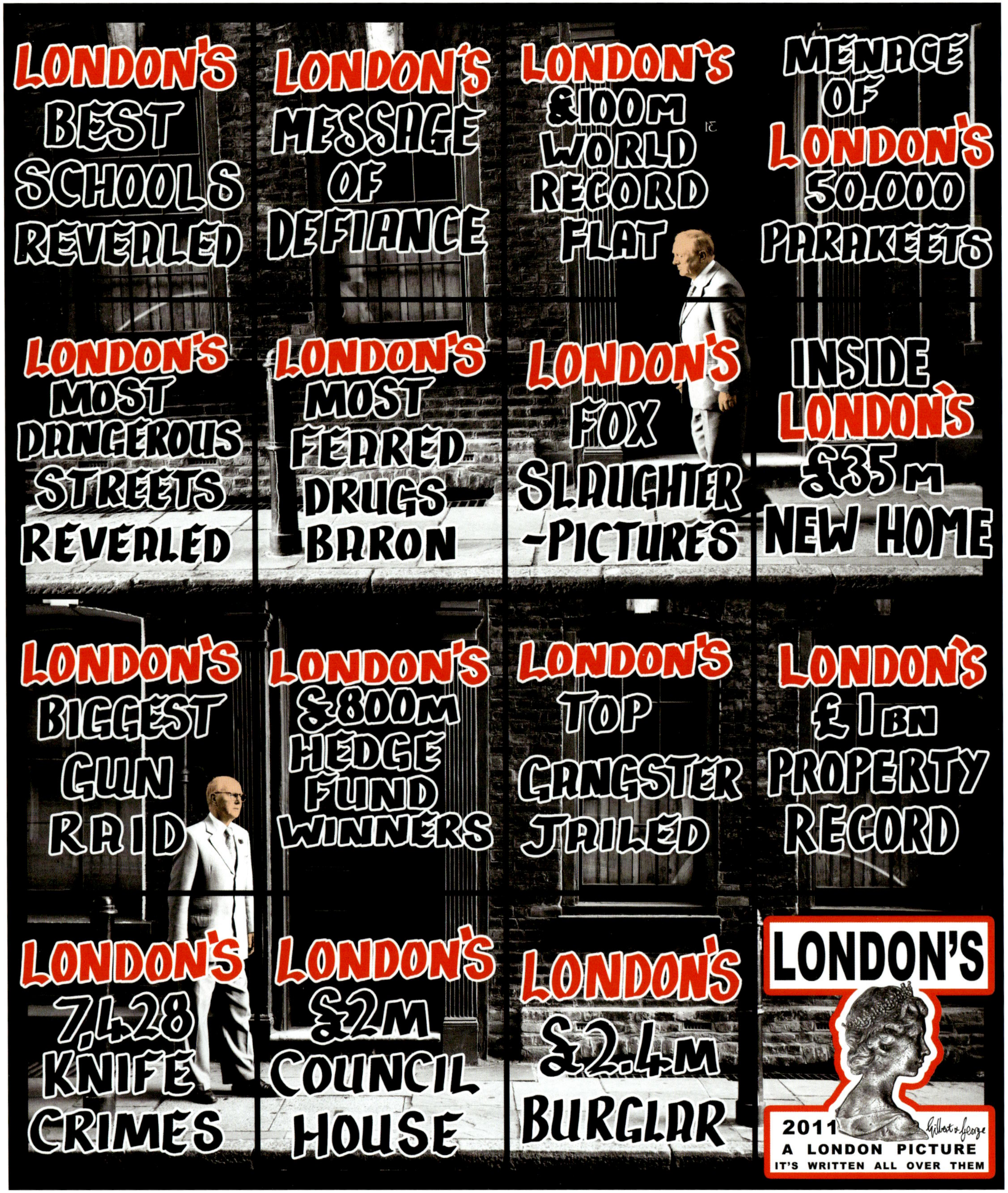
LONDON'S BEST SCHOOLS REVEALED
LONDON'S MESSAGE OF DEFIANCE
LONDON'S £100M WORLD RECORD FLAT
MENACE OF LONDON'S 50.000 PARAKEETS
LONDON'S MOST DANGEROUS STREETS REVEALED
LONDON'S MOST FEARED DRUGS BARON
LONDON'S FOX SLAUGHTER -PICTURES
INSIDE LONDON'S £35M NEW HOME
LONDON'S BIGGEST GUN RAID
LONDON'S £800M HEDGE FUND WINNERS
LONDON'S TOP GANGSTER JAILED
LONDON'S £1BN PROPERTY RECORD
LONDON'S 7,428 KNIFE CRIMES
LONDON'S £2M COUNCIL HOUSE
LONDON'S £2.4M BURGLAR
LONDON'S
2011
A LONDON PICTURE
IT'S WRITTEN ALL OVER THEM

LONDON'S

2011

302 x 254 cm

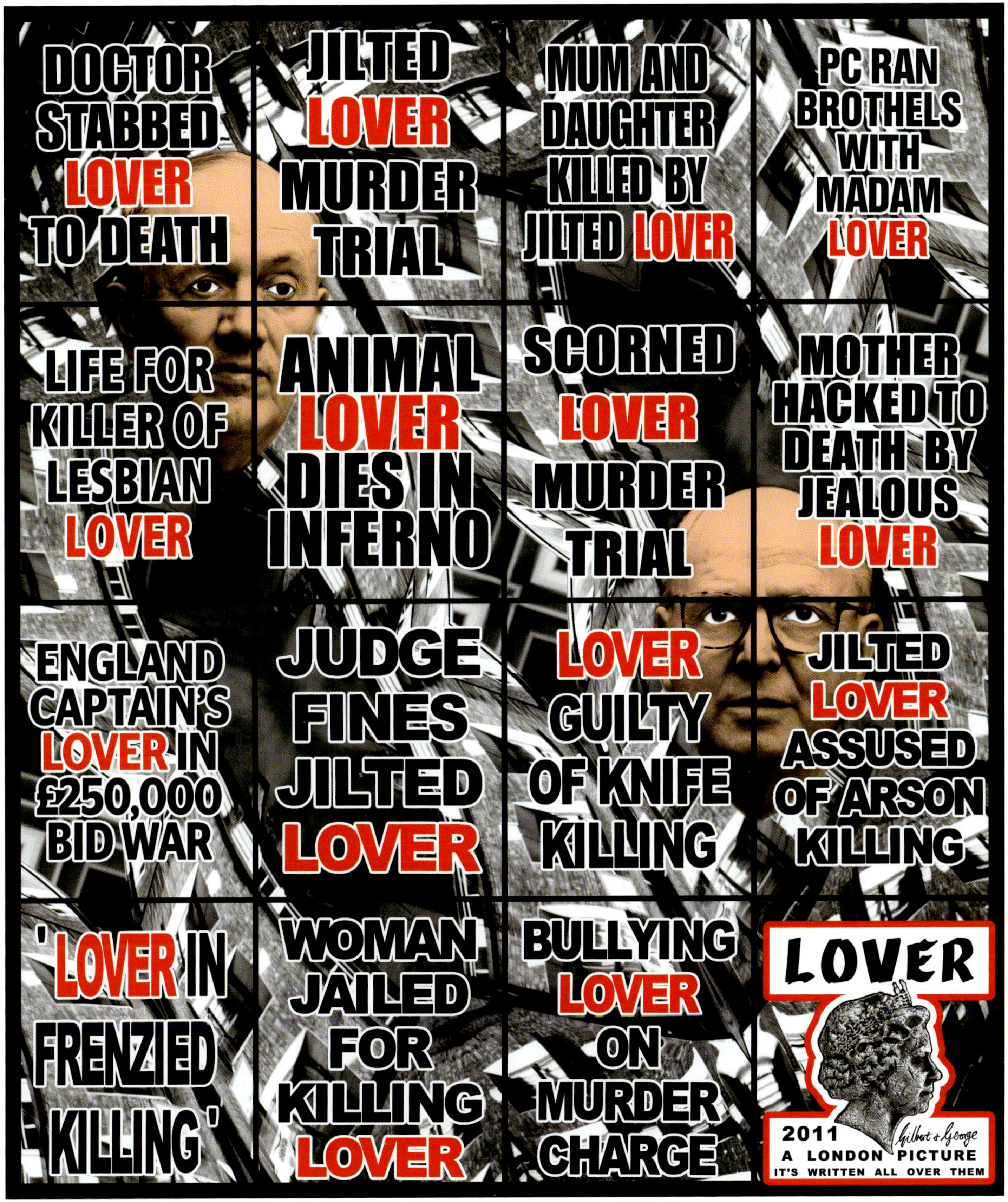
DOCTOR STABBED LOVER TO DEATH
JILTED LOVER MURDER TRIAL
MUM AND DAUGHTER KILLED BY JILTED LOVER
PC RAN BROTHELS WITH MADAM LOVER
LIFE FOR KILLER OF LESBIAN LOVER
ANIMAL LOVER DIES IN INFERNO
SCORNED LOVER MURDER TRIAL
MOTHER HACKED TO DEATH BY JEALOUS LOVER
ENGLAND CAPTAIN'S LOVER IN £250,000 BID WAR
JUDGE FINES JILTED LOVER
LOVER GUILTY OF KNIFE KILLING
JILTED LOVER ASSUSED OF ARSON KILLING
'LOVER IN FRENZIED KILLING'
WOMAN JAILED FOR KILLING LOVER
BULLYING LOVER ON MURDER CHARGE
LOVER
2011
A LONDON PICTURE
IT'S WRITTEN ALL OVER THEM
Gilbert & George

LOVER

2011

302 x 254 cm

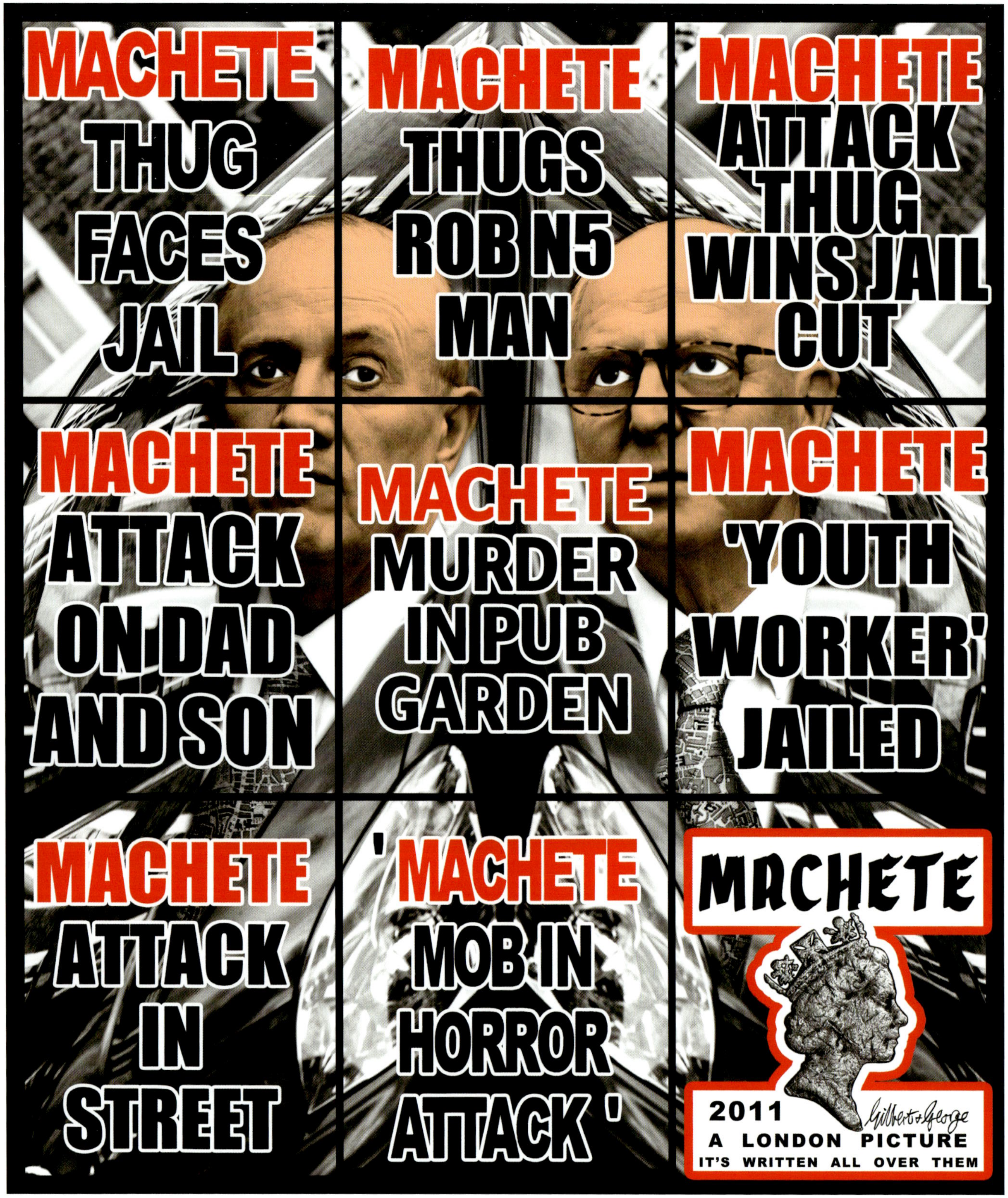
MACHETE THUG FACES JAIL
MACHETE THUGS ROB N5 MAN
MACHETE ATTACK THUG WINS JAIL CUT
MACHETE ATTACK ON DAD AND SON
MACHETE MURDER IN PUB GARDEN
MACHETE 'YOUTH WORKER' JAILED
MACHETE ATTACK IN STREET
'MACHETE MOB IN HORROR ATTACK'
MACHETE
2011
A LONDON PICTURE
IT'S WRITTEN ALL OVER THEM

MACHETE. 2011. 226 x 190 cm

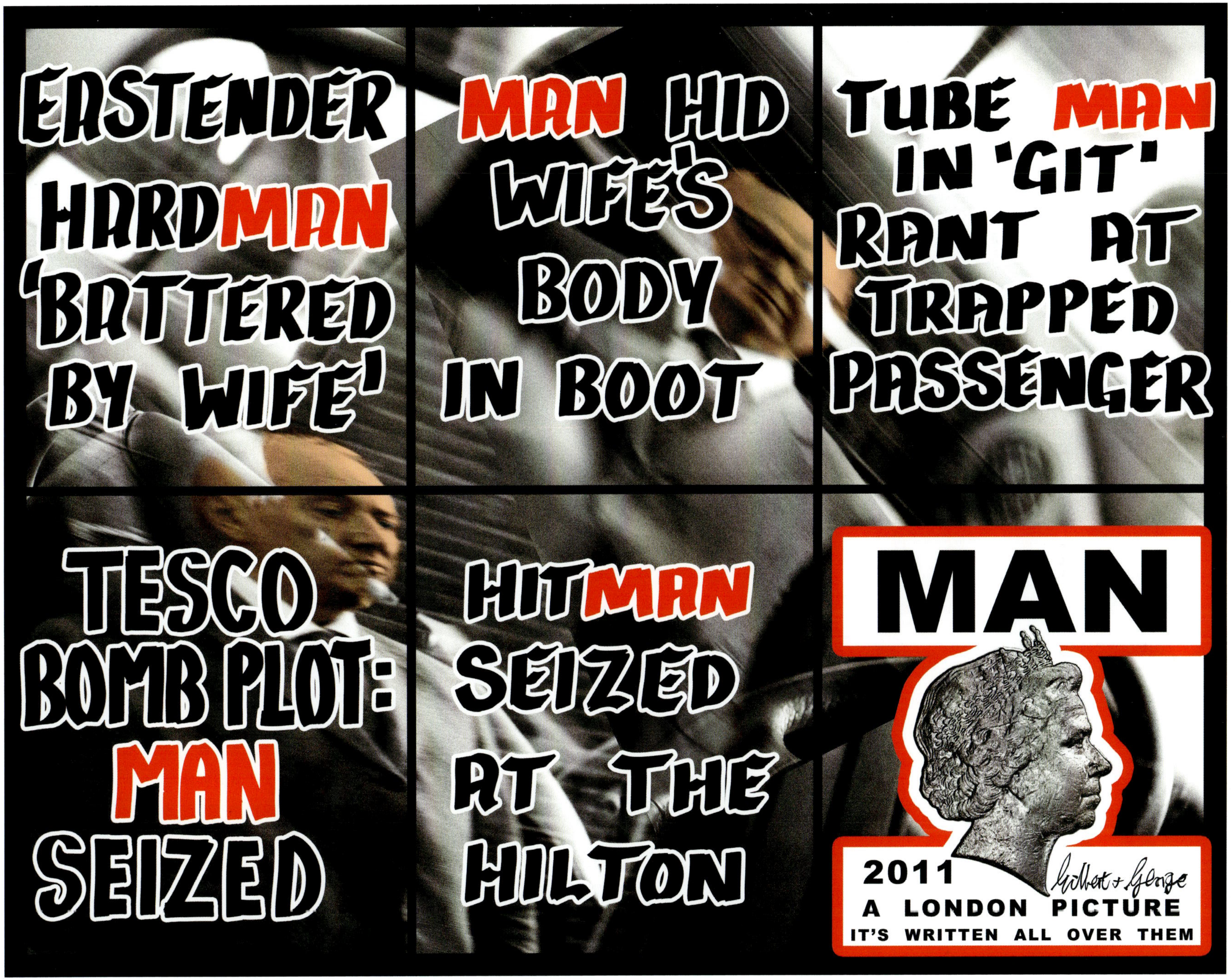
EASTENDER HARDMAN 'BATTERED BY WIFE'
MAN HID WIFE'S BODY IN BOOT
TUBE MAN IN 'GIT' RANT AT TRAPPED PASSENGER
TESCO BOMB PLOT: MAN SEIZED
HITMAN SEIZED AT THE HILTON
MAN
2011
A LONDON PICTURE
IT'S WRITTEN ALL OVER THEM

MAN. 2011. 151 x 190 cm

MAN, 22, DIES IN POLICE CUSTODY
MAN, 27 DIES IN STAB ATTACK
MAN, 45 HELD OVER WOMAN'S DEATH
MAN, 44, IN DEATH FALL TRAGEDY
MAN, 81, LEFT TIED UP BY BURGLAR
MAN, 32, ARRESTED OVER JO MURDER
MAN, 27, QUIZZED OVER DRIVE - BY SHOOTING
MAN, 24, DENIES 'BODY IN SUITCASE MURDER'
MAN, 81, DIES IN BLAZE
WOMAN ACCUSED OF KILLING MAN, 91
MAN, 87, IN FLATS DEATH PLUNGE
MAN AGED
2011
Gilbert & George
A LONDON PICTURE
IT'S WRITTEN ALL OVER THEM

MAN AGED. 2011. 226 x 254 cm

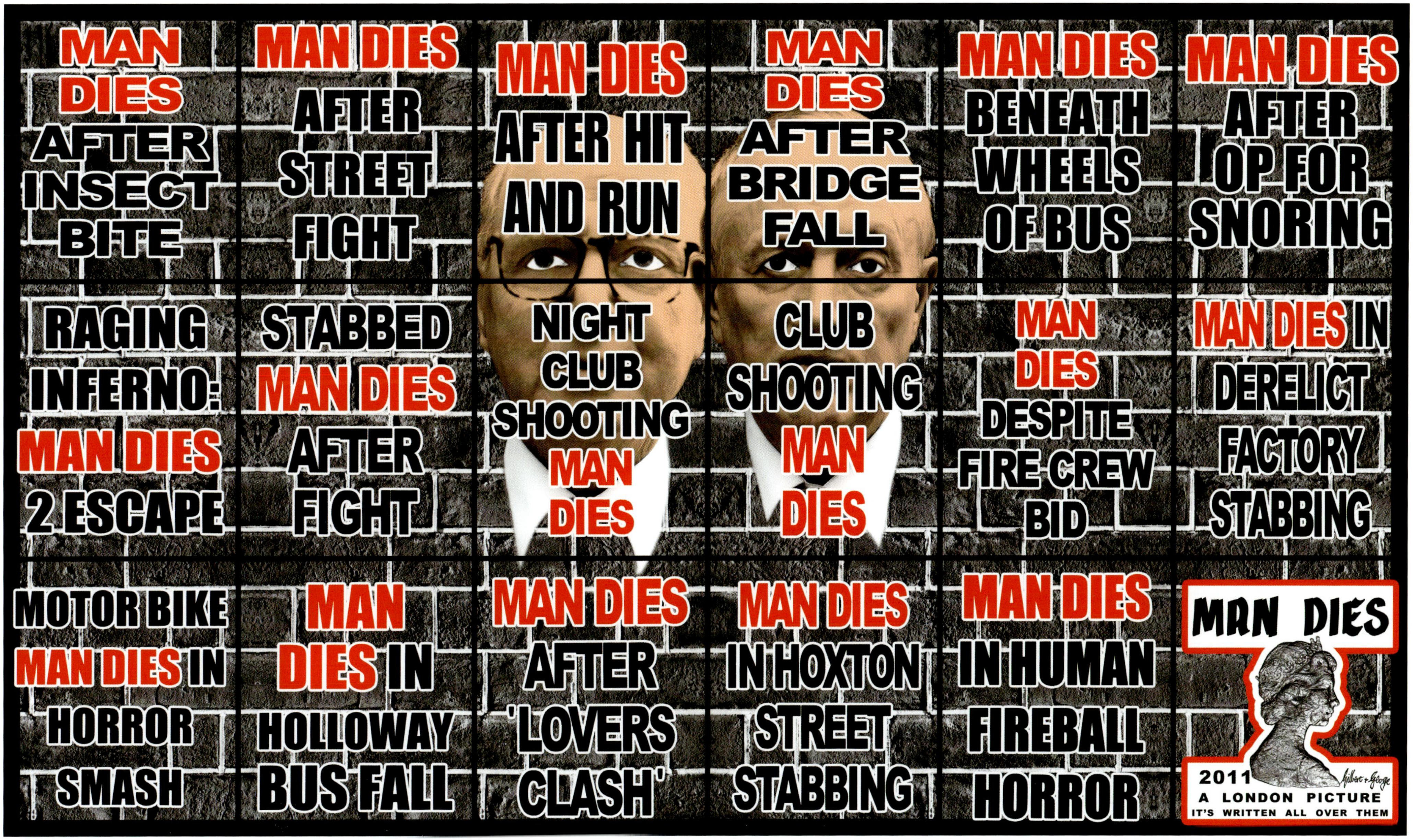
MAN DIES AFTER INSECT BITE
MAN DIES AFTER STREET FIGHT
MAN DIES AFTER HIT AND RUN
MAN DIES AFTER BRIDGE FALL
MAN DIES BENEATH WHEELS OF BUS
MAN DIES AFTER OP FOR SNORING
RAGING INFERNO: MAN DIES 2 ESCAPE
STABBED MAN DIES AFTER FIGHT
NIGHT CLUB SHOOTING MAN DIES
CLUB SHOOTING MAN DIES
MAN DIES DESPITE FIRE CREW BID
MAN DIES IN DERELICT FACTORY STABBING
MOTOR BIKE MAN DIES IN HORROR SMASH
MAN DIES IN HOLLOWAY BUS FALL
MAN DIES AFTER 'LOVERS CLASH'
MAN DIES IN HOXTON STREET STABBING
MAN DIES IN HUMAN FIREBALL HORROR
MAN DIES
2011
A LONDON PICTURE
IT'S WRITTEN ALL OVER THEM

MAN DIES. 2011. 226 x 381 cm

MAN STABBED NEAR CLUB
MAN STABBED IN FACE
MURDER MYSTERY OF MAN STABBED IN NECK
MAN STABBED IN MASS STREET BRAWL
MAN STABBED IN GANG ATTACK
N7 MAN STABBED IN NOISE BUST-UP
MAN STABBED IN FRENZIED ATTACK
MAN STABBED AT BUS STOP
MAN STABBED
2011
Gilbert + George
A LONDON PICTURE
IT'S WRITTEN ALL OVER THEM

MAN STABBED. 2011. 226 x 190 cm

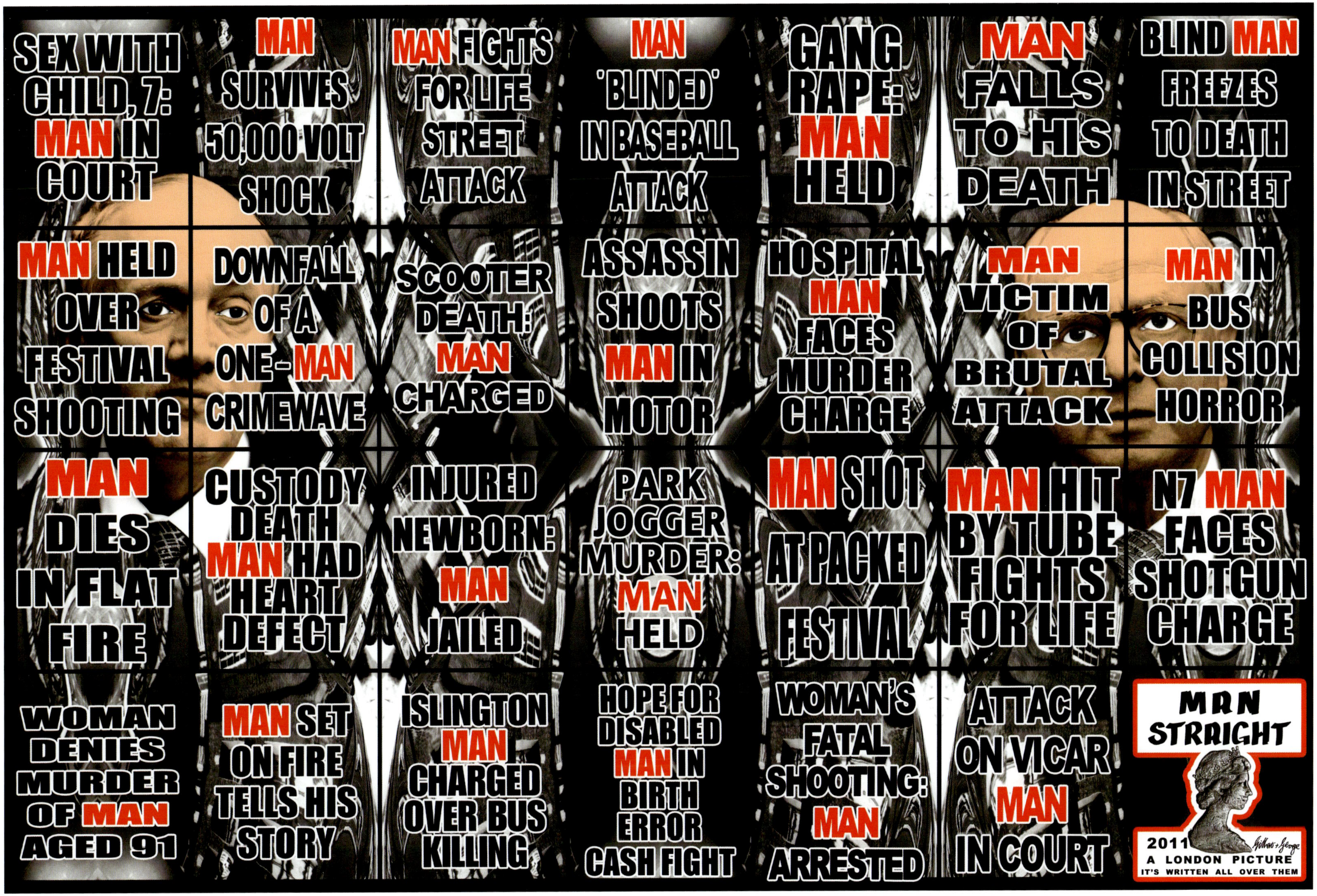
SEX WITH CHILD, 7: MAN IN COURT
MAN SURVIVES 50,000 VOLT SHOCK
MAN FIGHTS FOR LIFE STREET ATTACK
MAN 'BLINDED' IN BASEBALL ATTACK
GANG RAPE: MAN HELD
MAN FALLS TO HIS DEATH
BLIND MAN FREEZES TO DEATH IN STREET
MAN HELD OVER FESTIVAL SHOOTING
DOWNFALL OF A ONE-MAN CRIMEWAVE
SCOOTER DEATH: MAN CHARGED
ASSASSIN SHOOTS MAN IN MOTOR
HOSPITAL MAN FACES MURDER CHARGE
MAN VICTIM OF BRUTAL ATTACK
MAN IN BUS COLLISION HORROR
MAN DIES IN FLAT FIRE
CUSTODY DEATH MAN HAD HEART DEFECT
INJURED NEWBORN: MAN JAILED
PARK JOGGER MURDER: MAN HELD
MAN SHOT AT PACKED FESTIVAL
MAN HIT BY TUBE FIGHTS FOR LIFE
N7 MAN FACES SHOTGUN CHARGE
WOMAN DENIES MURDER OF MAN AGED 91
MAN SET ON FIRE TELLS HIS STORY
ISLINGTON MAN CHARGED OVER BUS KILLING
HOPE FOR DISABLED MAN IN BIRTH ERROR CASH FIGHT
WOMAN'S FATAL SHOOTING: MAN ARRESTED
ATTACK ON VICAR MAN IN COURT
MAN STRAIGHT
2011
A LONDON PICTURE
IT'S WRITTEN ALL OVER THEM

MAN STRAIGHT. 2011. 302 x 444 cm

MISSING CHILDREN FOUND SAFE AND WELL
MUM'S PLEA FOR MISSING SON
FEARS FOR MISSING HOLLOWAY GIRL, 15
PARENT'S FEAR FOR MISSING CLOWN GIRL
MISSING WOMAN'S REMAINS FOUND
MISSING WOMAN MURDER TRIAL LATEST
AXED BANKER MISSING WITH 2 SHOTGUNS
FEAR FOR MISSING WHITECHAPEL SEX WORKER
FEARS FOR MISSING CLAPTON MAN
MISSING 11-YEAR OLD IN HACKNEY
HUNT FOR MISSING FOSTER BROTHER & SISTER
MAN GOES MISING AT SHOPPING CENTRE
MISSING DVD SELLER MURDER CHARGE
VIOLENT MENTAL PATIENT MISSING
MISSING MUM'S BODY FOUND IN THAMES
MISSING
2011
A LONDON PICTURE
IT'S WRITTEN ALL OVER THEM

MISSING

2011

302 x 254 cm

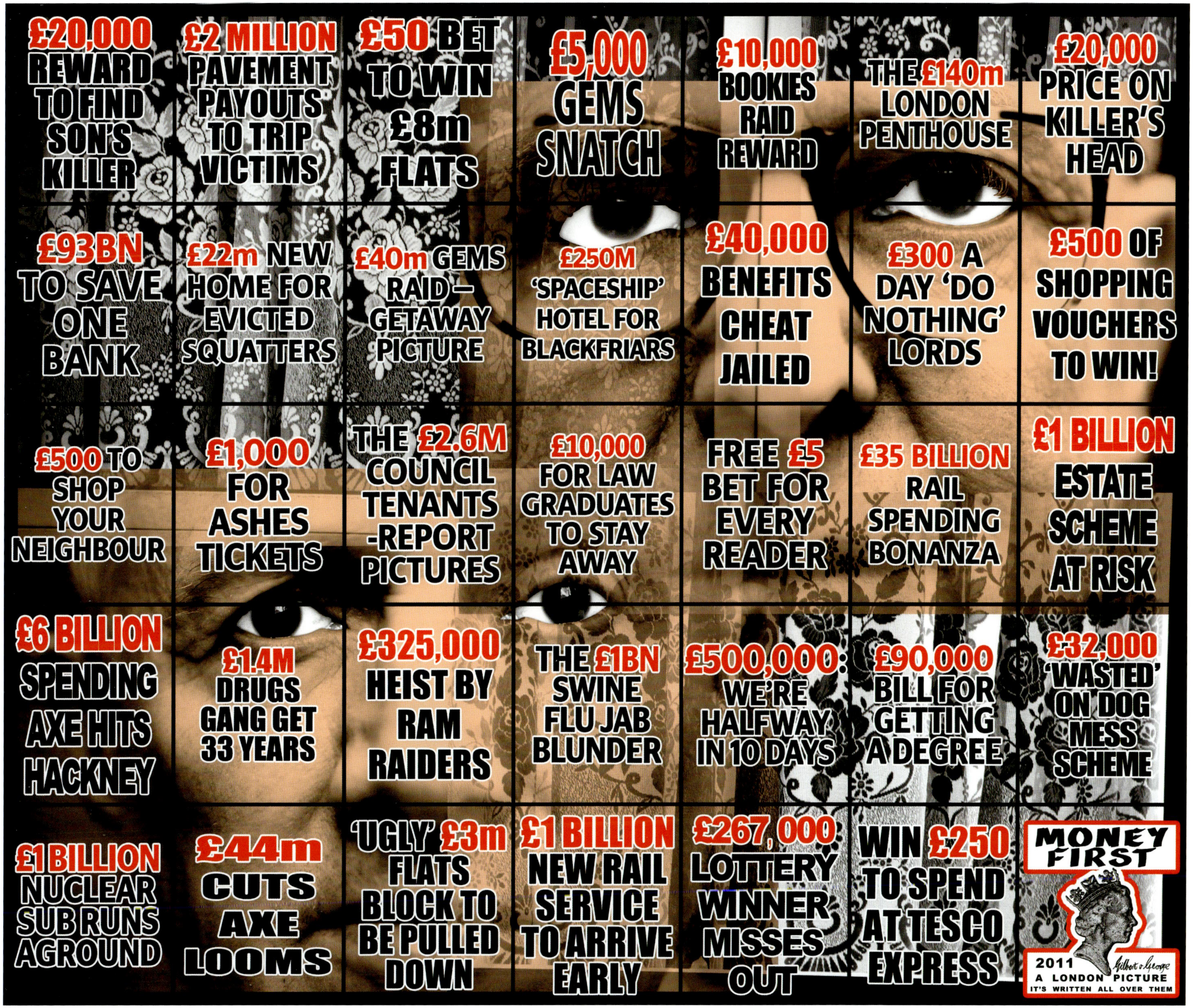
£20,000 REWARD TO FIND SON'S KILLER
£2 MILLION PAVEMENT PAYOUTS TO TRIP VICTIMS
£50 BET TO WIN £8m FLATS
£5,000 GEMS SNATCH
£10,000 BOOKIES RAID REWARD
THE £140m LONDON PENTHOUSE
£20,000 PRICE ON KILLER'S HEAD
£93BN TO SAVE ONE BANK
£22m NEW HOME FOR EVICTED SQUATTERS
£40m GEMS RAID – GETAWAY PICTURE
£250M 'SPACESHIP' HOTEL FOR BLACKFRIARS
£40,000 BENEFITS CHEAT JAILED
£300 A DAY 'DO NOTHING' LORDS
£500 OF SHOPPING VOUCHERS TO WIN!
£500 TO SHOP YOUR NEIGHBOUR
£1,000 FOR ASHES TICKETS
THE £2.6M COUNCIL TENANTS -REPORT PICTURES
£10,000 FOR LAW GRADUATES TO STAY AWAY
FREE £5 BET FOR EVERY READER
£35 BILLION RAIL SPENDING BONANZA
£1 BILLION ESTATE SCHEME AT RISK
£6 BILLION SPENDING AXE HITS HACKNEY
£1.4M DRUGS GANG GET 33 YEARS
£325,000 HEIST BY RAM RAIDERS
THE £1BN SWINE FLU JAB BLUNDER
£500,000: WE'RE HALFWAY IN 10 DAYS
£90,000 BILL FOR GETTING A DEGREE
£32,000 'WASTED' ON DOG MESS SCHEME
£1 BILLION NUCLEAR SUB RUNS AGROUND
£44m CUTS AXE LOOMS
'UGLY' £3m FLATS BLOCK TO BE PULLED DOWN
£1 BILLION NEW RAIL SERVICE TO ARRIVE EARLY
£267,000 LOTTERY WINNER MISSES OUT
WIN £250 TO SPEND AT TESCO EXPRESS
MONEY FIRST
2011
Gilbert & George
A LONDON PICTURE
IT'S WRITTEN ALL OVER THEM

MONEY FIRST. 2011. 377 x 444 cm

£50M RAID: FIRST E-FIT
£100bn TO STOP BANKS PANIC
TRADER'S £156M 'HANDCUFFS' DEAL
BANK GIANT'S £691M RECORD LOSS
£1.5M HOUSES FOR HOMELES
BA BOSS REJECTS £700,000 BONUS
BANK WORKER'S '£70M FRAUD PLOT'
PETROL FIRMS' £3M AN HOUR PROFIT
UBS CHIEF QUITS AFTER £9.6BN HIT
GOLDMA BANKER £12M BONANZ
JEREMY BEADLE'S £100M CHARITY LEGACY
CHELSEA: £240,000 FLAT AUCTION
£100bn GLOBAL BID TO RESCUE BANKS
ROGUE TRADER LOSES £3.6BN
HOW BROTHE LOST £560 M
MET CHIEF'S £400,000 GOODBYE
ANGER AT £10M WEST END BLACKOUT
ACCOUNTANT WHO STOLE £9M
RAVERS SEIZE £5M HOUSE -PICTURES
F1 BOS IN £2 bn DIVORC
£2,000 A YEAR POWER BILL WARNING
LAWYER GUILTY OF £7M BANK SWINDLE
CITY'S £5bn BONUS BONANZA
CANCER MAN'S £45M LOTTERY JOY
SUMMI $1trn BOOST F WORLD ECONOM

MONEY. 2011. 377 x 698 cm

RITISH £1bn OCKED IN CELAND
CRISIS BANK LOSES £10bn
£5bn CHELSEA HEIR FLEES POLICE
£25M CHARITY DINNER – FIRST PICTURES
ST PAUL'S UNVEILS £3.8M GARDEN
£1M CASH HAUL IN SECURITY BOX SWOOP
BANK'S £1.4BN ROGUE RADERS CANDAL
TUBE FIRM'S £144,000 TRACK WORKERS
HACKNEY: £500,000 CATWALK CLOTHES THEFT
MAYOR AIDE'S £100,000 FOR HIS 'DARLING'
RAIL CHIEF'S £1.4M FINE – AND A KNIGHTHOOD
WORST RAIL FIRM PAYS £29M PENALTY
ORTHERN ROCK: 25 BN ESCUE
BLACK MONDAY £60BN SHARES CRASH
ACTRESS WINS £5M SUPERBUG PAYOUT
TRAINEE BROKER'S £100,000 'SKIVVY' CLAIM
CHELSEA SIGN NEW STRIKER FOR £15M
£1.25bn TAKEOVER BID FOR ALLIANCE AND LEICESTER
RADER: WASN'T WORTH £1M ONUS
GLAXO CHARGES £6 FOR £1 SWINE FLU VACCINE
£10bn BID FOR CADBURY
TATE GALLERY'S £100M BONANZA
TORIES SQUEEZE £50,000 EARNERS
BORIS' £5 bn SAVINGS STUN TORIES
BANK IANT'S 691M ECORD LOSS
SHARES CRASH ANOTHER £30bn
ARSENAL FOOTBALL WIFE'S £10M DIVORCE
BRITAIN'S £500bn BAILOUT: SPECIAL EDITION
CRISIS BANK LOSES £10bn
MONEY
2011
A LONDON PICTURE
IT'S WRITTEN ALL OVER THEM

HUNT FOR £100,000 JEWELS THIEF
COUNCIL SPENDS £42K ON CELEBS
HOW I BLEW £100,000 ON CLUBS AND STRIPPERS
TRICKSTERS ROB N1 MAN OF £6,000 IN STREET
SHEIKH'S £1.5 BN QUICK PROFIT RECORD
TOWN HALL BOSSES £10K AWAY DAY
CLUB BOSSES JAILED FOR £2M BANK CON
WIN £50 CASH
MUM'S £30,000 BENEFITS FRAUD
'SLEAZE' PEER CLAIMS £400,000 EXPENSES
DUPED TRADER WINS £20m PAYOUT
AMERICAN IN £42m ARSENAL SHARES DEAL
COUNCIL FAT CATS KEEP £1M PENSIONS
AXED MET CHIEF'S £3,000 A WEEK PENSION
TAX CHEAT'S £42m 'PIGGY BANK'
HSBC BANKERS' £32m BONUSES
LONDON'S £1.2m EMPTY COUNCIL HOUSE
COUNCILS £440,000 TAXI BILL
PREPARE FOR £2.4BN INCREASE IN TAXES
BENEFITS CAP AT £26,000 A YEAR

MONEY STRAIGHT. 2011. 377 x 698 cm

EX-CON
INS £1m
COURT
BATTLE
SCOOTER GANG IN £12,000 N1 RAID
TOWN HALL'S £100,000 EARNERS
SMOKER FINED £50 FOR DROPPING CIG BUTT
NUN'S £900,000 DEATH BED GIFT
FATHER'S KNIFE KILLER: £20,000 REWARD
ANK BOSS
LEARED OF
EALING £1
MILLION
ROBIN HOOD TAX ON £1m HOUSES
HEROIN WORTH £4.5m SEIZED
CINEMA PLAN FOR MOTHBALLED £23m VENUE
LONDON'S £30M NEW SQUATS
TROUBLED BANK'S £300,000 WIMBLEDON 'SECRET'
OUNCIL
CHIEFS'
100,000
A YEAR
ENSIONS
STARS' £15m CHARITY FUND RAISER
ARSENAL TARGET £10M WONDER KID
JUDGE'S £300,000 TO STAY AT HOME
HISTORIC DAY FOR £16 bn CROSSRAIL
TOP HEAD HELD IN '£500,000 FRAUD' PROBE
FAILED
ANKER'S
500,000
A YEAR
ENSION
ARSENAL STARS' £500,000 HOSPITAL TARGET
CHELSEA STAR'S £120,000 BIRTHDAY PARTY
LIB-DEM U-TURN ON £1M MANSION TAX
PETCHEY £1m VESSEL SETS SAIL
CCTV TRAFFIC CARS NET £84k A YEAR
BLAIR'S
5M GIFT
TO WAR
OUNDED
LONDON, YOU DID IT: £1 MILLION RAISED
BENEFITS CHEAT MUM HAD £80,000 IN BANK
CRISIS THEATRE THROWN £4.5m LIFELINE
WIN A £100 MEAL AT TOP EATERY
MONEY STRAIGHT
2011
A LONDON PICTURE
IT'S WRITTEN ALL OVER THEM

OLD FOLK'S CENTRE TO BE SOLD FOR £5 MILLION
READERS RAISE AN INCREDIBLE £4.5M
BENEFITS CHEAT MUST PAY BACK £21,000
PAPER AND ENGLAND CAR FLAG £1
'FANTASY PLOT' TO SELL RITZ FOR £250M
CRASH VICTIM GETS £1M
PETROL BLOCKADE AS BP LOSES £11BILLION
BAIL-OUT OF BANKS TO COST £1.5 TRILLION
BANK RESCUE BOSS RACING TO £6m BONUS
SACKED TRADER SUES FOR £1.5M
AGENCY WORKERS COST COUNCIL £38m
LLOYDS BANK LOSES £4 BN
FIASCO AS MR BIG HOLDS ON TO £3m
CHARITY CHIEF STOLE £22,000
MONEY LAST
2011
Gilbert & George
A LONDON PICTURE
IT'S WRITTEN ALL OVER THEM

MONEY LAST. 2011. 226 x 317 cm

MOSQUE
BOMB
HOAXER
FACES
JAIL
MOSQUE
V
STUDIO
BATTLE
HOTS UP
DNA TRAPS
RAPIST
MOSQUE
'PREACHER'
YOBS IN
PIG'S HEAD
ATTACK ON
MOSQUE
MOSQUE
SLAMS
USA JET
TERROR
MOSQUE
2011
Gilbert & George
A LONDON PICTURE
IT'S WRITTEN ALL OVER THEM

MOSQUE. 2011. 151 x 190 cm

HACKNEY: MUSICAN'S FIGHT WITH MUGGER
£1M MUGGER WHO PREYED ON WOMEN
SERIAL MUGGER KNOCKS OUT 3 WOMEN
MUGGER
2011
A LONDON PICTURE
IT'S WRITTEN ALL OVER THEM

MUGGER. 2011. 151 x 127 cm

'TRANSEX MUGGER FACING JAIL'
MUGGER MUM FREED TO CARE FOR HER CHILD
N5 HUNT FOR ARMED MUGGER 'AGED 8'
MUGGER STRAIGHT
2011
Gilbert + George
A LONDON PICTURE
IT'S WRITTEN ALL OVER THEM

MUGGER STRAIGHT. 2011. 151 x 127 cm

HAVE-A-GO
VICTIM
TACKLES
MUGGERS
STRANGLE
THREAT
MUGGERS
HUNTED
FOR SALE
MUGGERS
GLUE N1
MAN'S
EYE
MUGGERS
2011
A LONDON PICTURE
IT'S WRITTEN ALL OVER THEM

MUGGERS. 2011. 151 x 127 cm

CCTV OF
MUGGING
SUSPECT
BRAVE
YOUTHS
RESCUE
MUGGING
VICTIM
BISHOP'S
MUGGING
– FIRST
INTERVIEW
HORROR OF
WOMAN IN
'SCISSORS
MUGGING'
MUSWELL
HILL
MUGGING
GANG
HUNTED
MUGGING
2011
A LONDON PICTURE
IT'S WRITTEN ALL OVER THEM

MUGGING. 2011. 151 x 190 cm

COPS LAUNCH BLITZ ON MUGGERS
BUS STAFF 'IGNORED MUGGED TEEN'S HELP PLEA'
GANG JAILED OVER MUGGINGS
ACTION CALL ON 'TUBE MUGGINGS'
MUGGED WOMAN HAS HEART ATTACK
MUGGY
2011
Gilbert & George
A LONDON PICTURE
IT'S WRITTEN ALL OVER THEM

MUGGY. 2011. 151 x 190 cm

GRIEVING
MUM
SLAMS
KILLER
UPPER ST
KILLING:
CAN'T FORGIV
SAYS MUM
MUM :
WHY I
SHOPPED
KILLER SON
MUM
2011
A LONDON PICTURE
IT'S WRITTEN ALL OVER THEM

MUM. 2011. 151 x 127 cm

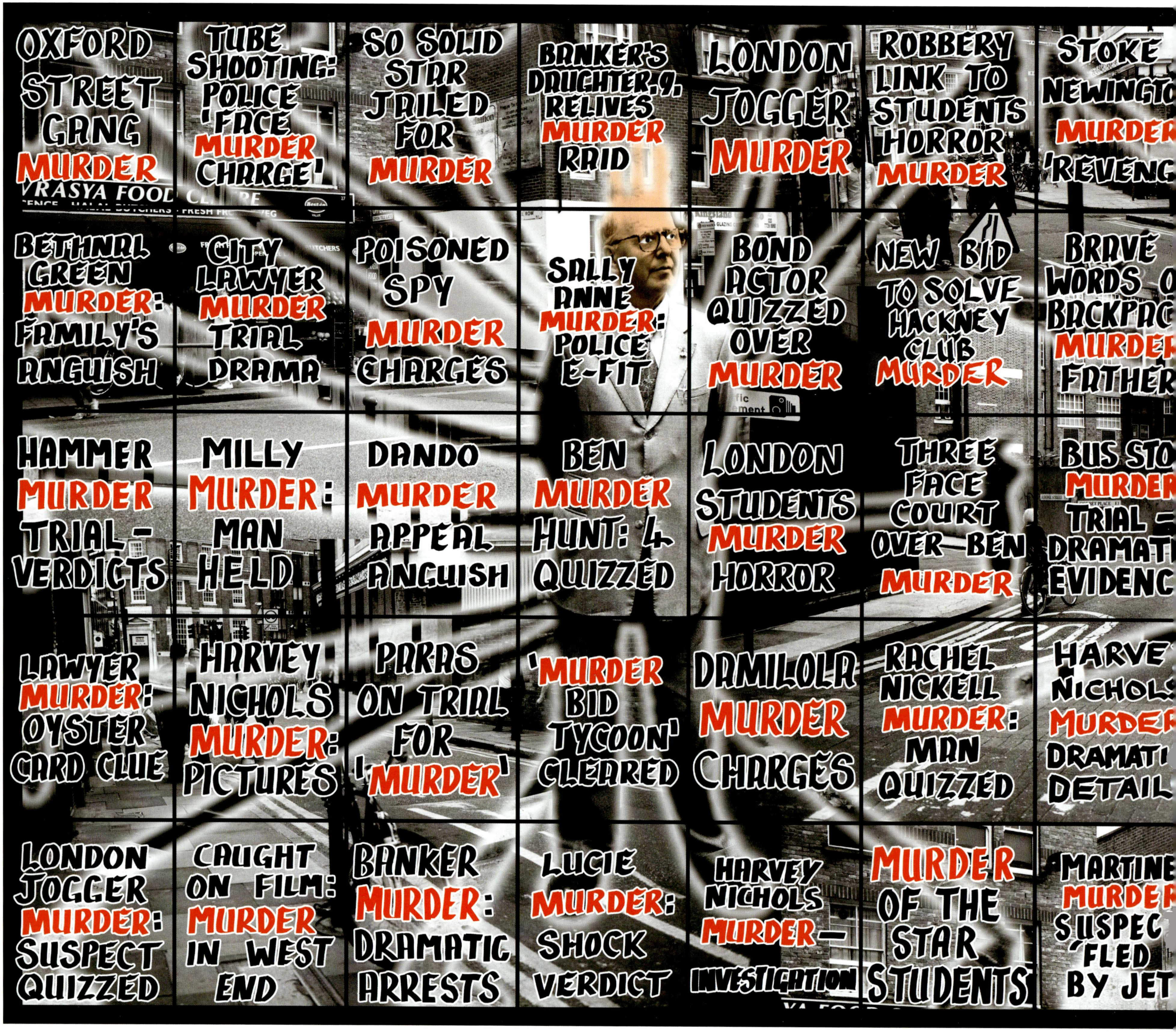
OXFORD STREET GANG MURDER
TUBE SHOOTING: POLICE 'FACE MURDER CHARGE'
SO SOLID STAR JAILED FOR MURDER
BANKER'S DAUGHTER, 9, RELIVES MURDER RAID
LONDON JOGGER MURDER
ROBBERY LINK TO STUDENTS HORROR MURDER
STOKE NEWINGTO MURDER 'REVENG
BETHNAL GREEN MURDER: FAMILY'S ANGUISH
CITY LAWYER MURDER TRIAL DRAMA
POISONED SPY MURDER CHARGES
SALLY ANNE MURDER: POLICE E-FIT
BOND ACTOR QUIZZED OVER MURDER
NEW BID TO SOLVE HACKNEY CLUB MURDER
BRAVE WORDS O BACKPAC MURDE FATHER
HAMMER MURDER TRIAL – VERDICTS
MILLY MURDER: MAN HELD
DANDO MURDER APPEAL ANGUISH
BEN MURDER HUNT: 4 QUIZZED
LONDON STUDENTS MURDER HORROR
THREE FACE COURT OVER BEN MURDER
BUS STO MURDER TRIAL – DRAMAT EVIDENC
LAWYER MURDER: OYSTER CARD CLUE
HARVEY NICHOLS MURDER: PICTURES
PARAS ON TRIAL FOR 'MURDER'
'MURDER BID TYCOON' CLEARED
DAMILOLA MURDER CHARGES
RACHEL NICKELL MURDER: MAN QUIZZED
HARVE NICHOLS MURDE DRAMATI DETAIL
LONDON JOGGER MURDER: SUSPECT QUIZZED
CAUGHT ON FILM: MURDER IN WEST END
BANKER MURDER: DRAMATIC ARRESTS
LUCIE MURDER: SHOCK VERDICT
HARVEY NICHOLS MURDER – INVESTIGATION
MURDER OF THE STAR STUDENTS
MARTINE MURDER SUSPEC 'FLED BY JET

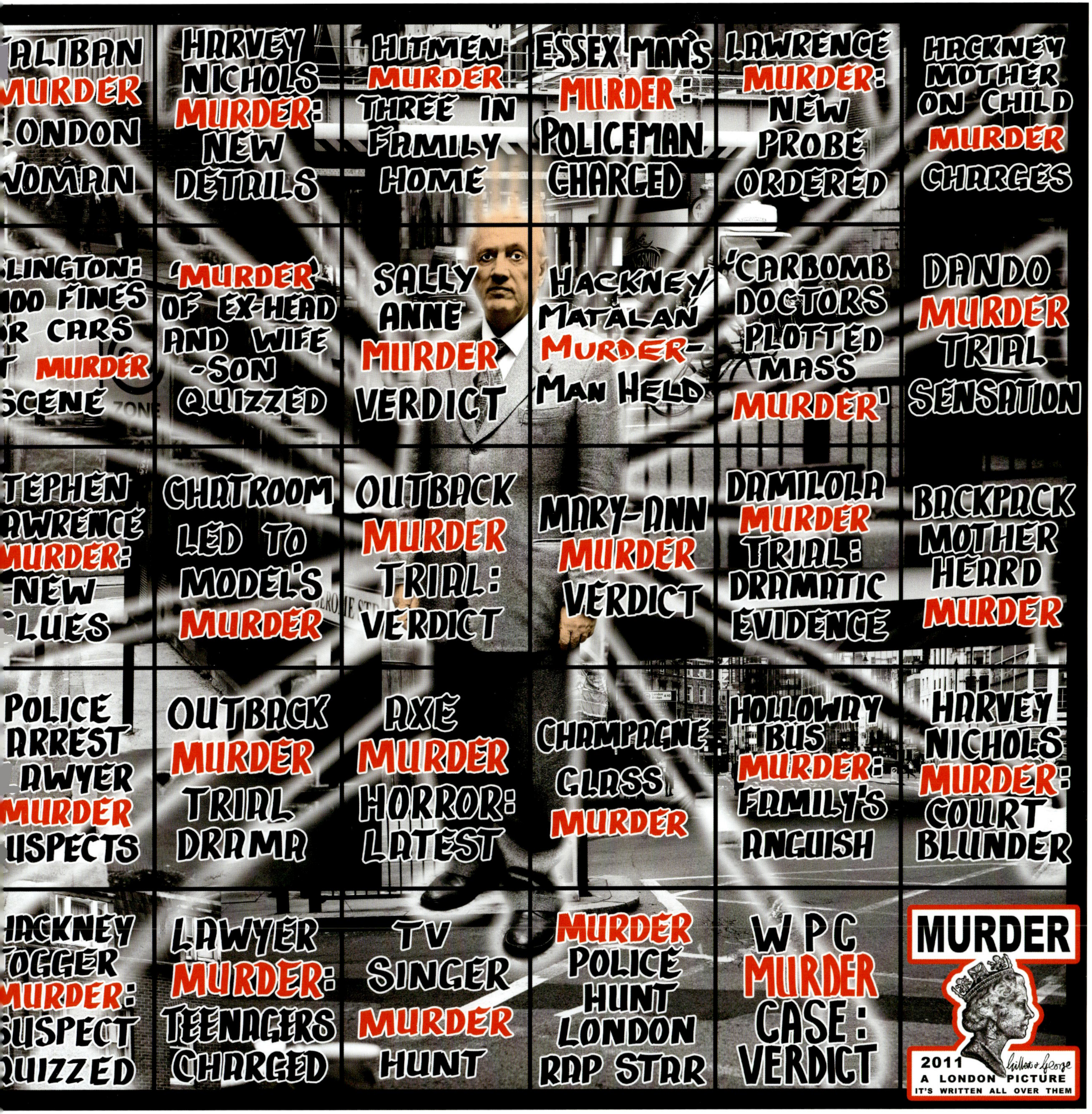
MURDER
NEW
MURDER
POLICE
MURDER
HARVEY NICHOLS MURDER: NEW DETAILS
'MURDER' OF EX-HEAD AND WIFE -SON QUIZZED
CHATROOM LED TO MODEL'S MURDER
OUTBACK MURDER TRIAL DRAMA
LAWYER MURDER: TEENAGERS CHARGED
HITMEN MURDER THREE IN FAMILY HOME
SALLY ANNE MURDER VERDICT
OUTBACK MURDER TRIAL: VERDICT
AXE MURDER HORROR: LATEST
TV SINGER MURDER HUNT
ESSEX MAN'S MURDER: POLICEMAN CHARGED
HACKNEY MATALAN MURDER-MAN HELD
MARY-ANN MURDER VERDICT
CHAMPAGNE GLASS MURDER
MURDER POLICE HUNT LONDON RAP STAR
LAWRENCE MURDER: NEW PROBE ORDERED
'CARBOMB DOCTORS PLOTTED MASS MURDER'
DAMILOLA MURDER TRIAL: DRAMATIC EVIDENCE
HOLLOWAY BUS MURDER: FAMILY'S ANGUISH
W P C MURDER CASE: VERDICT
HACKNEY MOTHER ON CHILD MURDER CHARGES
DANDO MURDER TRIAL SENSATION
BACKPACK MOTHER HEARD MURDER
HARVEY NICHOLS MURDER: COURT BLUNDER
MURDER
2011
A LONDON PICTURE
IT'S WRITTEN ALL OVER THEM

MURDER. 2011. 377 x 825 cm

CRICKET
COACH
MURDER
PROBE
LUCIE
PREGNANT
MUM
MURDER
BID
VERDICT
DAD'S
CHARGE
MATALAN
MURDER
TRIAL
LATEST
OF
MURDER:
POLICE
SEEK NEW
WITNESSES
LOVERS
FACE
MURDER
TRIAL
LEVY
MURDER
TRIAL
STARTS

MURDER STRAIGHT. 2011. 377 x 571 cm

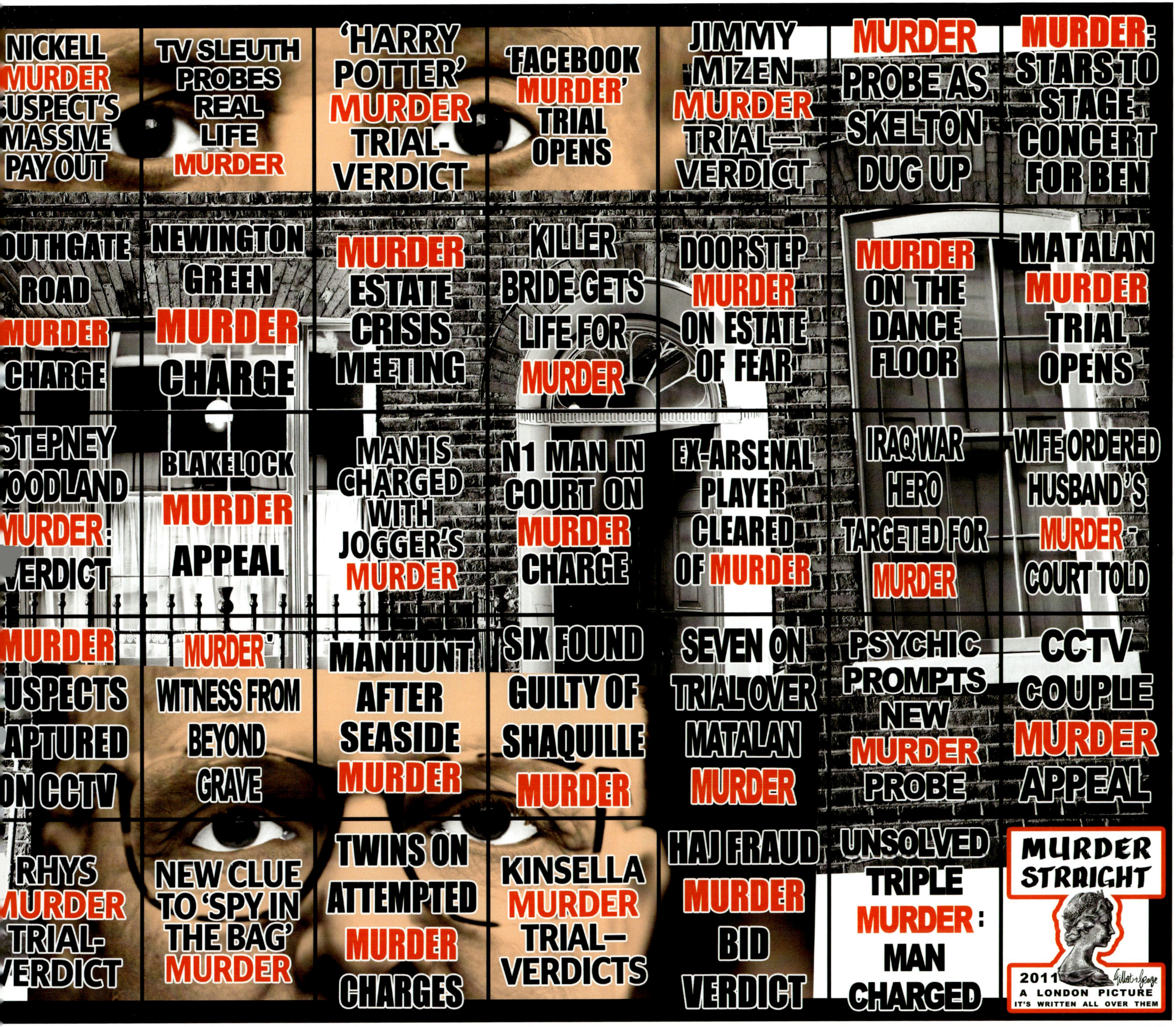
NICKELL MURDER USPECT'S MASSIVE PAY OUT
TV SLEUTH PROBES REAL LIFE MURDER
'HARRY POTTER' MURDER TRIAL- VERDICT
'FACEBOOK MURDER' TRIAL OPENS
JIMMY MIZEN MURDER TRIAL— VERDICT
MURDER PROBE AS SKELTON DUG UP
MURDER: STARS TO STAGE CONCERT FOR BEN
OUTHGATE ROAD MURDER CHARGE
NEWINGTON GREEN MURDER CHARGE
MURDER ESTATE CRISIS MEETING
KILLER BRIDE GETS LIFE FOR MURDER
DOORSTEP MURDER ON ESTATE OF FEAR
MURDER ON THE DANCE FLOOR
MATALAN MURDER TRIAL OPENS
STEPNEY OODLAND URDER: ERDICT
BLAKELOCK MURDER APPEAL
MAN IS CHARGED WITH JOGGER'S MURDER
N1 MAN IN COURT ON MURDER CHARGE
EX-ARSENAL PLAYER CLEARED OF MURDER
IRAQ WAR HERO TARGETED FOR MURDER
WIFE ORDERED HUSBAND'S MURDER - COURT TOLD
MURDER USPECTS APTURED ON CCTV
MURDER' WITNESS FROM BEYOND GRAVE
MANHUNT AFTER SEASIDE MURDER
SIX FOUND GUILTY OF SHAQUILLE MURDER
SEVEN ON TRIAL OVER MATALAN MURDER
PSYCHIC PROMPTS NEW MURDER PROBE
CCTV COUPLE MURDER APPEAL
RHYS URDER TRIAL- ERDICT
NEW CLUE TO 'SPY IN THE BAG' MURDER
TWINS ON ATTEMPTED MURDER CHARGES
KINSELLA MURDER TRIAL— VERDICTS
HAJ FRAUD MURDER BID VERDICT
UNSOLVED TRIPLE MURDER: MAN CHARGED
MURDER STRAIGHT
2011 A LONDON PICTURE
IT'S WRITTEN ALL OVER THEM

CITY BOSS MURDERED IN CHELSEA
FATHER MURDERED SAVING SON
HARROW SCHOOL: TEACHER'S DAUGHTER MURDERED
MURDERED FATHER: POLICE 'FAILURES'
MURDERED LAWYER'S FIANCEE: MY GRIEF
MURDERED CYCLIST -FIRST PICTURE
MAN MURDERED FOR MOBILE
MURDERED LAWYER: NEW CLUES
MOTHER AND BABY FOUND MURDERED
BOYS, 14 AND 16, MURDERED
N.LONDON: MAN MURDERED IN AMBULANCE
BUS PASSENGER MURDERED -PICTURE
MAN MURDERED IN AMBULANCE
NURSE MURDERED AT HOSPITAL
LONDON SOCCER FAN MURDERED
MURDERED -FOR FALLING IN LOVE
CITY LAWYER MURDERED
LONDON POLICE WOMAN MURDERED
LONDON AUTHOR MURDERED IN HOME
MURDERED
2011
A LONDON PICTURE
IT'S WRITTEN ALL OVER THEM

MURDERED. 2011. 302 x 317 cm

MURDERED WOMAN TYCOON — FIRST PICTURE
MAN MURDERED FOR BEING HAPPY
STEPMUM MURDERED IN BED
MURDERED TEENAGER 'REVENGE BEATING'
TRIBUTES PAID TO MURDERED POLICEMAN
MURDERED STRAIGHT
2011
Gilbert+George
A LONDON PICTURE
IT'S WRITTEN ALL OVER THEM

MURDERED STRAIGHT. 2011. 151 x 190 cm

LONDON STUDENT MURDERS -NEW ARREST
MARSHA AND AMELIE MURDERS: NEW DRAMA
FAMILY MURDERS: HITMEN GUILTY
SUFFOLK MURDERS: MAN IN COURT
'RIPPER' MURDERS -LATEST
CHILD MURDERS -FIRST PICTURE
'TARANTINO' MURDERS: NEW ARRESTS
SUFFOLK MURDERS: MAN HELD
MURDERS
2011
A LONDON PICTURE
IT'S WRITTEN ALL OVER THEM

MURDERS. 2011. 226 x 190 cm

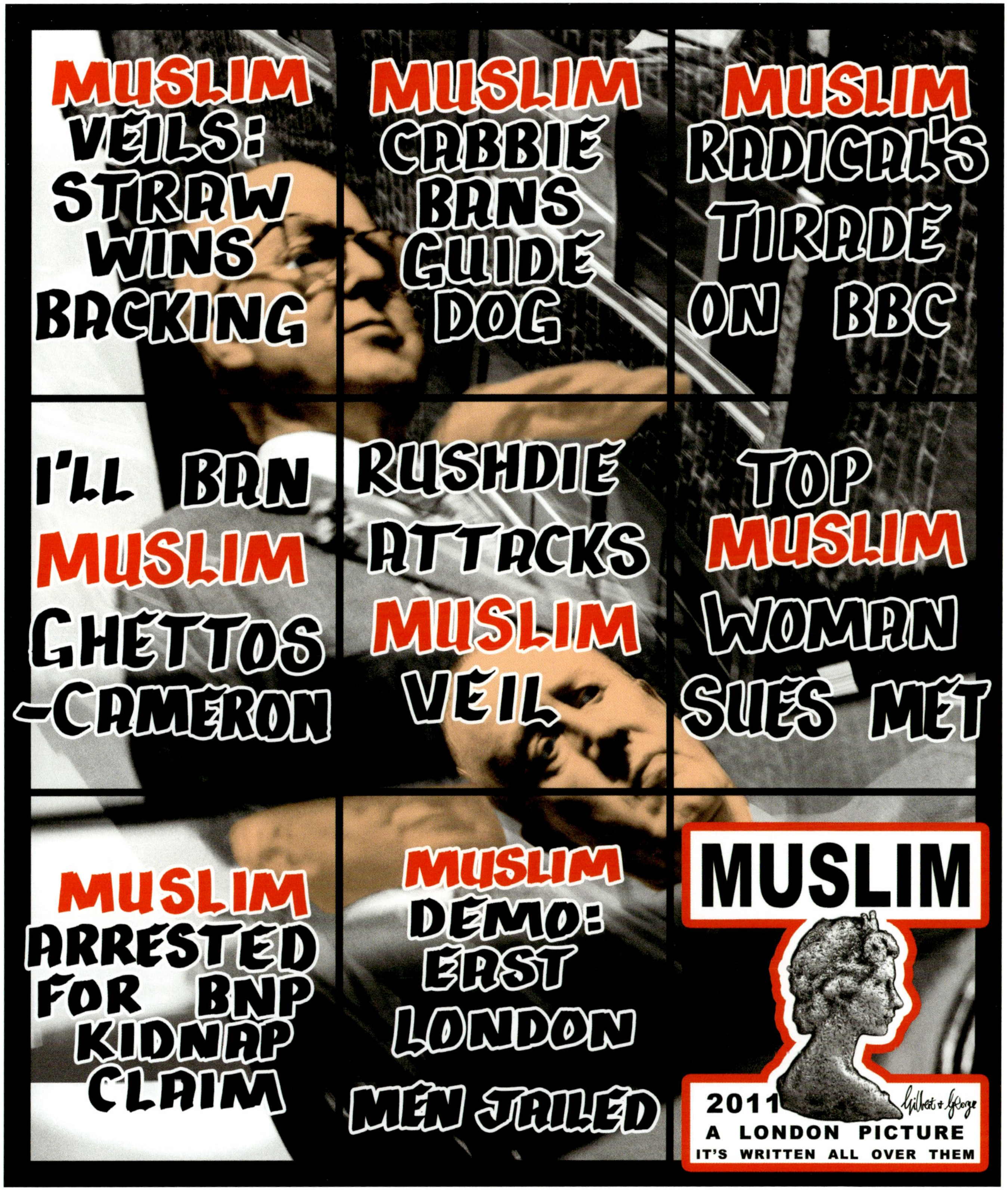
MUSLIM VEILS: STRAW WINS BACKING
MUSLIM CABBIE BANS GUIDE DOG
MUSLIM RADICAL'S TIRADE ON BBC
I'LL BAN MUSLIM GHETTOS -CAMERON
RUSHDIE ATTACKS MUSLIM VEIL
TOP MUSLIM WOMAN SUES MET
MUSLIM ARRESTED FOR BNP KIDNAP CLAIM
MUSLIM DEMO: EAST LONDON MEN JAILED
MUSLIM
2011
A LONDON PICTURE
IT'S WRITTEN ALL OVER THEM

MUSLIM. 2011. 226 x 190 cm

SECRET
'MUSLIM DRINKERS'
EXPOSED
MUSLIM
SECT
ATTACK
B'DESHI
VOTERS
MUSLIM
BABY
BATTERER
WALKS
FREE
MUSLIM
PROTEST:
COURT
SETBACK
DEATH
THREAT TO
MUSLIM
WOMAN
MUSLIM
STRAIGHT
2011
A LONDON PICTURE
IT'S WRITTEN ALL OVER THEM

MUSLIM STRAIGHT. 2011. 151 x 190 cm

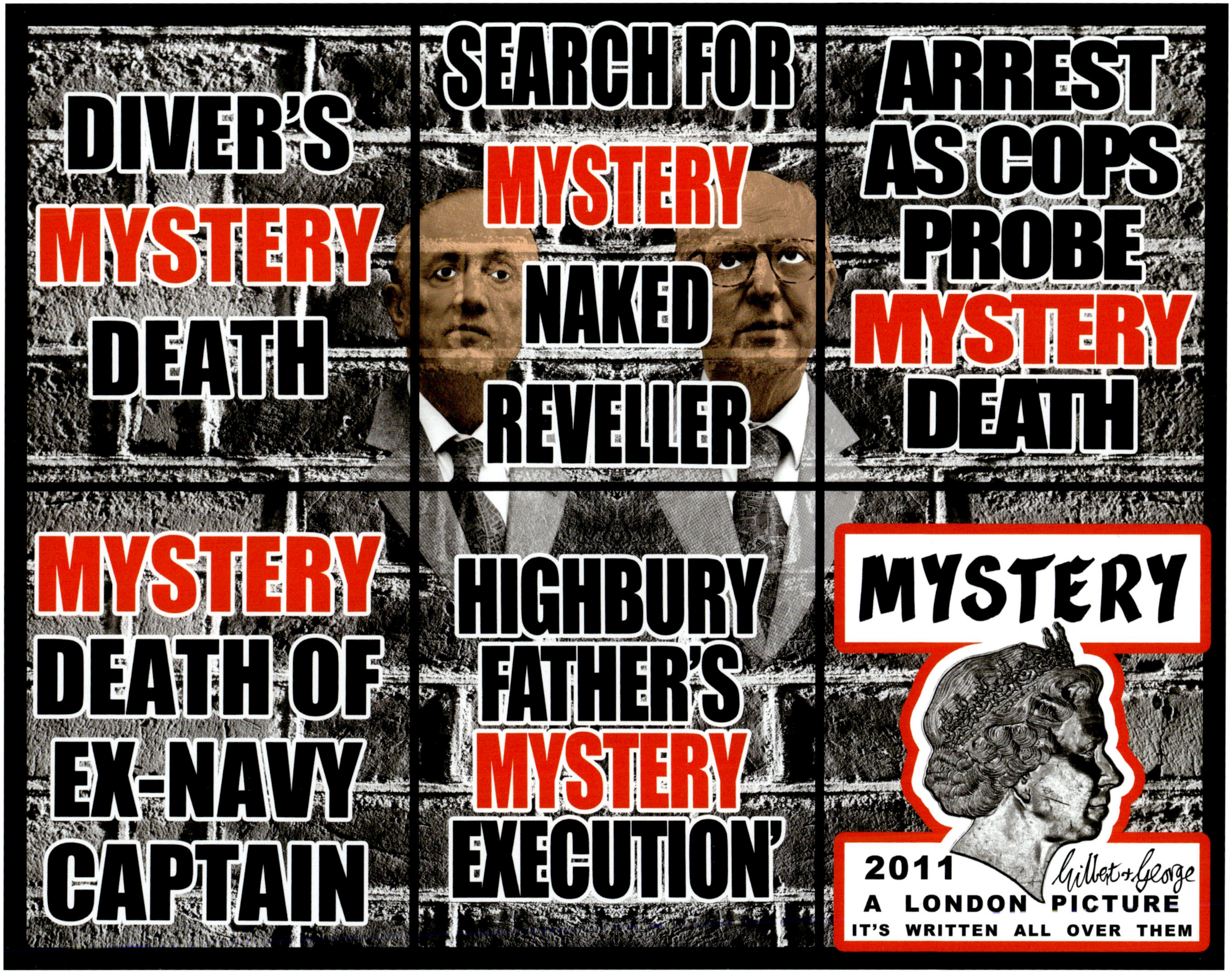
DIVER'S MYSTERY DEATH
SEARCH FOR MYSTERY NAKED REVELLER
ARREST AS COPS PROBE MYSTERY DEATH
MYSTERY DEATH OF EX-NAVY CAPTAIN
HIGHBURY FATHER'S MYSTERY EXECUTION'
MYSTERY
2011
A LONDON PICTURE
IT'S WRITTEN ALL OVER THEM
Gilbert & George

MYSTERY. 2011. 151 x 190 cm

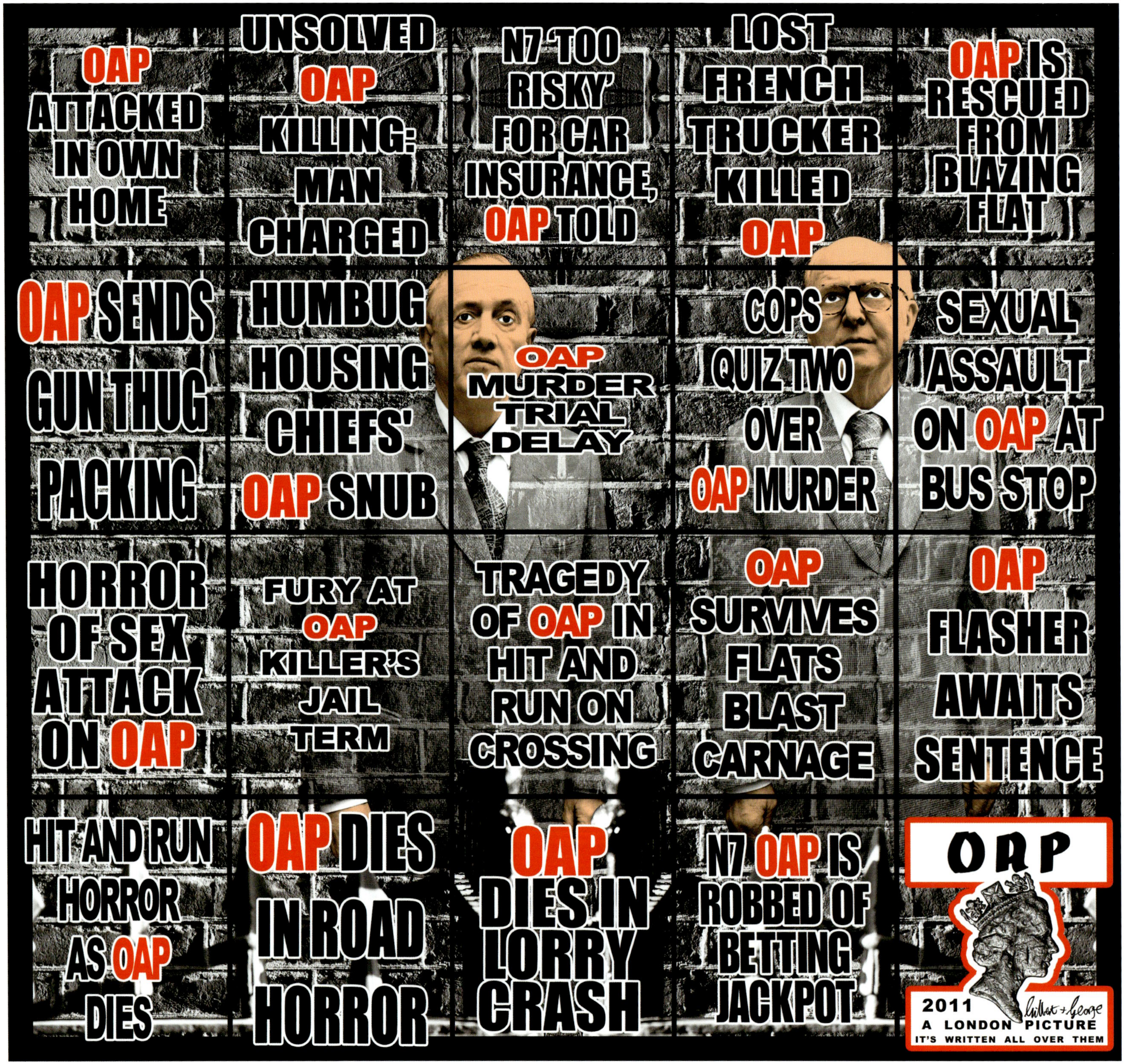
OAP ATTACKED IN OWN HOME
UNSOLVED OAP KILLING: MAN CHARGED
N7 'TOO RISKY' FOR CAR INSURANCE, OAP TOLD
LOST FRENCH TRUCKER KILLED OAP
OAP IS RESCUED FROM BLAZING FLAT
OAP SENDS GUN THUG PACKING
HUMBUG HOUSING CHIEFS' OAP SNUB
OAP MURDER TRIAL DELAY
COPS QUIZ TWO OVER OAP MURDER
SEXUAL ASSAULT ON OAP AT BUS STOP
HORROR OF SEX ATTACK ON OAP
FURY AT OAP KILLER'S JAIL TERM
TRAGEDY OF OAP IN HIT AND RUN ON CROSSING
OAP SURVIVES FLATS BLAST CARNAGE
OAP FLASHER AWAITS SENTENCE
HIT AND RUN HORROR AS OAP DIES
OAP DIES IN ROAD HORROR
OAP DIES IN LORRY CRASH
N7 OAP IS ROBBED OF BETTING JACKPOT
OAP
2011
A LONDON PICTURE
IT'S WRITTEN ALL OVER THEM

OAP. Abbreviation for old-age pensioner. 2011. 302 x 317 cm

MAN CHARGED WITH OAPS KILLING
ESSEX ROAD 'BAR HELL' FOR OAPS
RAPE TERROR OF OAPs
OAPS FLAT RAID FURY
TRAGEDY OF OAPS ROAD DEATH
OAPs TERROR IN CARE HOME
CONMEN STEAL OAPS £17,000 SAVINGS
OAPS £42,000 BENEFITS VICTORY PAYOUT
OAPS BLAZE DEATH TRAGEDY
OAPS POLICE SWOOP SHOCK
THIEVES STEAL £27k – AND OAPS DINNER
AXE FALLS ON OAPS BUS SERVICE
DRIVER CHARGED AFTER OAPS DEATH
OAPS BUS SERVICE FACES THE AXE
OAPS HEAD "USED AS FOOTBALL"
WOMAN CHARGED WITH OAPS KILLING
OAPS DISABLED PARKING MISERY
SCANDAL OF OAPS FLAT BLAZE DEATH
OAPS FLEE DEATH BLAZE
OAPS
2011
A LONDON PICTURE
IT'S WRITTEN ALL OVER THEM

OAPS. Abbreviation for old-age pensioners. 2011. 302 x 317 cm

PAEDO PERVERT DIES IN PRISON
INTERNET PAEDO WALKS FREE FROM COURT
PROTECT US PLEA AS PAEDO GOES MISSING
MISSING PAEDO SPLASHED ON WEBSITE
HATE CAMPAIGN OVER ALLEGED PAEDO
CUTE KIDS 2007 SEE INSIDE FOR ENTRY COUPON
SICK PAEDO CAGED
PAEDO COP FACES JAIL
NEW SWIM POOL: PAEDO FEAR
5 YEARS FOR PAEDO PERVERT
MISSING PAEDO ARRESTED AT AIRPORT
INTERNET PAEDO FACES THE MUSIC
INTERNET PAEDO GROOMED SECOND VICTIM
REVIEW OF SCHOOLS PAEDO CHECKS URGED
PAEDO FAILS IN COUNCIL FLAT APPEAL
PAEDO
2011
A LONDON PICTURE
IT'S WRITTEN ALL OVER THEM

PAEDO. 2011. 226 x 317 cm

£20,000
BOUNTY
TO CATCH
PARK
KILLER
TUFNELL
PARK
GUN
ROBBERY
MAN SHOT
IN PARK
FESTIVAL
CLASH
BRUTAL
ATTACK
ON PARK
KEEPER
MOTHER IN
PARK SEX
ATTACK
ORDEAL
'PARK RAPE'
TRIAL
VERDICT
FIREBUGS
TORCH
PARK
AVIARY
PARK
KILLER:
£20K
REWARD
PARK
2011
A LONDON PICTURE
IT'S WRITTEN ALL OVER THEM

PARK. 2011. 226 x 190 cm

ALDGATE PENSIONER MURDER: NEW ARRESTS
PENSIONER TRIED TO SELL GUN ON MARKET STALL
PENSIONER IN DEATH PLUNGE MYSTERY
DRUG-RUN PENSIONER IS JAILED
PENSIONER KILLED IN ROAD CRASH TRAGEDY
PENSIONER DIES AFTER BURGLARY
DEATH ROBS PENSIONER OF COURT VICTORY
TERROR ORDEAL OF HAMMER ATTACK PENSIONER
PENSIONER ROBBED OF LIFE SAVINGS IN STREET
PENSIONER ROBBED OF CASH FOR SON'S GRAVE
PENSIONER COLLAPSES AND DIES AFTER EVICTION
MANHUNT FOR CROOK WHO TERRORISED PENSIONER
PENSIONER DRAGGED UNDER WHEELS OF LORRY
PENSIONER MURDER: VERDICT
PENSIONER
2011
A LONDON PICTURE
IT'S WRITTEN ALL OVER THEM

PENSIONER. 2011. 226 x 317 cm

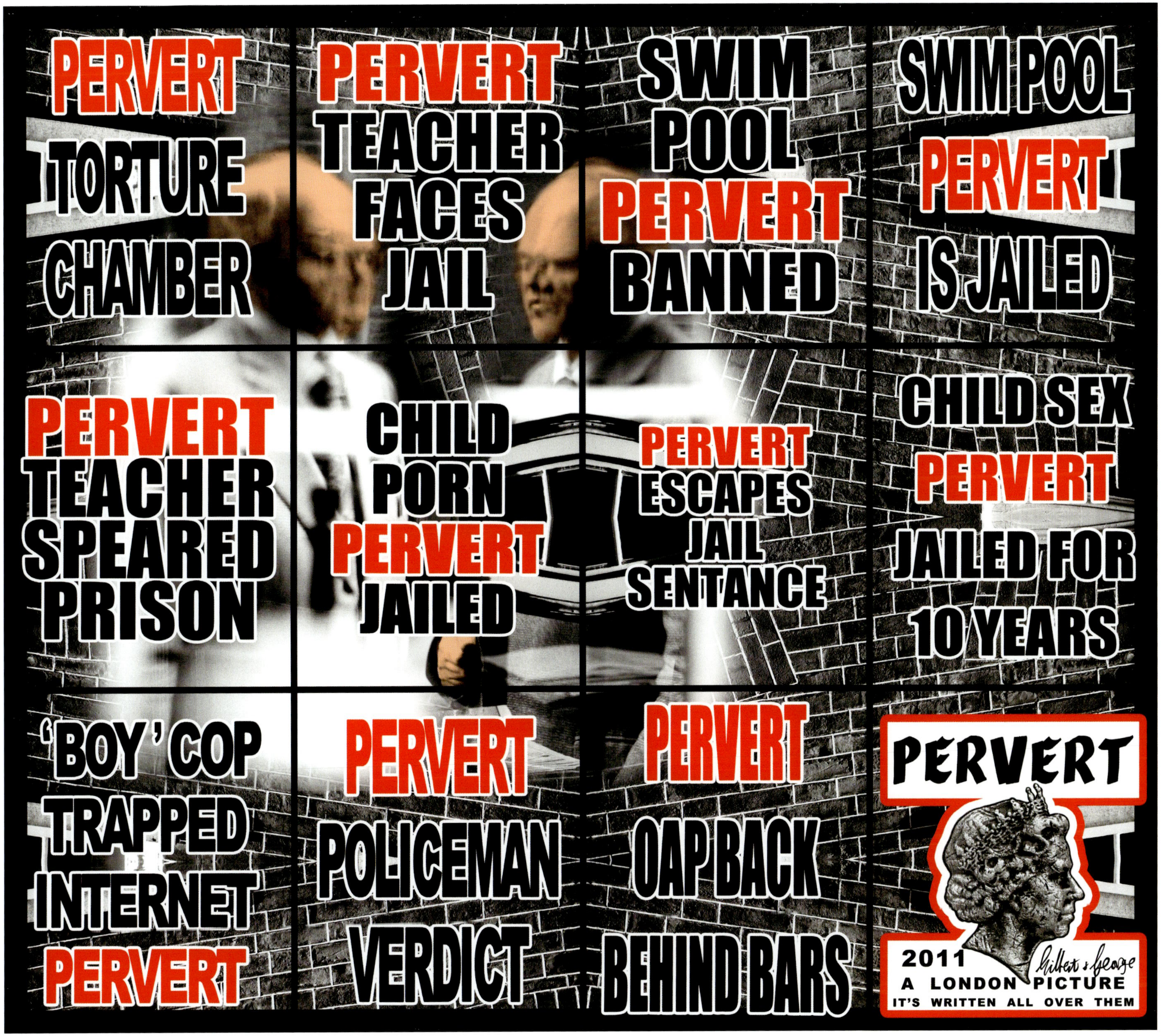
PERVERT
TORTURE
CHAMBER
PERVERT
TEACHER
FACES
JAIL
SWIM
POOL
PERVERT
BANNED
SWIM POOL
PERVERT
IS JAILED
PERVERT
TEACHER
SPEARED
PRISON
CHILD
PORN
PERVERT
JAILED
PERVERT
ESCAPES
JAIL
SENTANCE
CHILD SEX
PERVERT
JAILED FOR
10 YEARS
'BOY' COP
TRAPPED
INTERNET
PERVERT
PERVERT
POLICEMAN
VERDICT
PERVERT
OAP BACK
BEHIND BARS
PERVERT
2011
A LONDON PICTURE
IT'S WRITTEN ALL OVER THEM

PERVERT. 2011. 226 x 254 cm

WOMAN'S REVENGE ATTACK ON PLAYBOY
PLAYBOY FACES LIFE FOR MURDER
ROYAL PLAYBOY DIES
PLAYBOY
2011
Gilbert & George
A LONDON PICTURE
IT'S WRITTEN ALL OVER THEM

PLAYBOY. 2011. 151 x 127 cm

PLOT. 2011. 151 x 127 cm

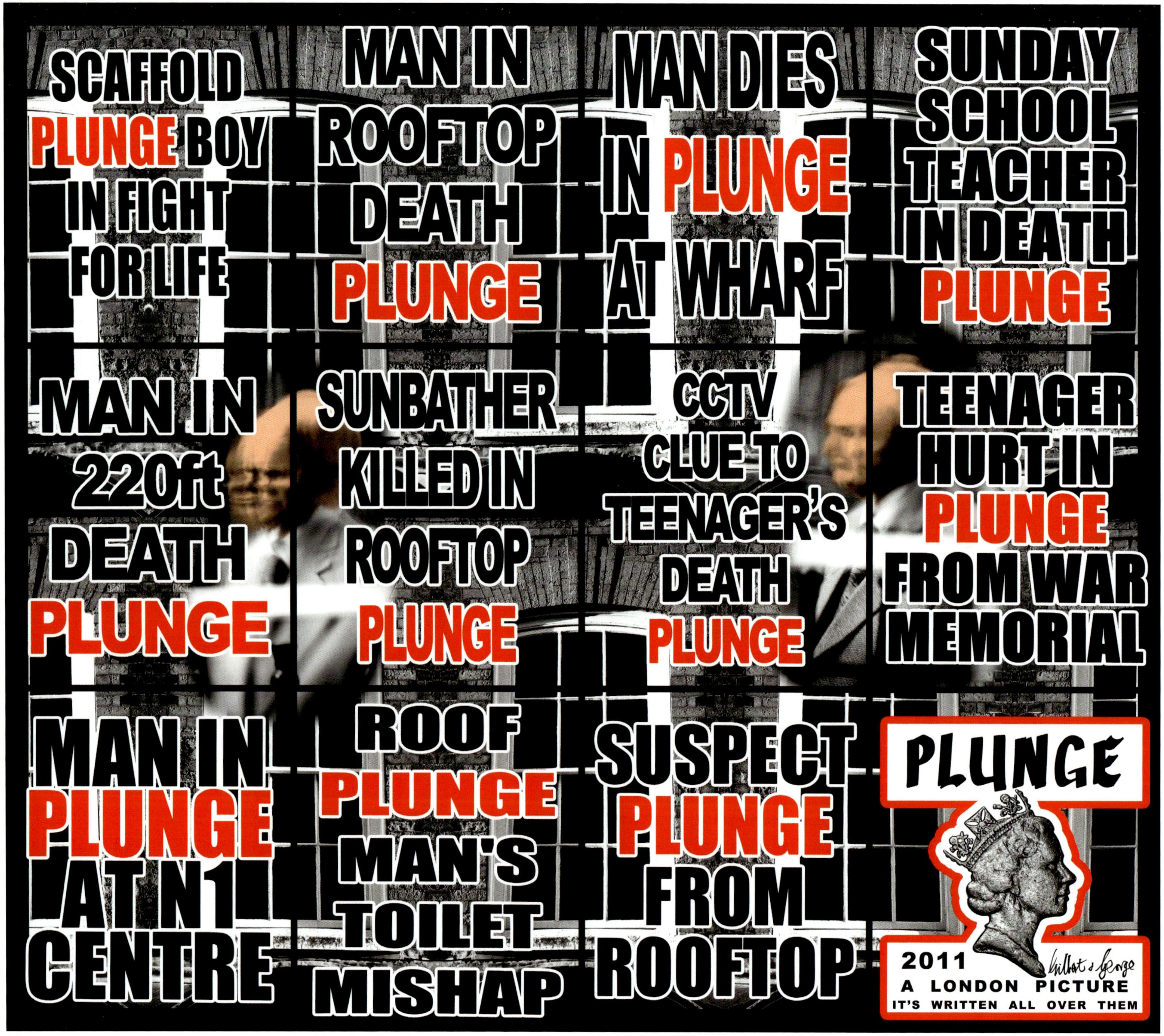
SCAFFOLD PLUNGE BOY IN FIGHT FOR LIFE
MAN IN ROOFTOP DEATH PLUNGE
MAN DIES IN PLUNGE AT WHARF
SUNDAY SCHOOL TEACHER IN DEATH PLUNGE
MAN IN 220ft DEATH PLUNGE
SUNBATHER KILLED IN ROOFTOP PLUNGE
CCTV CLUE TO TEENAGER'S DEATH PLUNGE
TEENAGER HURT IN PLUNGE FROM WAR MEMORIAL
MAN IN PLUNGE AT N1 CENTRE
ROOF PLUNGE MAN'S TOILET MISHAP
SUSPECT PLUNGE FROM ROOFTOP
PLUNGE
2011
Gilbert & George
A LONDON PICTURE
IT'S WRITTEN ALL OVER THEM

PLUNGE. 2011. 226 x 254 cm

ARMED
POLICE
FLOOD
LONDON
LONDON
POLICE
FIND
MISSING
£7M
LONDON
POLICE
FIND
MISSING
MILLIONS
LONDON
ARMED
POLICE
HUNT
'GIANT CAT'
KNIFEMAN
SLASHES
LONDON
POLICE
OFFICER
POLICE
DIG FOR
CHILDREN'S
BODIES:
PICTURES
POLICE
SORRY
OVER 2
RAPISTS
LONDON
POLICE
WORK AS
MASSEURS
POLICE
HUNT
THREE
MISSING
BOYS
ARMED
POLICE
HUNT
'GIANT
BEAST'
MADDY
POLICE
SEEK
BRITON
POLICE
HUNT
MISSING
LORD
POLICE
HUNT
MISSING
POISON
100
RIOT
POLICE
EVICT
SQUATTERS
POLICE
ARREST
BATMAN
HACKNEY:
POLICE
CLOSE
DOWN
NIGHTCLUB
POLICE
LOSE
'BOMBS'
ON TRAIN
POLICE
2011
A LONDON PICTURE
IT'S WRITTEN ALL OVER THEM

POLICE. 2011. 226 x 381 cm

POLICE
WOMAN
IS JAILED
OVERWEIGHT
POLICE
WON'T BE
HYPNOTISED
SCHOOLS
POLICE
TEAM
SLASHED
POLICE
CAR
CRASH
PROBE
POLICE
'BABY'
COPYRIGHT
ROW'
POLICE
RAID
SUSPECT
SEX DEN
POLICE
SWOOP
IN DAWN
DRUGS
RAIDS
POLICE
SWOOP
SUSPECTS
POLICE
BREAK
UP LIDO
TROUBLE
SEX CASE
POLICE
OFFICER
SACKED
POLICE
RAID ON
'HOUSE OF
HORROR'
POLICE
SWOOP
FRAUD'
CAMPAIGN
AGAINST
NOISY
POLICE
SIRENS
POLICE
CHIEF
GUILTY OF
FIT-UP
'DANGER'
RIDERS
TARGETED
BY CYCLE
POLICE
ANGER

POLICE STRAIGHT. 2011. 302 x 571 cm

20 DEATH: POLICE COULD FACE CHARGES
POLICE CALLED TO ALLY PALLY SNOW RIOT
LONDON'S £100,000 A YEAR POLICE CONSTABLE
SQUATTERS LOCK THEMSELVES IN POLICE STATION
TURKISH MOB BESIEGE POLICE STATION
POLICE SQUADS WOOP ON CRIME ESTATES
POLICE TARGET DOMESTIC VIOLENCE
POLICE RAPPED OVER DEATH IN CUSTODY
POLICE CHIEF'S PLEDGE OVER MURDER
POLICE SMASH PEOPLE SMUGGLING RING
POLICE PROBE OTING RAUD'
POLICE CHIEF QUITS IN TERROR BLUNDER
POLICE WOMAN SUES FOR SEX BIAS
POLICE DOCTORS PAID £200,000 A YEAR
POLICE GET TOUGH WITH ASIAN DRUG GANGS
BORIS LEDGES MORE POLICE ON BEAT
POLICE RAID 22 HOMES FOR DOGS
TERRORISM OFFICER TO POLICE BOROUGH
GUN POLICE TARGET CARS: 15 HELD
POLICE STRAIGHT
2011
A LONDON PICTURE
IT'S WRITTEN ALL OVER THEM
Gilbert & George

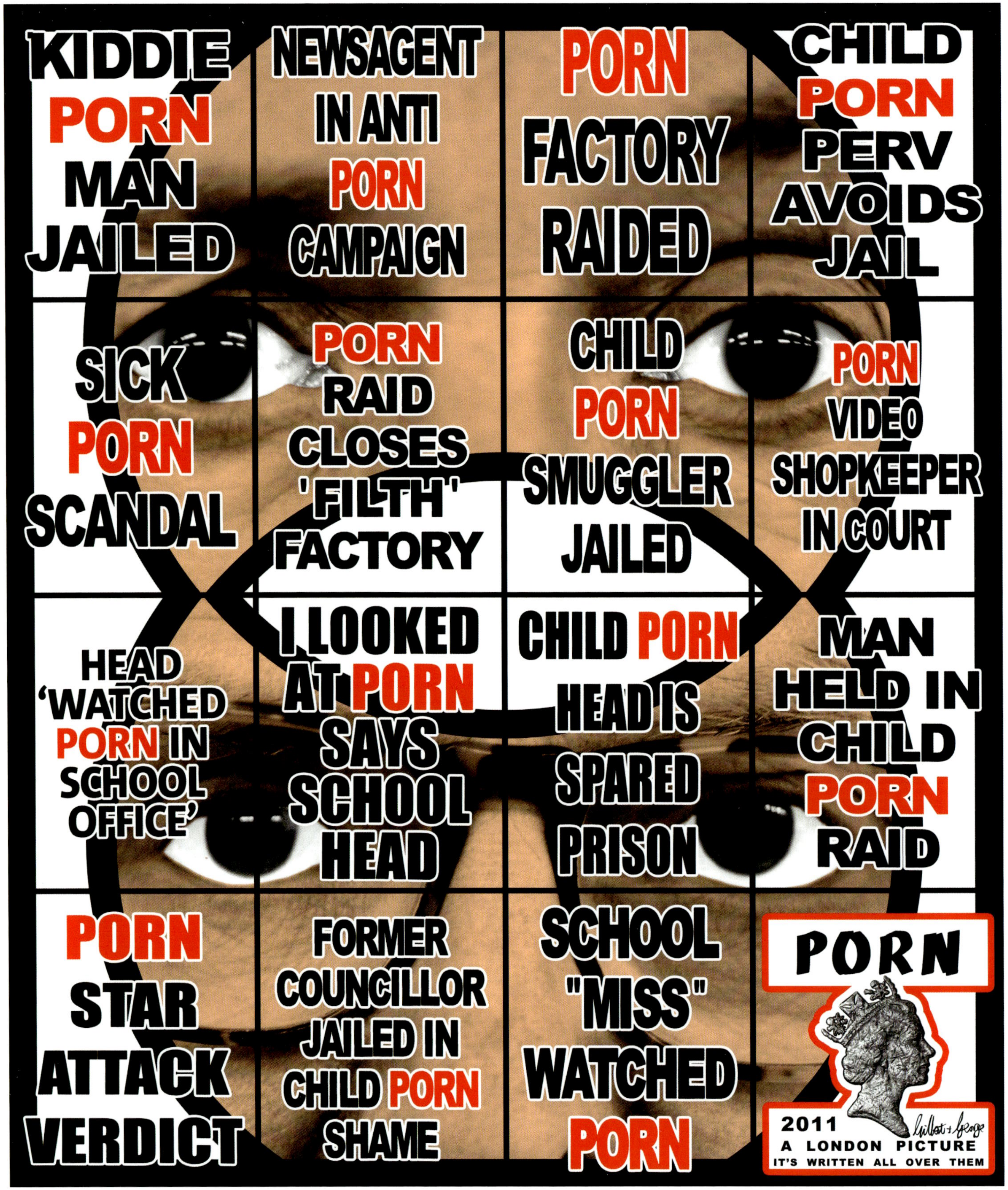
KIDDIE PORN MAN JAILED
NEWSAGENT IN ANTI PORN CAMPAIGN
PORN FACTORY RAIDED
CHILD PORN PERV AVOIDS JAIL
SICK PORN SCANDAL
PORN RAID CLOSES 'FILTH' FACTORY
CHILD PORN SMUGGLER JAILED
PORN VIDEO SHOPKEEPER IN COURT
HEAD 'WATCHED PORN IN SCHOOL OFFICE'
I LOOKED AT PORN SAYS SCHOOL HEAD
CHILD PORN HEAD IS SPARED PRISON
MAN HELD IN CHILD PORN RAID
PORN STAR ATTACK VERDICT
FORMER COUNCILLOR JAILED IN CHILD PORN SHAME
SCHOOL "MISS" WATCHED PORN
PORN
2011
A LONDON PICTURE
IT'S WRITTEN ALL OVER THEM

PORN

2011

302 x 254 cm

PREACHER. 2011. 151 x 127 cm

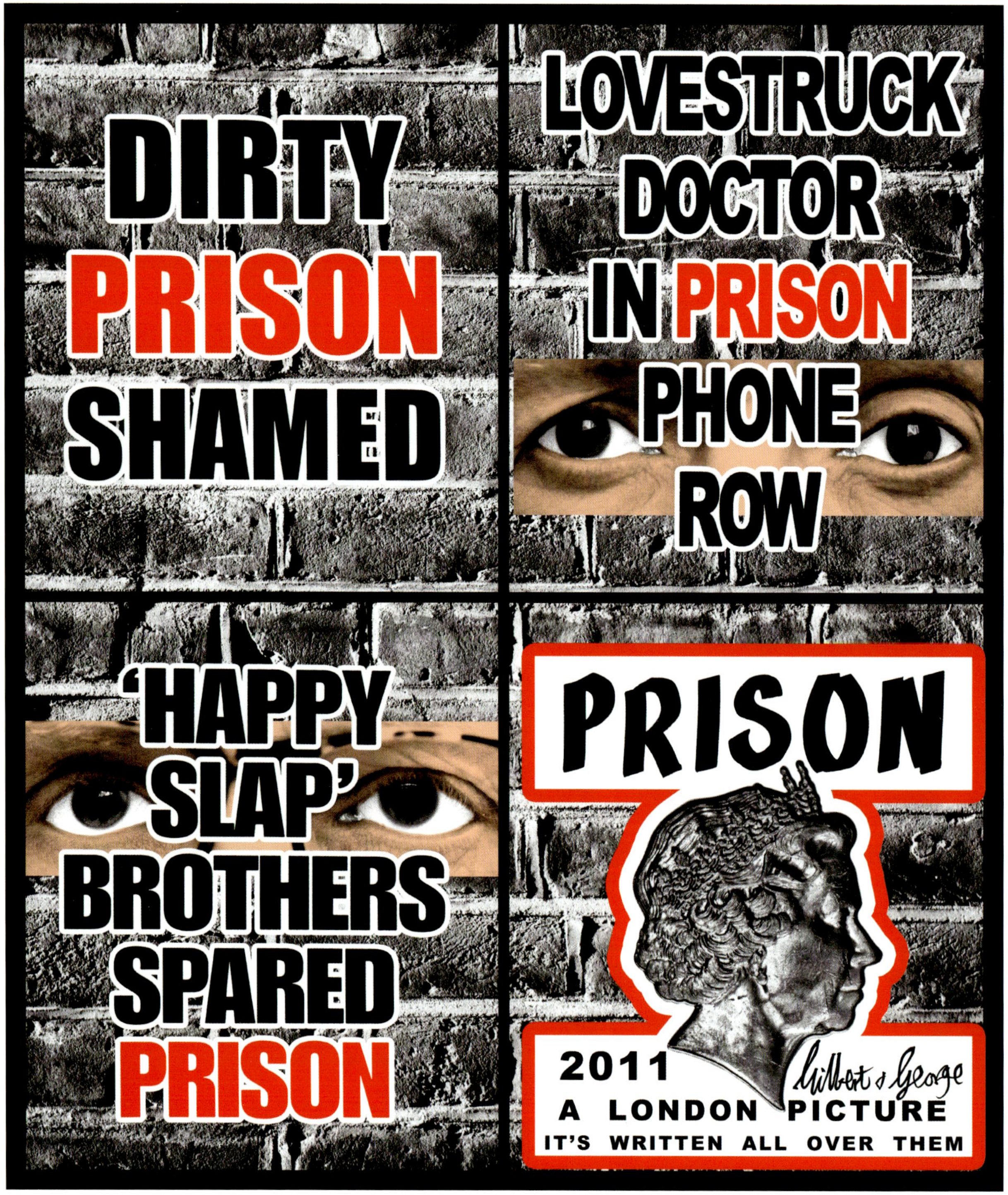
DIRTY
PRISON
SHAMED
LOVESTRUCK
DOCTOR
IN PRISON
PHONE
ROW
'HAPPY
SLAP'
BROTHERS
SPARED
PRISON
PRISON
2011
Gilbert & George
A LONDON PICTURE
IT'S WRITTEN ALL OVER THEM

PRISON. 2011. 151 x 127 cm

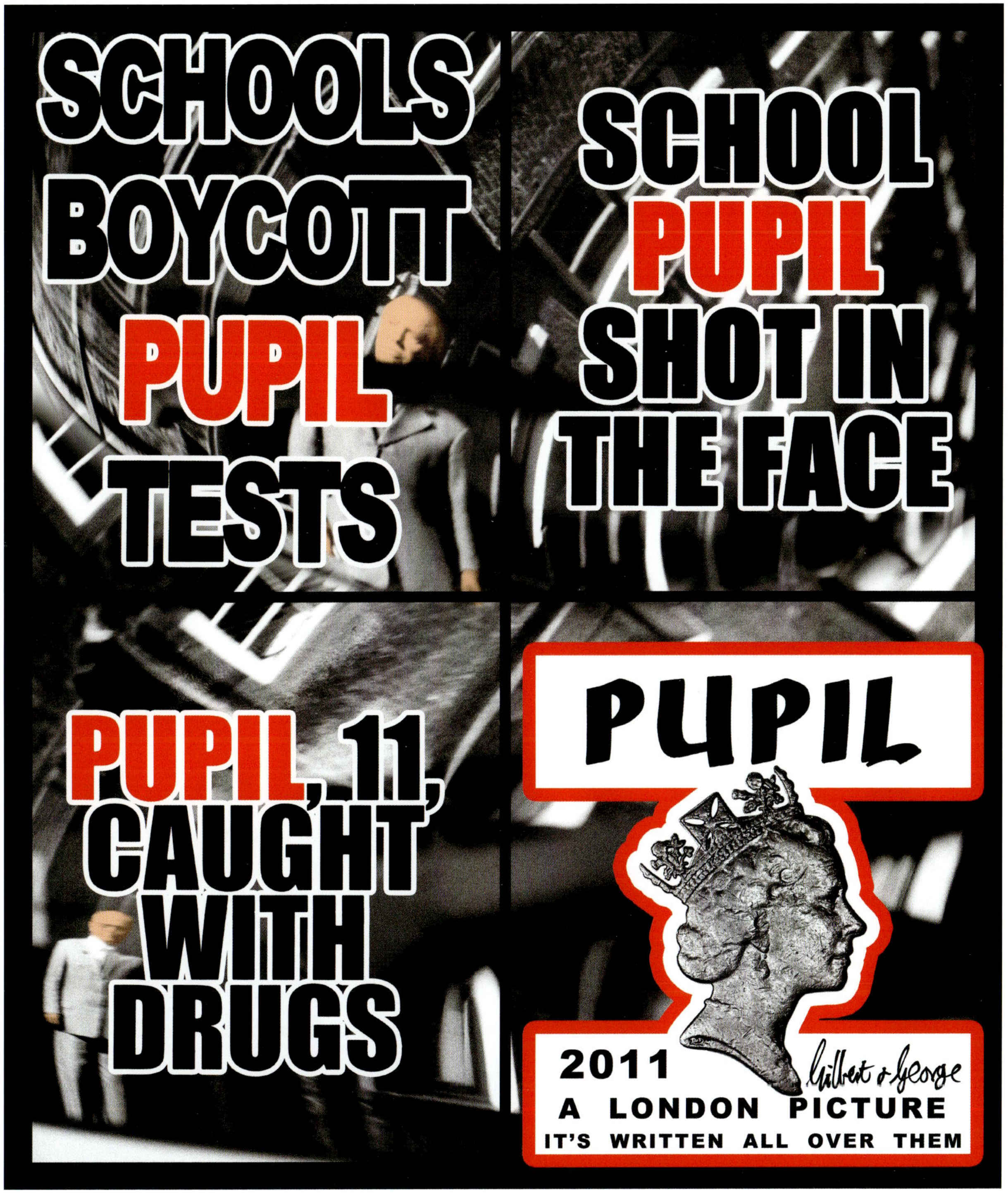
SCHOOLS
BOYCOTT
PUPIL
TESTS
SCHOOL
PUPIL
SHOT IN
THE FACE
PUPIL, 11,
CAUGHT
WITH
DRUGS
PUPIL
2011
Gilbert & George
A LONDON PICTURE
IT'S WRITTEN ALL OVER THEM

PUPIL. 2011. 151 x 127 cm

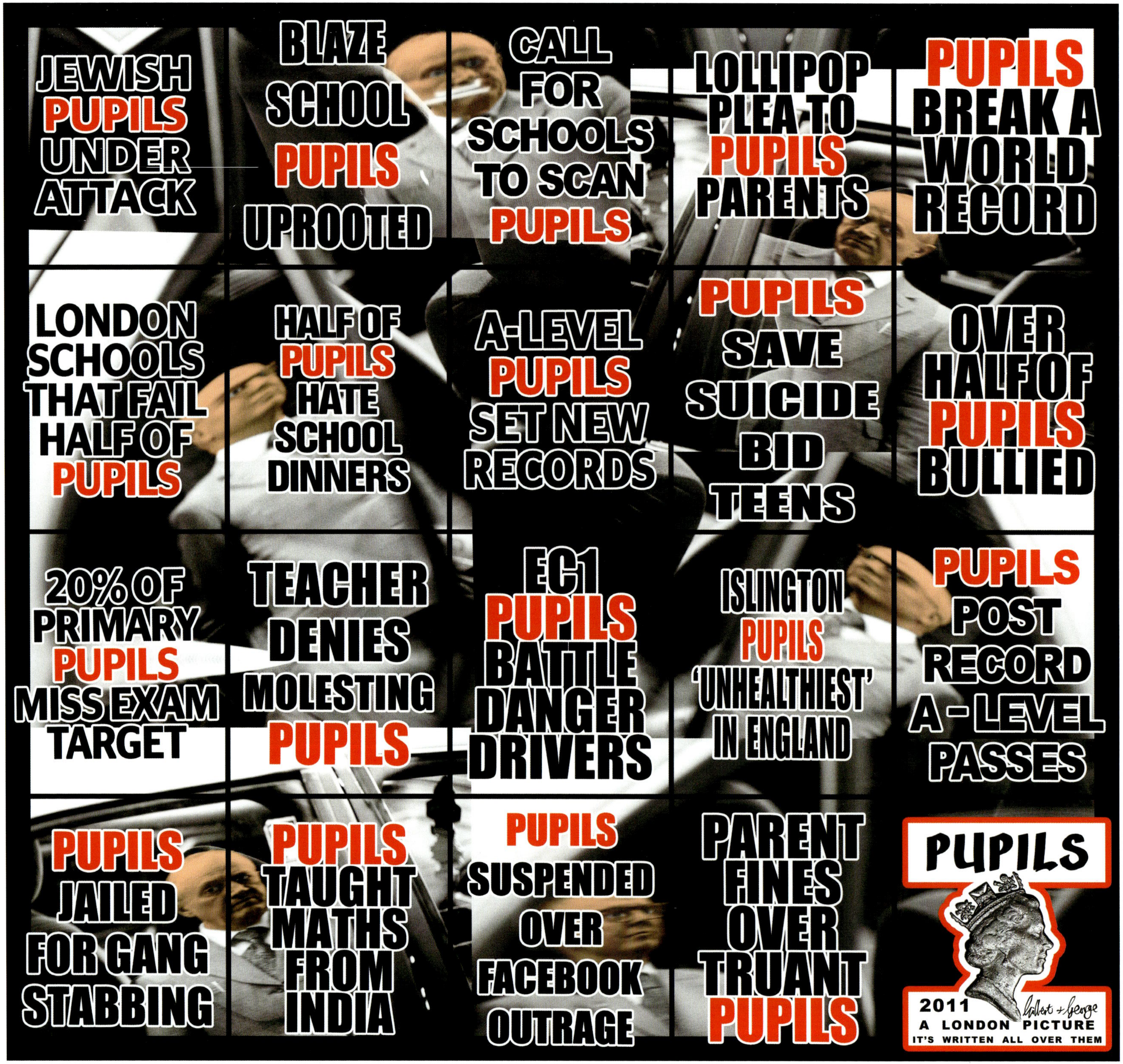
JEWISH PUPILS UNDER ATTACK
BLAZE SCHOOL PUPILS UPROOTED
CALL FOR SCHOOLS TO SCAN PUPILS
LOLLIPOP PLEA TO PUPILS PARENTS
PUPILS BREAK A WORLD RECORD
LONDON SCHOOLS THAT FAIL HALF OF PUPILS
HALF OF PUPILS HATE SCHOOL DINNERS
A-LEVEL PUPILS SET NEW RECORDS
PUPILS SAVE SUICIDE BID TEENS
OVER HALF OF PUPILS BULLIED
20% OF PRIMARY PUPILS MISS EXAM TARGET
TEACHER DENIES MOLESTING PUPILS
EC1 PUPILS BATTLE DANGER DRIVERS
ISLINGTON PUPILS 'UNHEALTHIEST' IN ENGLAND
PUPILS POST RECORD A-LEVEL PASSES
PUPILS JAILED FOR GANG STABBING
PUPILS TAUGHT MATHS FROM INDIA
PUPILS SUSPENDED OVER FACEBOOK OUTRAGE
PARENT FINES OVER TRUANT PUPILS
PUPILS
2011
A LONDON PICTURE
IT'S WRITTEN ALL OVER THEM

PUPILS. 2011. 302 x 317 cm

RACE MURDER REPORT: FULL DETAILS
BNP CHIEF'S RACE HATE TRIAL: VERDICT
RACE BACKLASH AGAINST MET CHIEF
BORIS CHIEF SACKED FOR RACE SLUR
RACE ROW MET CHIEF: DRAMATIC SHOWDOWN
RACE ROW ROCKS YARD
RACE CLASHES AT OLD BAILEY
OPEN WARFARE IN POLICE RACE ROW
HACKNEY-BOY'S 'RACE' NIGHTMARE
RACE MURDER SCANDAL
RACE CLASHES HIT WINDSOR
RACE MURDER: SOCCER STAR'S TV APPEAL
RACE REVOLT HITS YARD
BOAT RACE CAPTAIN ARRESTED
MET CHIEF IN RACE BATTLE
RACE
2011
A LONDON PICTURE
IT'S WRITTEN ALL OVER THEM

RACE

2011

302 x 254 cm

'HATE' MEETING CALLED OFF
BAN EAST END 'HATE MARCH' CALL
'HATE' CLERIC'S BOOKS BANNED
RACE HATE FUELS GANG ATTACK
XMAS HATE POSTER FURY
JEWISH SCHOOL BROKE RACE LAWS
BOY, 10, ACCUSED OF RACE HATE RAMPAGE
WE'RE STILL IN THE RACE – ARSENAL BOSS
FASHION STAR HELD OVER RACE OUTBURST
MAYORAL RACE: LABOUR AXE RAHMAN
MAN SLASHED IN RACE ATTACK
RACIST NEIGHBOUR JAILED OVER HATE CAMPAIGN
RACE TO CATCH TWO BOMBERS
'BIN BOY' IN RACE ROW
RACE HATE MAILSHOT OUTRAGE
RACE HATE
2011
A LONDON PICTURE
IT'S WRITTEN ALL OVER THEM

RACE HATE

2011

302 x 254 cm

NEWSAGENT
BEATEN IN
RACIST
ATTACK
RACIST
GANG
IN N1
ATTACK
RACIST
THUGS
STREET
TERROR
RACIST
2011
A LONDON PICTURE
IT'S WRITTEN ALL OVER THEM

RACIST. 2011. 151 x 127 cm

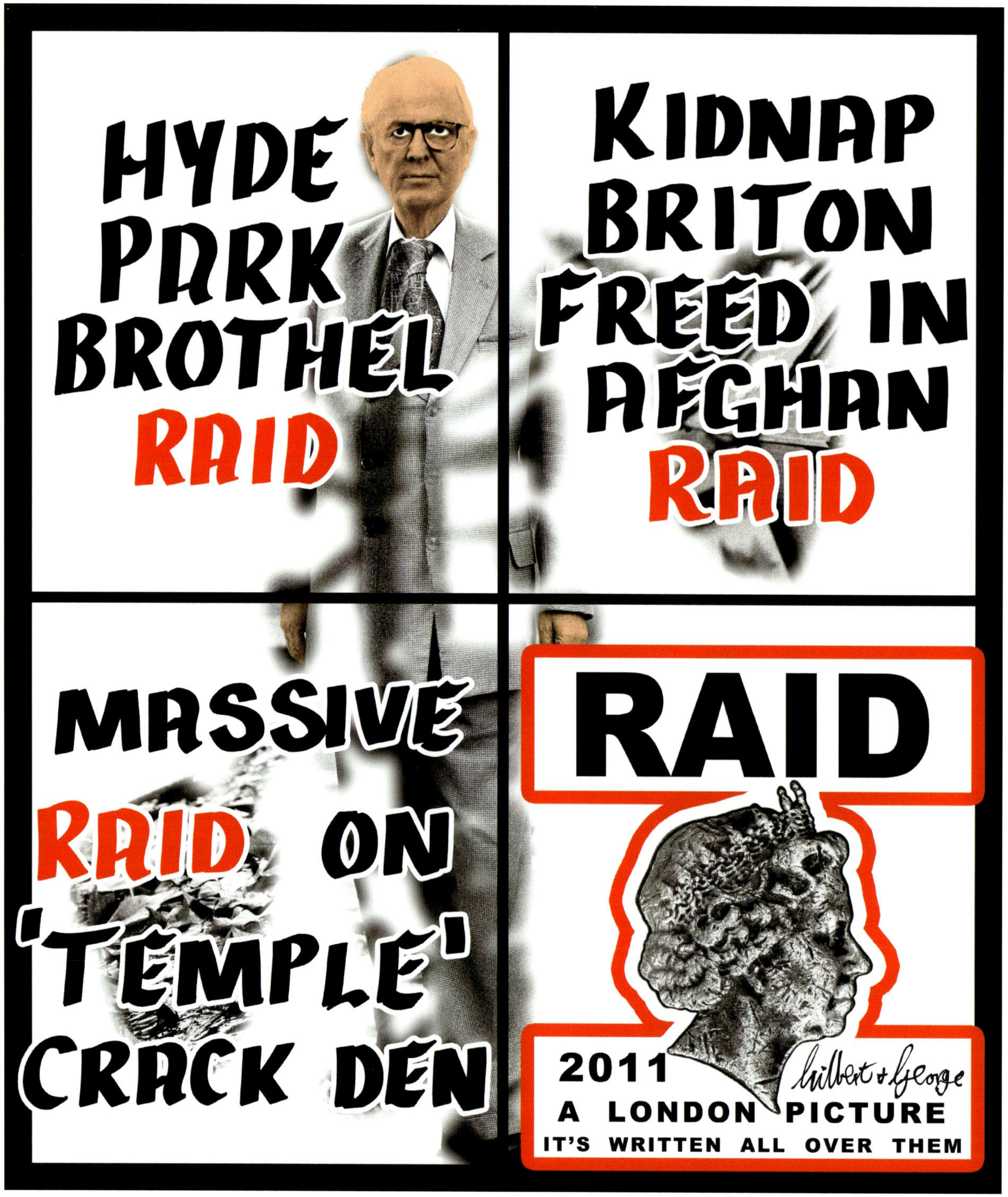
HYDE PARK BROTHEL RAID
KIDNAP BRITON FREED IN AFGHAN RAID
MASSIVE RAID ON 'TEMPLE' CRACK DEN
RAID
2011
Gilbert & George
A LONDON PICTURE
IT'S WRITTEN ALL OVER THEM

RAID. 2011. 151 x 127 cm

MAYFAIR £40m GEMS RAID
£1/2M DRUKS 'FACTORY' RAID
UPPER ST BET SHOP RAID – £10,000 REWARD
OAPS TARGET OF TERROR RAID GANG
EC1 DRUGS DEN SHUT AFTER POLICE RAID
POST OFFICE CASH VAN RAID
SECOND RAID ON JEWEL STORE
AXEMEN IN N7 GEMS RAID
RAID STRAIGHT
2011
Gilbert & George
A LONDON PICTURE
IT'S WRITTEN ALL OVER THEM

RAID STRAIGHT. 2011. 226 x 190 cm

£100,000 BANK RAIDERS HUNTED
ARCHWAY CASH RAIDERS HUNTED
DIAMOND RAIDERS HIT THE JACKPOT
ARMED RAIDERS FOILED BY KICK BOXER
REVEALED: £40m GEMS RAIDERS DISGUISE
PERFUME RAIDERS SNATCH £7,000 HAUL
HOLLOWAY RAIDERS IN £20,000 CASH SNATCH
ARMED RAIDERS SNATCH £15,000
'SHOCK AND AWE' RAIDERS JAILED
CHINESE GANG RAIDERS JAILED
HEROES CATCH ESSEX RD KNIFE RAIDERS
RAIDERS
2011
A LONDON PICTURE
IT'S WRITTEN ALL OVER THEM

RAIDERS. 2011. 226 x 254 cm

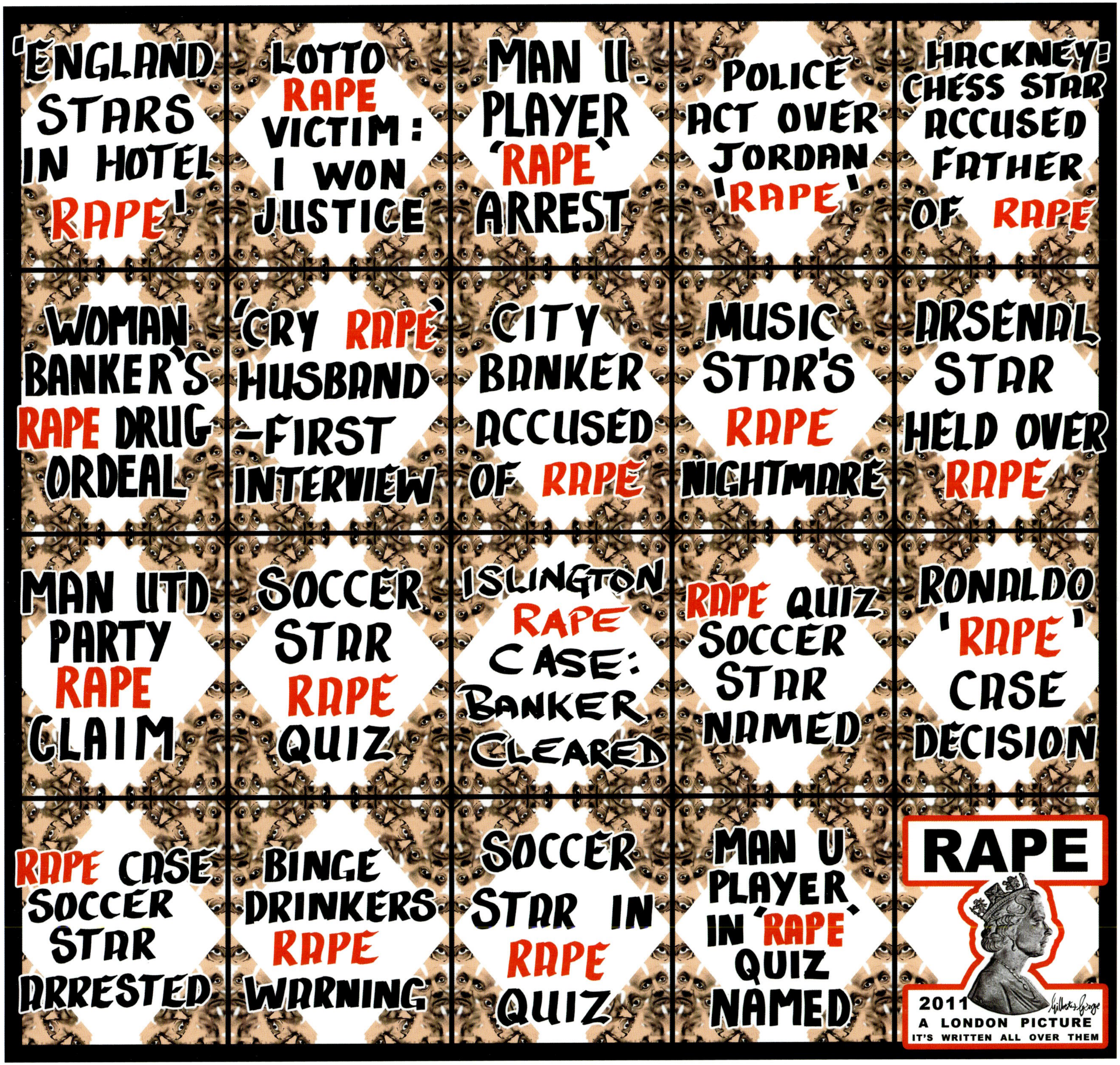
'ENGLAND STARS IN HOTEL RAPE'
LOTTO RAPE VICTIM: I WON JUSTICE
MAN U. PLAYER 'RAPE' ARREST
POLICE ACT OVER JORDAN 'RAPE'
HACKNEY: CHESS STAR ACCUSED FATHER OF RAPE
WOMAN BANKER'S RAPE DRUG ORDEAL
'CRY RAPE' HUSBAND -FIRST INTERVIEW
CITY BANKER ACCUSED OF RAPE
MUSIC STAR'S RAPE NIGHTMARE
ARSENAL STAR HELD OVER RAPE
MAN UTD PARTY RAPE CLAIM
SOCCER STAR RAPE QUIZ
ISLINGTON RAPE CASE: BANKER CLEARED
RAPE QUIZ SOCCER STAR NAMED
RONALDO 'RAPE' CASE DECISION
RAPE CASE SOCCER STAR ARRESTED
BINGE DRINKERS RAPE WARNING
SOCCER STAR IN RAPE QUIZ
MAN U PLAYER IN 'RAPE' QUIZ NAMED
RAPE
2011
A LONDON PICTURE
IT'S WRITTEN ALL OVER THEM

RAPE. 2011. 302 x 317 cm

ANGER AT CASH CUT TO CENTRES FOR RAPE VICTIMS
BRAVE RAPE VICTIM TELLS OF ORDEAL
DANGER MAN IS JAILED FOR RAPE HORROR
RAPE VICTIM SEES HER ATTACKER JAILED
CLERK CLEARED OF DATE RAPE
RAPE LAWYER WINS TOP HONOUR
GIRL'S 'BLINDFOLD RAPE ORDEAL'
FATHER CLEARED OF RAPE CHARGES
HORROR OF GANG RAPE ATTACK
GANG RAPE: MAN HELD
GANG-RAPE BID MEN SENTENCED
STEPNEY TRAINEE LAWYER IN DOCK FOR RAPE
SCHOOLBOYS CONVICTED OF GANG RAPE
GIRL'S KIDNAP RAPE ORDEAL
NIGHT CLUB MAN JAILED FOR RAPE ATTACK
STRANDED MUM'S RAPE ORDEAL
HOLLOWAY POSTMAN JAILED FOR RAPE
ESTATE AGENT JAILED FOR RAPE
DISC JOCKEY RECORDED RAPE ON HIS CAMCORDER
CAB RAPE VICTIM'S HORROR RIDE
WOMAN'S 'HOSTAGE AND RAPE' ORDEAL
CAMDEN PASSAGE RAPE HORROR
'GURU' JAILED FOR RAPE RAMPAGE
MAN CHARGED WITH N4 RAPE
TONGUE BITE SNARES RAPE FIEND
BRUTAL GANG RAPE OF GIRL, 16
NINE JAILED FOR GANG RAPE OF GIRL. 14
RAPE STRAIGHT
2011
A LONDON PICTURE
IT'S WRITTEN ALL OVER THEM

RAPE STRAIGHT. 2011. 302 x 444 cm

CLUBBER IS GANG RAPED IN MINICAB
WOMAN RAPED BY THE POSTMAN
HIGHBURY SINGER 'RAPED AT GUNPOINT'
'I WAS RAPED ON PUB FLOOR' – COURT TOLD
WOMAN RAPED IN MUSUEM GARDENS
WOMAN IS RAPED AT KNIFEPOINT
BOY OF 7 'RAPED IN BUSHES BY TEENAGER'
TEENAGER RAPED BY SERIAL SEX ATTACKER
GIRL, 11, RAPED IN PARK
FACE OF FIEND WHO RAPED OAP
GIRL, 12 RAPED ON WAY TO SCHOOL
GIRL, 4, RAPED BY N1 SEX BEAST
POPHAM ROAD MAN RAPED GIRL, 10
FIEND RAPED ELDERLY GRANNY
TEEN RAPED IN NIGHTMARE ATTACK
RAPED
2011
A LONDON PICTURE
IT'S WRITTEN ALL OVER THEM

RAPED

2011

302 x 254 cm

10 LIFE SENTENCES FOR SUBURBAN RAPIST
CAMDEN RICKSHAW RAPIST JAILED
HUNT FOR WHITECHAPEL RAPIST
X FACTOR WINNER'S RAPIST FATHER
HUNT FOR SERIAL RAPIST
RAPIST LINKED TO 11 MURDERS
BLACK CAB RAPIST: VERDICTS
SERIAL RAPIST TARGETED SUBURBS
RAPIST
2011
A LONDON PICTURE
IT'S WRITTEN ALL OVER THEM

RAPIST. 2011. 226 x 190 cm

'SERIAL RAPIST' DENIES LATEST ATTACK
CAR WASH BOSS RAPIST JAILED
GRANNY RAPIST JAILED FOR LIFE
E.LONDON: MASS DNA TESTS TO CATCH RAPIST
RAPIST WARNING AFTER WOMAN ATTACKED
RAPIST 'FORCED SCISSORS DOWN MY THROAT'
SIX YEARS FOR RAPIST
CONVICTED RAPIST AWAITS SENTENCE
RAPIST JAILED AFTER 11 YEARS
RAPIST SAID HE WAS LULU'S SON
BRUTAL PARTY RAPIST JAILED
ESSEX RD ALLEY RAPIST JAILED
POLICE HUNT SERIAL RAPIST
WANTED: GUNMAN AND RAPIST
DOUBLE RAPIST GETS 14 YEARS
RAPIST BEAST JAILED
SODA RAPIST GIVEN 8 MORE YEARS
SERIAL RAPIST STALKS BOW
RAPIST JAILED FOR NEW SEX ATTACK
RAPIST STRAIGHT
2011
A LONDON PICTURE
IT'S WRITTEN ALL OVER THEM

RAPIST STRAIGHT. 2011. 302 x 317 cm

FOOD BOSS IN RAT PLAGUE
RAT RUN ROAD CLOSURE RUCKUS
LOVE RAT STRANGLES GIRLFRIEND WITH FLEX
RAT
2011
Gilbert + George
A LONDON PICTURE
IT'S WRITTEN ALL OVER THEM

RAT. 2011. 151 x 127 cm

MAILBOXES SEALED AFTER POSTIES ROBBED
SHOP MAN BEATEN, ROBBED
LIFT DEATH BANKER'S HUSBAND 'ROBBED OF JUSTICE'
ELDERLY COUPLE ROBBED OF LIFE SAVINGS
GRANNY ROBBED OF XMAS CASH IN CEMETERY
'KILLERS ROBBED ME OF MY FAMILY'
DISABLED MAN ROBBED AT GUNPOINT
ROBBED
2011
A LONDON PICTURE
IT'S WRITTEN ALL OVER THEM

ROBBED. 2011. 151 x 254 cm

TRAVEL AGENT ROBBER GETS 5 YEARS
STORE ATTACK ROBER JAILED
JUDGE'S AMAZING LET-OFF FOR 'CAR ROBBER'
NI JAW BREAK ROBBER JAILED
ROBBER HOLDS KNIFE TO SHOPPER'S THROAT
ROBBER
2011
A LONDON PICTURE
IT'S WRITTEN ALL OVER THEM

ROBBER. 2011. 151 x 190 cm

VIOLENT ROBBERS ATTACK LONE WOMAN
SECURITY VAN ROBBERS JAILED
ROBBERS GRAB £10,000 IN BANK AMBUSH
WOMEN ROBBERS ATTACK GRANDAD
FATHER AND SON ROBBERS JAILED
ROBBERS STEAL DRUGS FROM PHARMACY
GRAVE ROBBERS WARNING
ROBBERS BEAT JEWELLER TO DEATH
AIRPORT ROBBERS GUILTY IN CASE THAT COST £25m
HAVE-A-GO HEROINE ROUTS ROBBERS WITH MOP
MASKED ROBBERS ATTACK PREGNANT WOMAN
ROBBERS
2011
A LONDON PICTURE
IT'S WRITTEN ALL OVER THEM
Gilbert & George

ROBBERS. 2011. 226 x 254 cm

PROTESTS AT RAIL FARES 'ROBBERY'
£50m ROBBERY: CCTV PICTURE
ROBBERY WITNESS £7m DEATH THREAT
£40m ROBBERY -LATEST
100 POLICE SMASH ROBBERY GANG
£53 MILLION SECURITAS ROBBERY VERDICTS
£50m ROBBERY: NEW DETAILS
ARMED ROBBERY CASES SOAR
ROBBERY
2011
A LONDON PICTURE
IT'S WRITTEN ALL OVER THEM

ROBBERY. 2011. 226 x 190 cm

YOUTHS ON CANAL ROBBERY CHARGES
JEWELLERS CAUGHT IN ROBBERY SCAM
CANAL TOWPATH ROBBERY GANG WARNING
MOPED RIDERS IN HIGHWAY ROBBERY
POST OFFICE ROBBERY WARNING TO OAPS
ROBBERY STRAIGHT
2011
Gilbert & George
A LONDON PICTURE
IT'S WRITTEN ALL OVER THEM

ROBBERY STRAIGHT. 2011. 151 x 190 cm

SCHOOL JANITOR ARREST SHOCK
SCHOOL HEPATITUS ALERT
SEX CLINIC TO OPEN NEXT TO SCHOOL
BULLIES' VICTIM: MY SCHOOL HELL
SECURITY FEAR AT 'SCHOOL OF FEAR'
BONES FIND HOLDS UP SCHOOL MOVE
SCHOOL BAN ON ICE CREAM VAN
DOUBLE DISASTER HITS SCHOOL
MORE STRIKES LOOM AT CRISIS SCHOOL
SCHOOL PARKING PERIL SPARKS CLASH
£2 MILLION SPORTS HALL FOR SCHOOL
SCHOOL SET TO WAKE THE DEAD
MP IN SCHOOL VIDEO BACKLASH
STRIKE THREAT OVER SCHOOL DEADLOCK
SCHOOL GETS TOPS MARKS
£95,000 A YEAR FOR PRIMARY SCHOOL HEAD
EC1 SCHOOL SET TO CLOSE
GO-AHEAD FOR £13M SCHOOL MOVE
TOP CHURCHMAN VISITS SCHOOL
SCHOOL CHIEFS SLAM CLOSURE PLANS

SCHOOL STRAIGHT. 2011. 377 x 635 cm

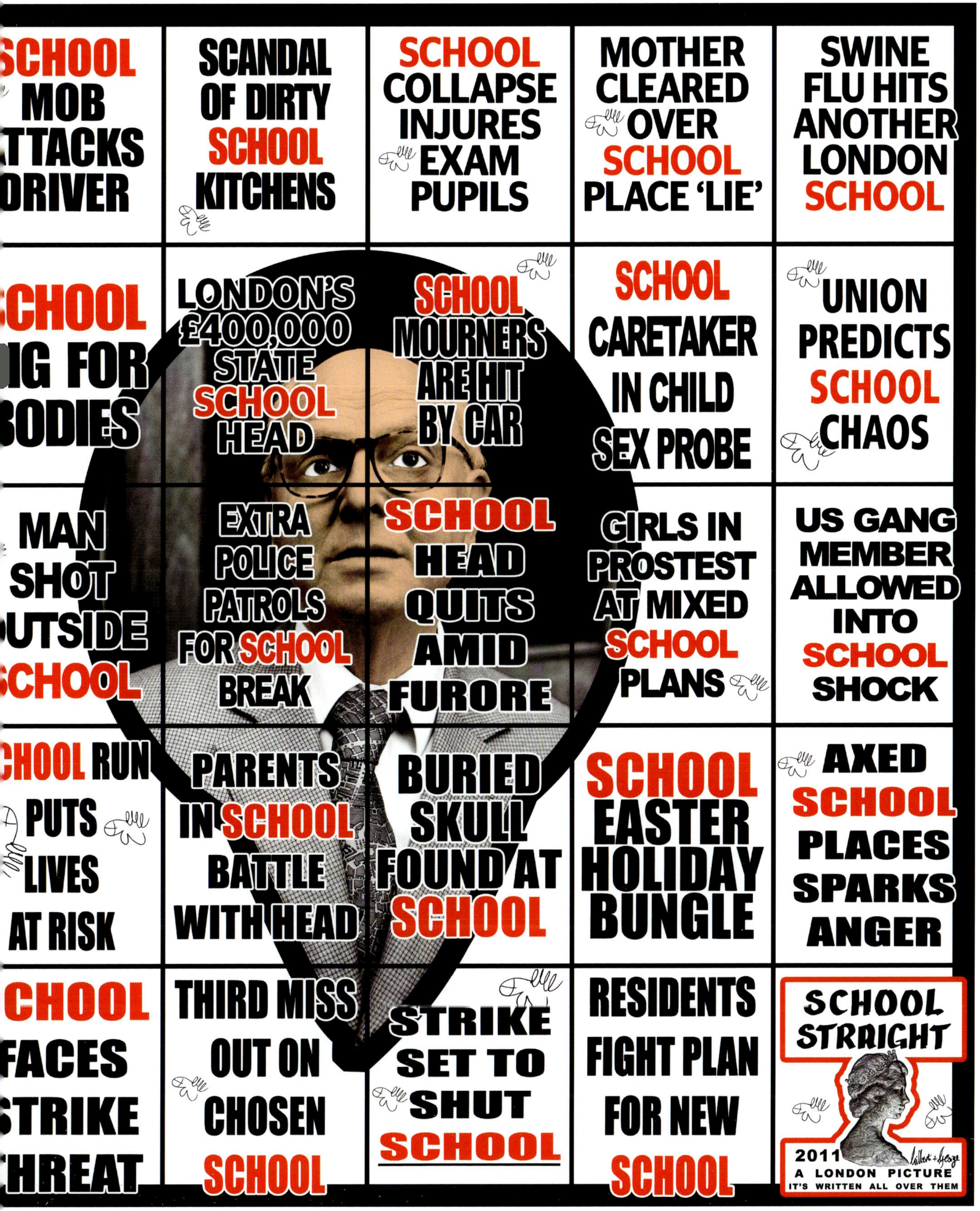
MOB
SCANDAL OF DIRTY SCHOOL KITCHENS
SCHOOL COLLAPSE INJURES EXAM PUPILS
MOTHER CLEARED OVER SCHOOL PLACE 'LIE'
SWINE FLU HITS ANOTHER LONDON SCHOOL
LONDON'S £400,000 STATE SCHOOL HEAD
SCHOOL MOURNERS ARE HIT BY CAR
SCHOOL CARETAKER IN CHILD SEX PROBE
UNION PREDICTS SCHOOL CHAOS
MAN SHOT
EXTRA POLICE PATROLS FOR SCHOOL BREAK
SCHOOL HEAD QUITS AMID FURORE
GIRLS IN PROSTEST AT MIXED SCHOOL PLANS
US GANG MEMBER ALLOWED INTO SCHOOL SHOCK
PUTS LIVES AT RISK
PARENTS IN SCHOOL BATTLE WITH HEAD
BURIED SKULL FOUND AT SCHOOL
SCHOOL EASTER HOLIDAY BUNGLE
AXED SCHOOL PLACES SPARKS ANGER
FACES
THIRD MISS OUT ON CHOSEN SCHOOL
STRIKE SET TO SHUT SCHOOL
RESIDENTS FIGHT PLAN FOR NEW SCHOOL
SCHOOL STRAIGHT
2011
A LONDON PICTURE
IT'S WRITTEN ALL OVER THEM

WOMAN MURDERED OUTSIDE LONDON SCHOOL
SCHOOL MASSACRE – FIRST DETAILS OF KILLER
HARROW SCHOOL MURDER – LATEST
SCHOOL RAPIST'S PAST REVEALED
SCHOOL SHOOTING MASSACRE – FULL DETAILS
LONDON SCHOOL HAS 100 SPY CAMERAS
SCHOOL TRIP DROWNING TRAGEDY
HARROW SCHOOL TRAGEDY – LATEST
TV CHEF'S SCHOOL MEALS VICTORY
SCHOOL BUS MASSACRE IN IRAQ
3 GIRLS RAPED ON SCHOOL TRIP
ISLINGTON SCHOOL ROW DEEPENS
SCHOOL SEX INSULTS BANNED
SCHOOL PERVERTS ROW GROWS
SCHOOL TRIP DRINK TRAGEDY
HEFTY FINES FOR SCHOOL PLACE CHEATS
SCHOOL PORN SCANDAL
PILOT CRASH-LANDS ON SCHOOL FIELD
50.000 LONDON PUPILS WITH NO SCHOOL
SCHOOL
2011
A LONDON PICTURE
IT'S WRITTEN ALL OVER THEM

SCHOOL. 2011. 302 x 317 cm

SCHOOLBOY
KNIFED
IN PARK
ATTACK
SCHOOLBOY
ROBBED BY
KNIFE GANG
SCHOOLBOY
WINS WORLD
TITLE
SCHOOLBOY
STABBED BY
KNIFE GANG
THOUSANDS
MOURN
SCHOOLBOY
STABBING
VICTIM
SCHOOLBOY
STABBED
AT BUS
STOP
SCHOOLBOY
CHARGED
WITH
MURDER
SCHOOLBOY
2011
A LONDON PICTURE
IT'S WRITTEN ALL OVER THEM

SCHOOLBOY. 2011. 151 x 254 cm

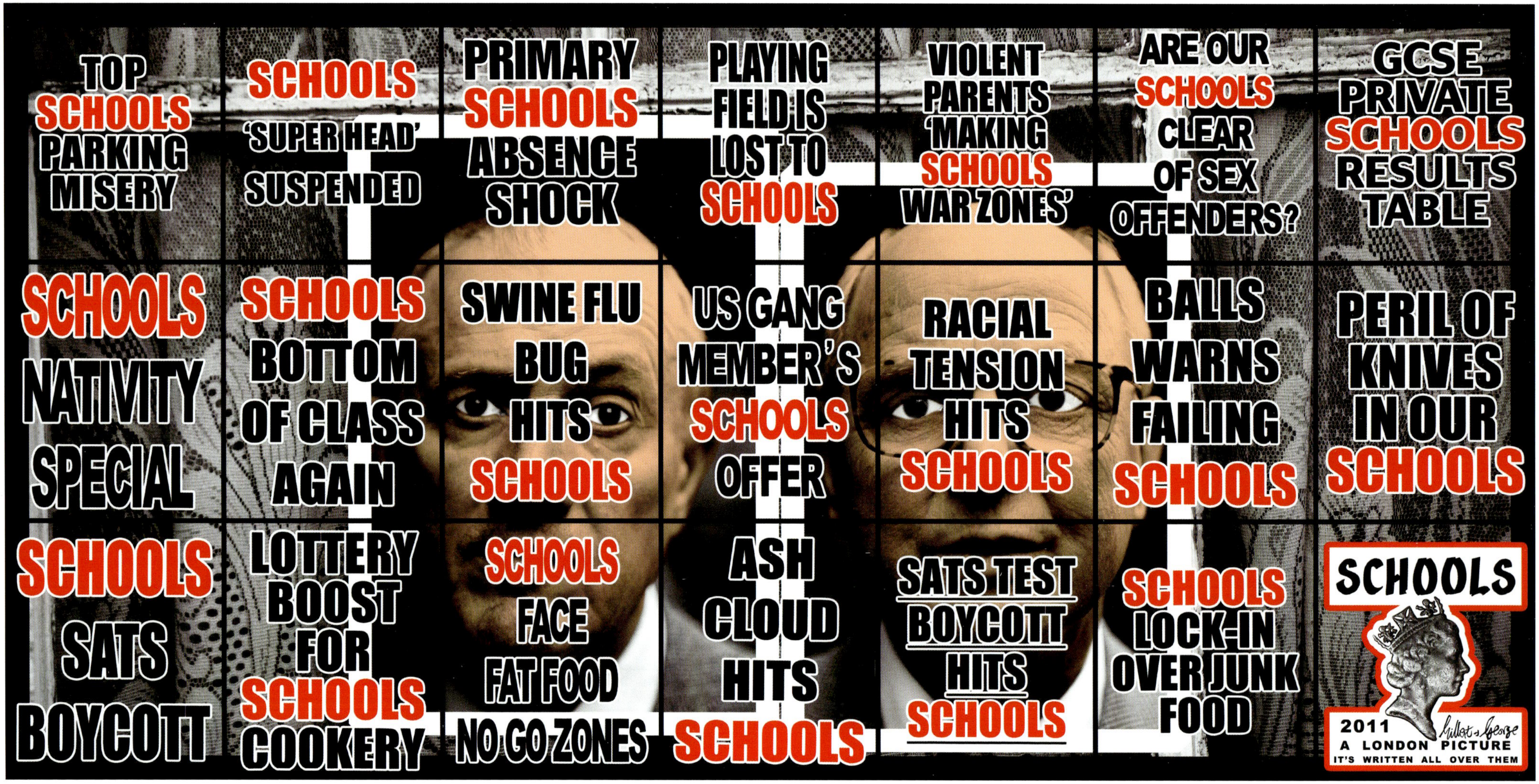
TOP SCHOOLS PARKING MISERY
SCHOOLS 'SUPER HEAD' SUSPENDED
PRIMARY SCHOOLS ABSENCE SHOCK
PLAYING FIELD IS LOST TO SCHOOLS
VIOLENT PARENTS 'MAKING SCHOOLS WAR ZONES'
ARE OUR SCHOOLS CLEAR OF SEX OFFENDERS?
GCSE PRIVATE SCHOOLS RESULTS TABLE
SCHOOLS NATIVITY SPECIAL
SCHOOLS BOTTOM OF CLASS AGAIN
SWINE FLU BUG HITS SCHOOLS
US GANG MEMBER'S SCHOOLS OFFER
RACIAL TENSION HITS SCHOOLS
BALLS WARNS FAILING SCHOOLS
PERIL OF KNIVES IN OUR SCHOOLS
SCHOOLS SATS BOYCOTT
LOTTERY BOOST FOR SCHOOLS COOKERY
SCHOOLS FACE FAT FOOD NO GO ZONES
ASH CLOUD HITS SCHOOLS
SATS TEST BOYCOTT HITS SCHOOLS
SCHOOLS LOCK-IN OVER JUNK FOOD
SCHOOLS
2011
A LONDON PICTURE
IT'S WRITTEN ALL OVER THEM

SCHOOLS. 2011. 226 x 444 cm

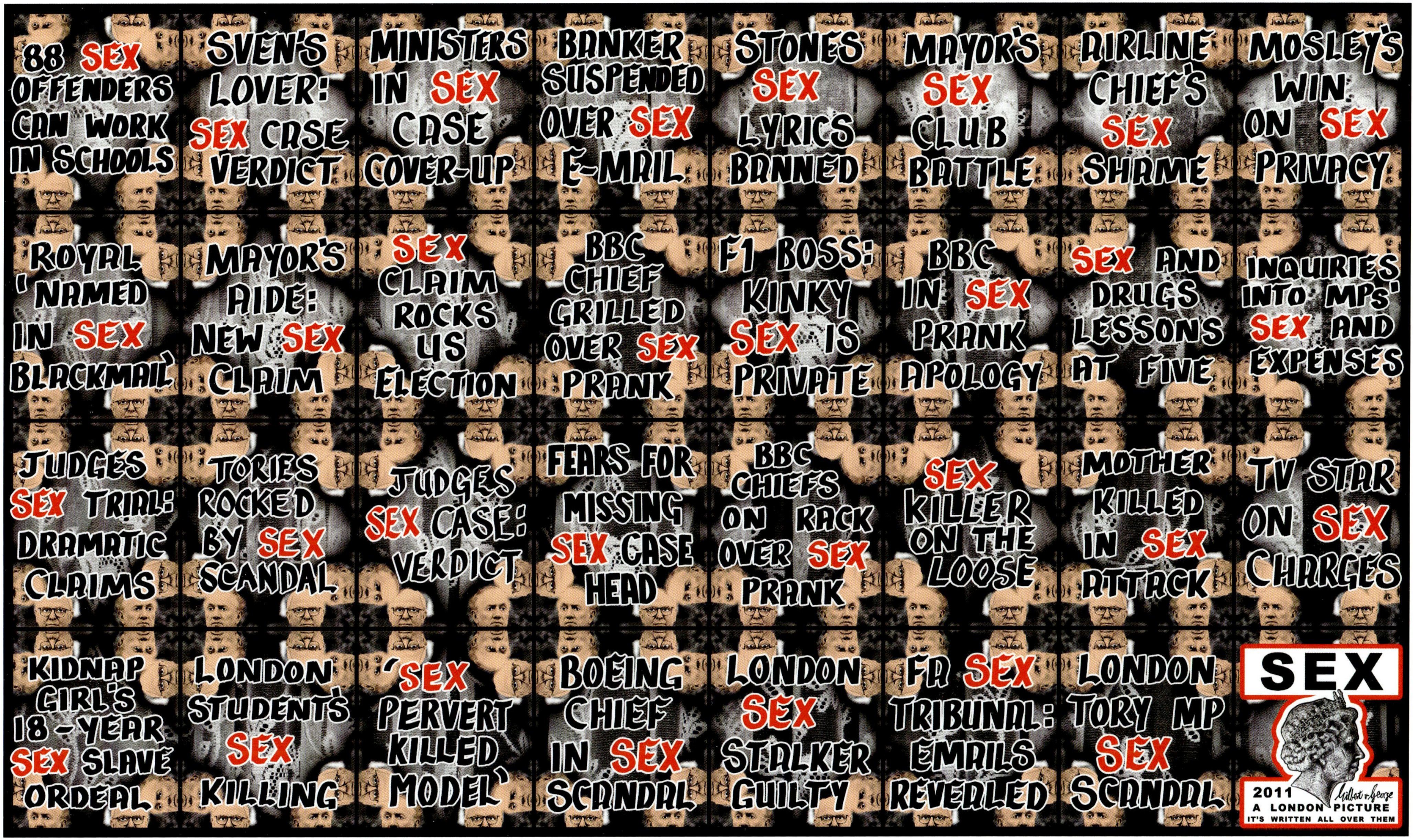
88 SEX OFFENDERS CAN WORK IN SCHOOLS
SVEN'S LOVER: SEX CASE VERDICT
MINISTERS IN SEX CASE COVER-UP
BANKER SUSPENDED OVER SEX E-MAIL
STONES SEX LYRICS BANNED
MAYOR'S SEX CLUB BATTLE
AIRLINE CHIEF'S SEX SHAME
MOSLEY'S WIN ON SEX PRIVACY
ROYAL 'NAMED IN SEX BLACKMAIL'
MAYOR'S AIDE: NEW SEX CLAIM
SEX CLAIM ROCKS US ELECTION
BBC CHIEF GRILLED OVER SEX PRANK
F1 BOSS: KINKY SEX IS PRIVATE
BBC IN SEX PRANK APOLOGY
SEX AND DRUGS LESSONS AT FIVE
INQUIRIES INTO MPS' SEX AND EXPENSES
JUDGES SEX TRIAL: DRAMATIC CLAIMS
TORIES ROCKED BY SEX SCANDAL
JUDGES SEX CASE: VERDICT
FEARS FOR MISSING SEX CASE HEAD
BBC CHIEFS ON RACK OVER SEX PRANK
SEX KILLER ON THE LOOSE
MOTHER KILLED IN SEX ATTACK
TV STAR ON SEX CHARGES
KIDNAP GIRL'S 18-YEAR SEX SLAVE ORDEAL
LONDON STUDENT'S SEX KILLING
'SEX PERVERT KILLED MODEL'
BOEING CHIEF IN SEX SCANDAL
LONDON SEX STALKER GUILTY
FA SEX TRIBUNAL: EMAILS REVEALED
LONDON TORY MP SEX SCANDAL
SEX
2011
A LONDON PICTURE
IT'S WRITTEN ALL OVER THEM

SEX. 2011. 302 x 508 cm

TV STAR'S £100,000 SEX SLUR
WOMAN BANKER'S £10M SEX CASE
WAITRESS IN £124,000 SEX BATTLE
CITY BANKER'S £11M SEX CLAIM
SEX VICTIM: £3M AWARD
BANKER'S £5M SEX CASE
£800M CITY SEX CASE
MP: I WAS OFFERED £10,000 FOR SEX
SEX & MONEY
2011
A LONDON PICTURE
IT'S WRITTEN ALL OVER THEM

SEX & MONEY. 2011. 226 x 190 cm

CRAZED SEX ATTACKER HUNTED
N1 CHAT ROOM SEX ATTACKER FACES JAIL
STATION SEX ATTACKER HUNTED
REIGN OF TERROR BY SEX ATTACKER
MUM'S SEX ATTACKER WINS JAIL CUT
SEX ATTACKER
2011
A LONDON PICTURE
IT'S WRITTEN ALL OVER THEM

SEX ATTACKER. 2011. 151 x 190 cm

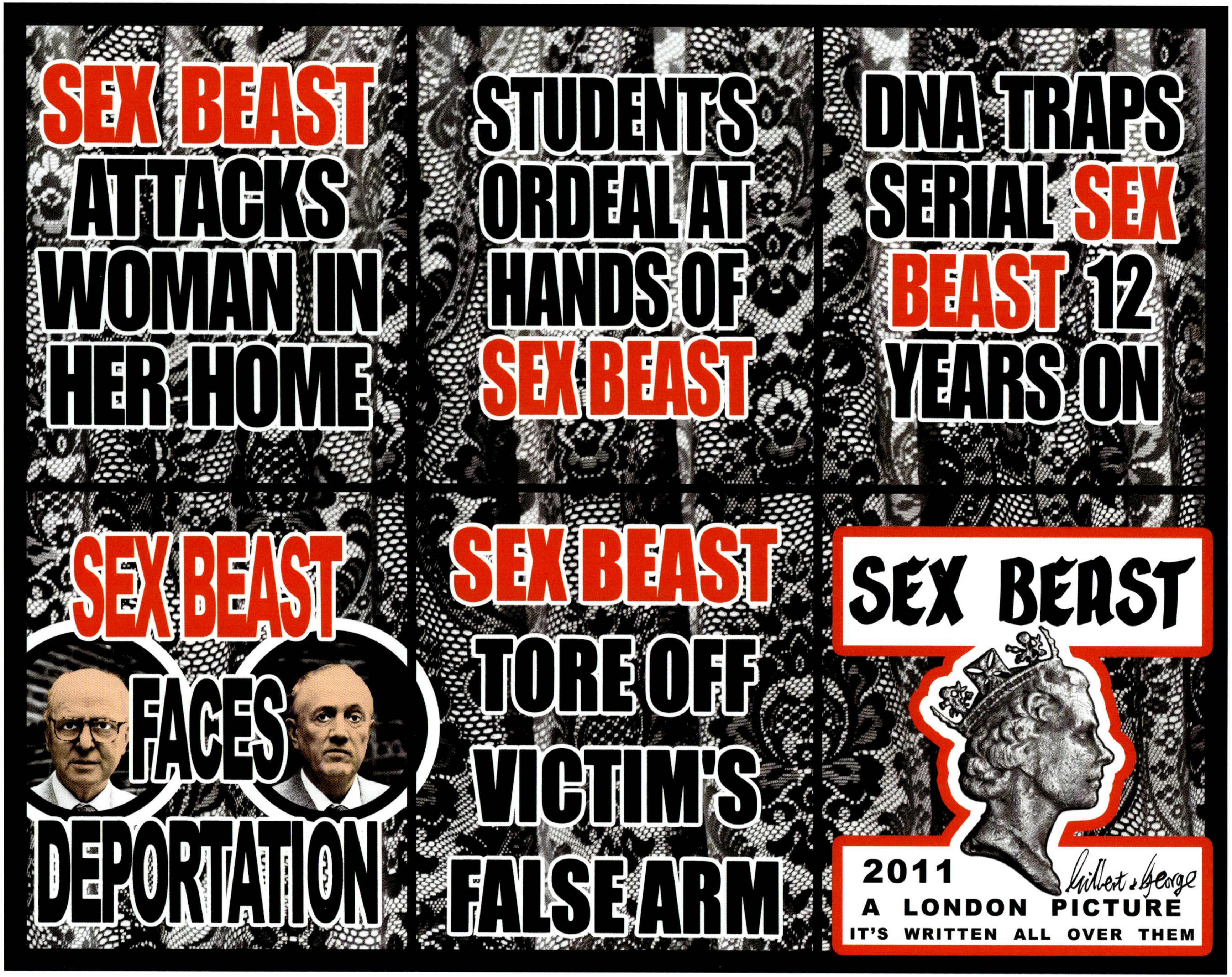
SEX BEAST ATTACKS WOMAN IN HER HOME
STUDENTS ORDEAL AT HANDS OF SEX BEAST
DNA TRAPS SERIAL SEX BEAST 12 YEARS ON
SEX BEAST FACES DEPORTATION
SEX BEAST TORE OFF VICTIM'S FALSE ARM
SEX BEAST
2011
A LONDON PICTURE
IT'S WRITTEN ALL OVER THEM
Gilbert & George

SEX BEAST. 2011. 151 x 190 cm

SEX PEST. 2011. 151 x 127 cm

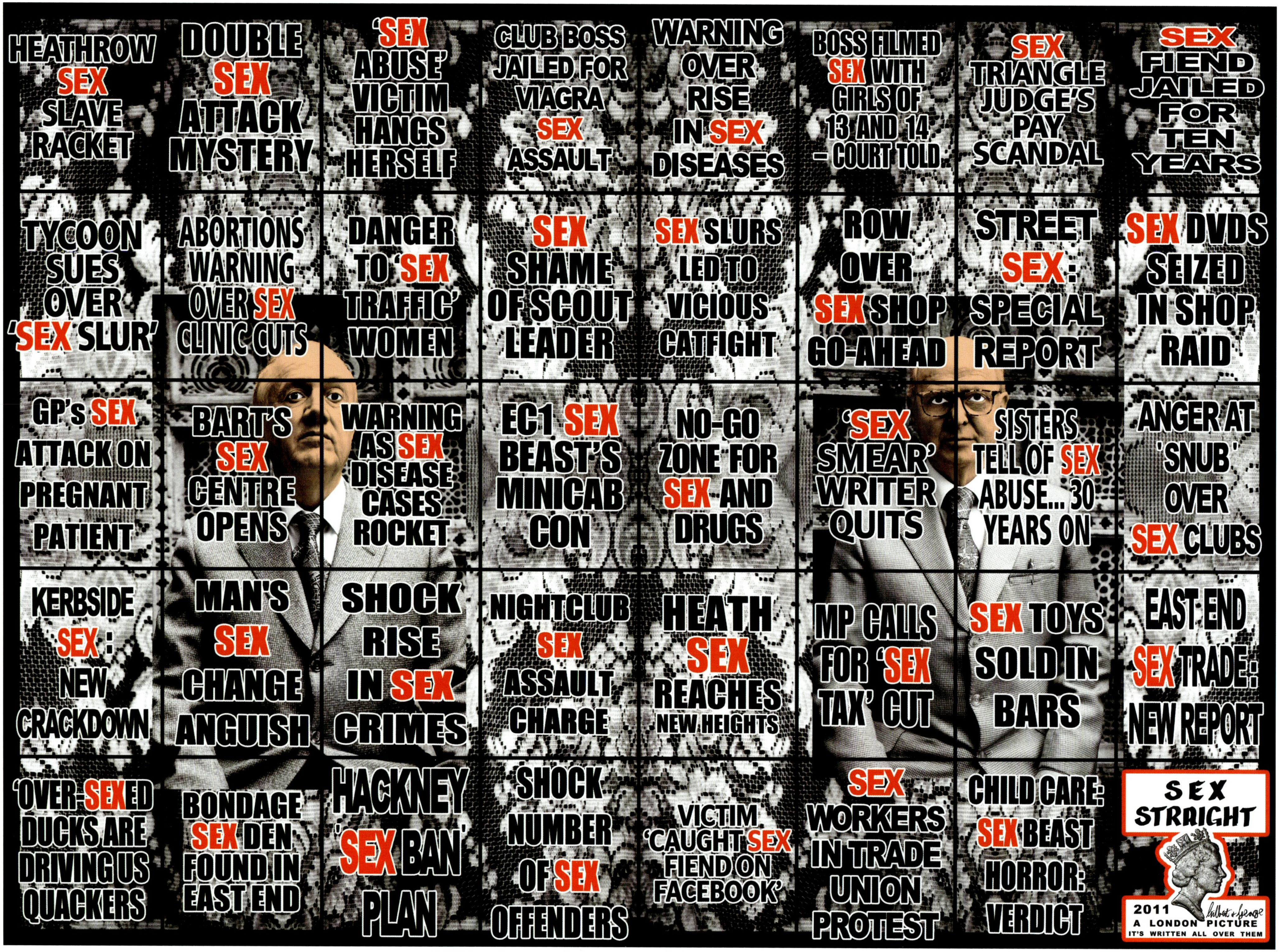
HEATHROW SEX SLAVE RACKET
DOUBLE SEX ATTACK MYSTERY
'SEX ABUSE' VICTIM HANGS HERSELF
CLUB BOSS JAILED FOR VIAGRA SEX ASSAULT
WARNING OVER RISE IN SEX DISEASES
BOSS FILMED SEX WITH GIRLS OF 13 AND 14 – COURT TOLD
SEX TRIANGLE JUDGE'S PAY SCANDAL
SEX FIEND JAILED FOR TEN YEARS
TYCOON SUES OVER 'SEX SLUR'
ABORTIONS WARNING OVER SEX CLINIC CUTS
DANGER TO 'SEX TRAFFIC' WOMEN
SEX SHAME OF SCOUT LEADER
SEX SLURS LED TO VICIOUS CATFIGHT
ROW OVER SEX SHOP GO-AHEAD
STREET SEX: SPECIAL REPORT
SEX DVDS SEIZED IN SHOP RAID
GP's SEX ATTACK ON PREGNANT PATIENT
BART'S SEX CENTRE OPENS
WARNING AS SEX DISEASE CASES ROCKET
EC1 SEX BEAST'S MINICAB CON
NO-GO ZONE FOR SEX AND DRUGS
'SEX SMEAR' WRITER QUITS
SISTERS TELL OF SEX ABUSE... 30 YEARS ON
ANGER AT 'SNUB' OVER SEX CLUBS
KERBSIDE SEX: NEW CRACKDOWN
MAN'S SEX CHANGE ANGUISH
SHOCK RISE IN SEX CRIMES
NIGHTCLUB SEX ASSAULT CHARGE
HEATH SEX REACHES NEW HEIGHTS
MP CALLS FOR 'SEX TAX' CUT
SEX TOYS SOLD IN BARS
EAST END SEX TRADE: NEW REPORT
'OVER-SEXED DUCKS ARE DRIVING US QUACKERS
BONDAGE SEX DEN FOUND IN EAST END
HACKNEY 'SEX BAN' PLAN
SHOCK NUMBER OF SEX OFFENDERS
VICTIM 'CAUGHT SEX FIEND ON FACEBOOK'
SEX WORKERS IN TRADE UNION PROTEST
CHILD CARE: SEX BEAST HORROR: VERDICT
SEX STRAIGHT
2011 A LONDON PICTURE
IT'S WRITTEN ALL OVER THEM

SEX STRAIGHT. 2011. 377 x 508 cm

MOTORBIKE
SHOOT OUT
TRIAL
'SHOOT
OUT'
GANGS
JAILED
STREET
SHOOT OUT
DUO
JAILED
SHOOT OUT
2011
A LONDON PICTURE
IT'S WRITTEN ALL OVER THEM

SHOOT OUT. 2011. 151 x 127 cm

HACKNEY SHOOTING VICTIM LURED TO DEATH
M^cDONALDS SHOOTING TERROR -PICTURE
MENEZES SHOOTING: POLICE COVER-UP
POLICE CHIEF RAPPED FOR TUBE SHOOTING
CHELSEA SHOOTING: POLICE 'CLEARED'
KENT: FATAL POLICE SHOOTING
TUBE SHOOTING: WOMAN'S AMAZING ESCAPE
POLICE TUBE SHOOTING DRAMA
TUBE SHOOTING REPORT KEPT SECRET
ISLINGTON SHOOTING HORROR
CLAPTON DOUBLE SHOOTING
TUBE SHOOTING -POLICE MAY FACE CHARGES
POLICE 'LIED' OVER SHOOTING -VICTIM'S FAMILY
POLICE SHOOTING -NEW DETAILS
MENEZES SHOOTING: VERDICT ON MET
POLICE SHOOTING: TUBE CAMERAS 'WERE WORKING'
OFFICIAL: POLICE FACE TUBE SHOOTING CHARGES
POLICE TUBE SHOOTING: NEW DRAMA
TUBE SHOOTING: FATAL ERRORS REVEALED
TUBE SHOOTING: NEW INQUIRY
MENEZES SHOOTING: DRAMATIC NEW DETAILS
TUBE POLICE SHOOTING — NEW DETAILS
ISLINGTON SHOOTING -DRAMATIC ARRESTS
LONDON PEACE ACTIVIST SHOOTING -VERDICT
MUSIC STARS ON RUN AFTER SHOOTING
MENEZES SHOOTING: EXCLUSIVE REPORT
STATION SHOOTING TERROR
SHOOTING
2011
A LONDON PICTURE
IT'S WRITTEN ALL OVER THEM

SHOOTING. 2011. 302 x 444 cm

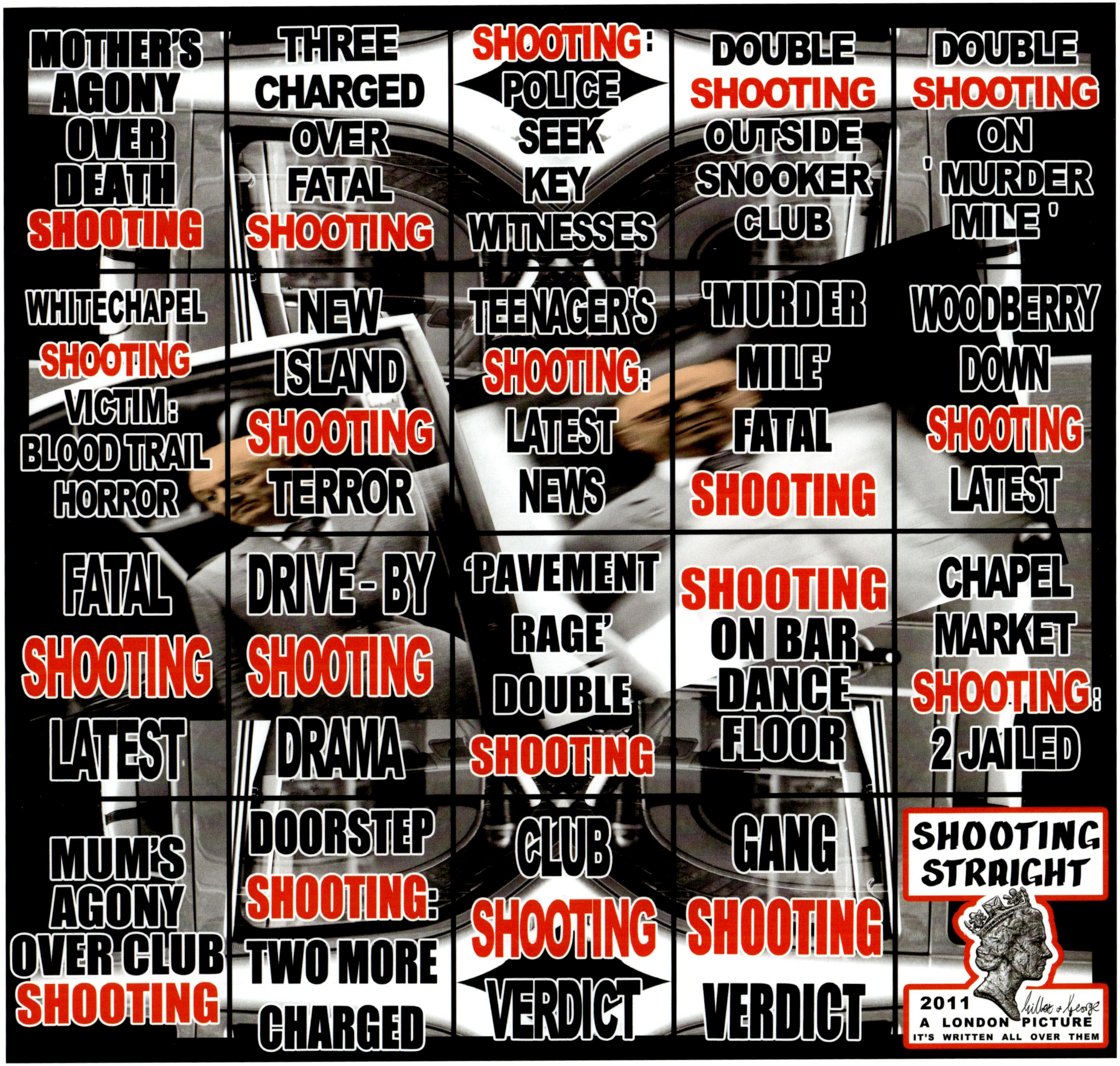
MOTHER'S AGONY OVER DEATH SHOOTING
THREE CHARGED OVER FATAL SHOOTING
SHOOTING: POLICE SEEK KEY WITNESSES
DOUBLE SHOOTING OUTSIDE SNOOKER CLUB
DOUBLE SHOOTING ON 'MURDER MILE'
WHITECHAPEL SHOOTING VICTIM: BLOOD TRAIL HORROR
NEW ISLAND SHOOTING TERROR
TEENAGER'S SHOOTING: LATEST NEWS
'MURDER MILE' FATAL SHOOTING
WOODBERRY DOWN SHOOTING LATEST
FATAL SHOOTING LATEST
DRIVE-BY SHOOTING DRAMA
'PAVEMENT RAGE' DOUBLE SHOOTING
SHOOTING ON BAR DANCE FLOOR
CHAPEL MARKET SHOOTING: 2 JAILED
MUM'S AGONY OVER CLUB SHOOTING
DOORSTEP SHOOTING: TWO MORE CHARGED
CLUB SHOOTING VERDICT
GANG SHOOTING VERDICT
SHOOTING STRAIGHT
2011
A LONDON PICTURE
IT'S WRITTEN ALL OVER THEM

SHOOTING STRAIGHT. 2011. 302 x 317 cm

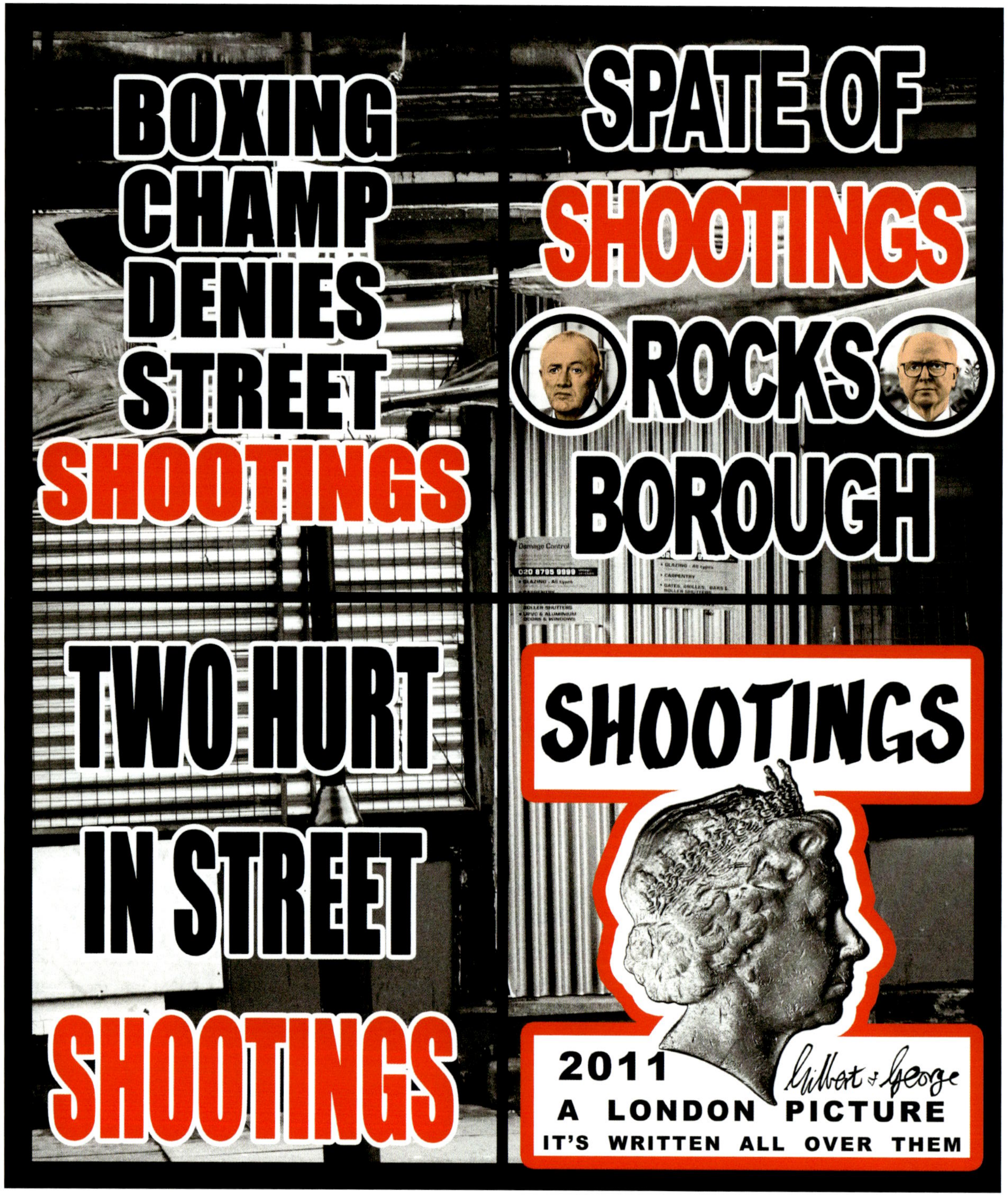
BOXING CHAMP DENIES STREET SHOOTINGS
SPATE OF SHOOTINGS ROCKS BOROUGH
TWO HURT IN STREET SHOOTINGS
SHOOTINGS
2011
A LONDON PICTURE
IT'S WRITTEN ALL OVER THEM
Gilbert & George

SHOOTINGS. 2011. 151 x 127 cm

SHOP MAN
STABBED
IN APPLE
'THEFT'
ROW
BETTING
SHOP
ATTACKED
SHOP
BOSS
KILLING:
YOUTH, 16
ARRESTED
SHOP
2011
A LONDON PICTURE
IT'S WRITTEN ALL OVER THEM

SHOP. 2011. 151 x 127 cm

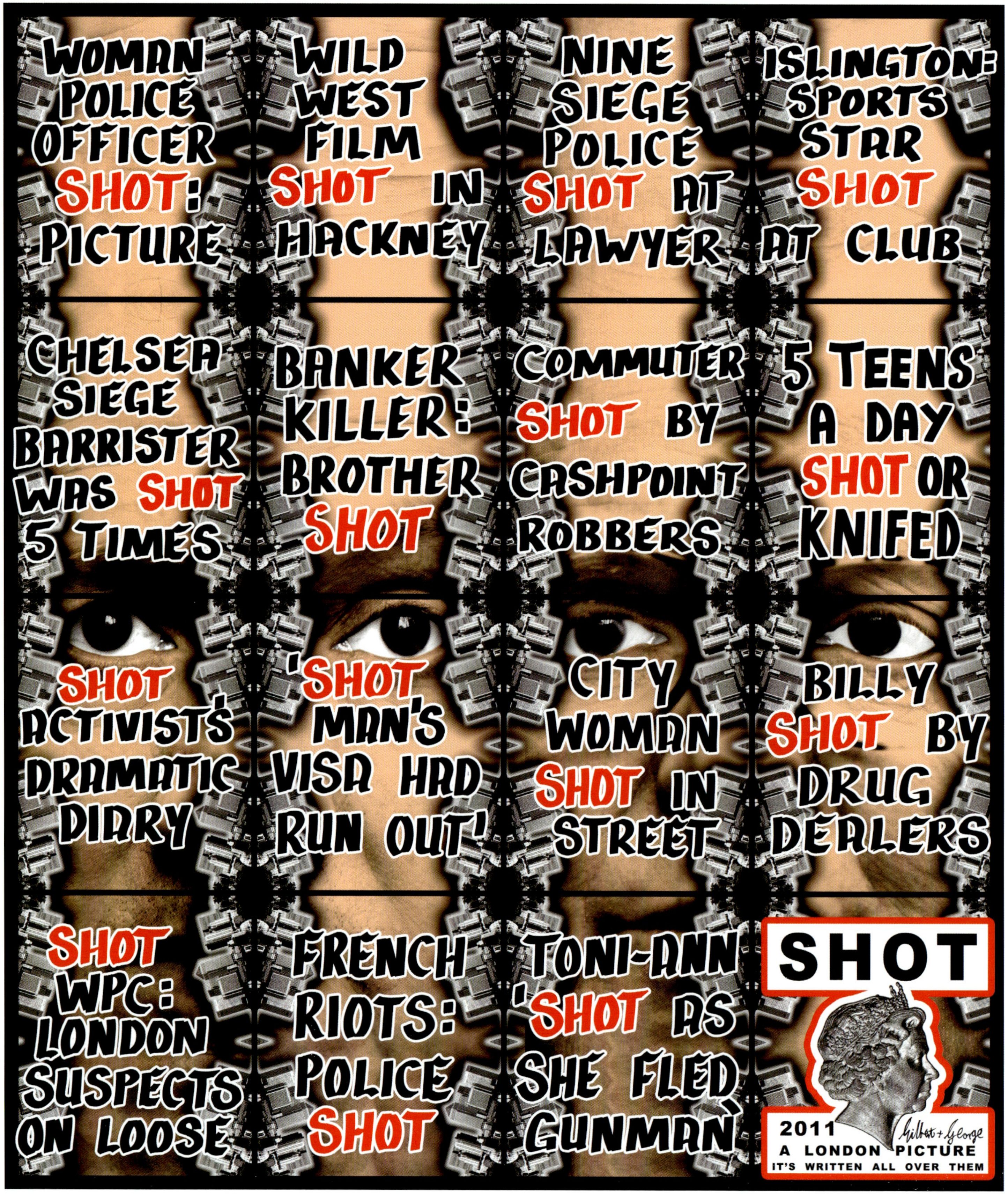
WOMAN POLICE OFFICER SHOT: PICTURE
WILD WEST FILM SHOT IN HACKNEY
NINE SIEGE POLICE SHOT AT LAWYER
ISLINGTON: SPORTS STAR SHOT AT CLUB
CHELSEA SIEGE BARRISTER WAS SHOT 5 TIMES
BANKER KILLER: BROTHER SHOT
COMMUTER SHOT BY CASHPOINT ROBBERS
5 TEENS A DAY SHOT OR KNIFED
SHOT ACTIVIST'S DRAMATIC DIARY
'SHOT MAN'S VISA HAD RUN OUT'
CITY WOMAN SHOT IN STREET
BILLY SHOT BY DRUG DEALERS
SHOT WPC: LONDON SUSPECTS ON LOOSE
FRENCH RIOTS: POLICE SHOT
TONI-ANN 'SHOT AS SHE FLED GUNMAN'
SHOT
2011
A LONDON PICTURE
IT'S WRITTEN ALL OVER THEM

SHOT

2011

302 x 254 cm

BARRISTER SHOT DEAD IN CHELSEA SIEGE
BOY, 11, SHOT DEAD -FIRST PICTURE
BRITISH BRIDE SHOT DEAD
SHOT DEAD
2011
A LONDON PICTURE
IT'S WRITTEN ALL OVER THEM

SHOT DEAD. 2011. 151 x 127 cm

THREE SHOT IN GUN ATTACK
TWO SHOT IN GUN VIOLENCE
TWO SHOT AS GUN GANGS RAMPAGE
SHOT GUN
2011
A LONDON PICTURE
IT'S WRITTEN ALL OVER THEM

SHOT GUN. 2011. 151 x 127 cm

WOMAN SHOT OUTSIDE AWARDS SHOW
TERROR OF BOY SHOT WHILE PLAYING
NEW YEAR REVELLER SHOT DEAD
FILM CREW FLEE AS MAN SHOT
SHOT DAD HAD BEEN INVOLVED IN ROAD RAGE ATTACK
BOY SHOT IN STREET
MAN SHOT IN CALLY ROAD ATTACK
TWO SHOT IN DRIVE - BY ATTACK
JOURNALIST 'SHOT' IN GAZA HELL
TWO SHOT IN STREET GUN BATTLE
TWO MEN ARE SHOT IN STREET GUNFIGHT
MAN SHOT BY N1 GUN GANG
NIGHT CLUB MAN IS SHOT
SHOT MUM AND KIDS WIN FIGHT TO STAY
N1 MAN SHOT SITTING IN HIS CAR
THREE SHOT IN GANG FEUD
HUNDREDS SAY FAREWELL TO SHOT SCHOOLGIRL
TERROR LEADER SHOT DEAD
SHOT FOR SAYING 'STOP SMOKING'
SHOT STRAIGHT
2011
A LONDON PICTURE
IT'S WRITTEN ALL OVER THEM

SHOT STRAIGHT. 2011. 302 x 317 cm

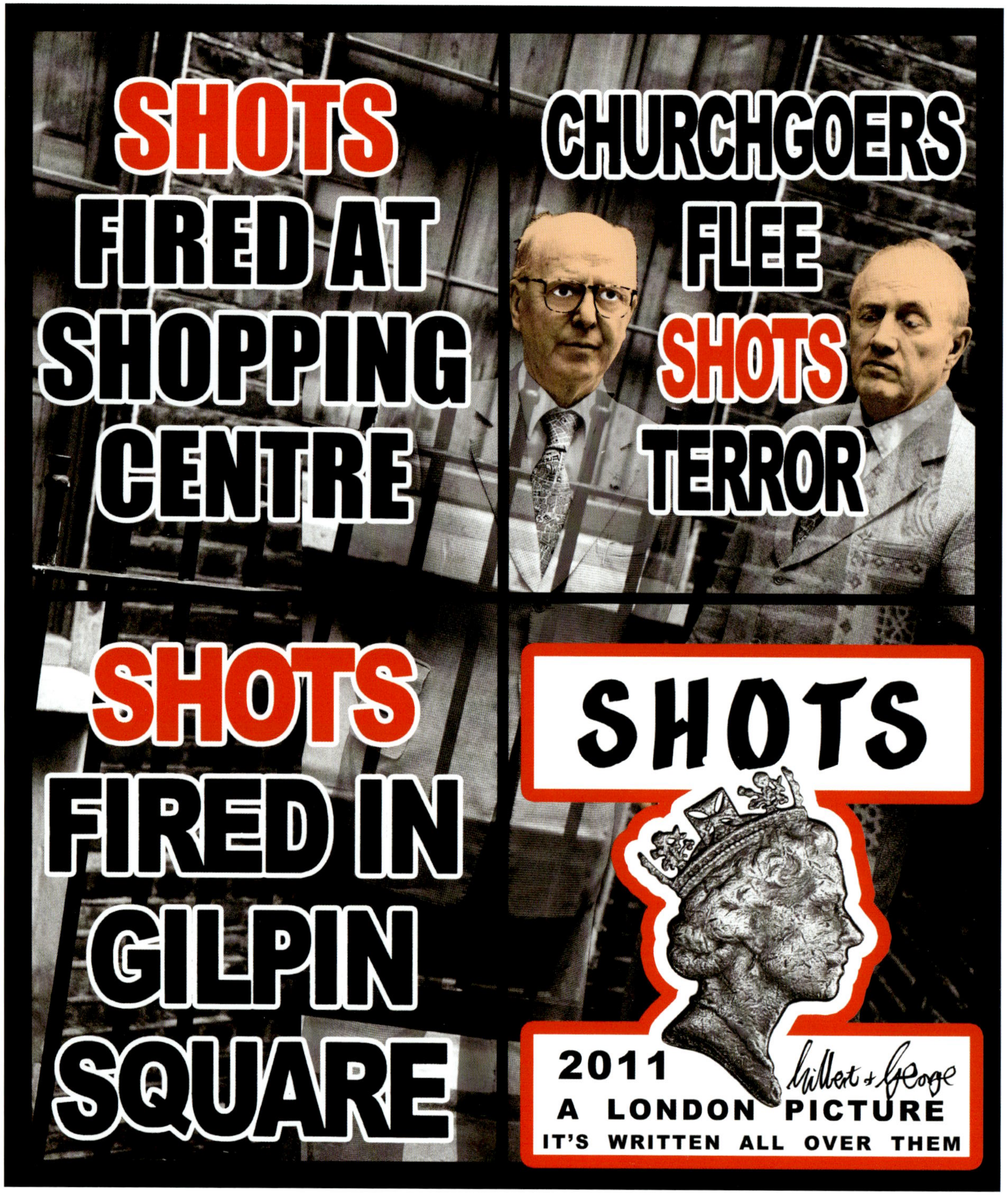
SHOTS
FIRED AT
SHOPPING
CENTRE
CHURCHGOERS
FLEE
SHOTS
TERROR
SHOTS
FIRED IN
GILPIN
SQUARE
SHOTS
2011
A LONDON PICTURE
IT'S WRITTEN ALL OVER THEM

SHOTS. 2011. 151 x 127 cm

SOCCER STAR'S HOME RAIDED
ADDICT TERRORISED SOCCER STAR'S FAMILY
SOCCER BOSS CHARGED WITH BLACKMAIL
SOCCER BOSSES FACE SEX CLAIMS
SOCCER STAR'S BROTHER: MURDER VERDICT
MIDDLE CLASS SOCCER THUGS JAILED
SOCCER STAR'S BURGLARY ORDEAL
SOCCER
2011
A LONDON PICTURE
IT'S WRITTEN ALL OVER THEM

SOCCER. 2011. 151 x 254 cm

BEACH SOCCER AXED OVER GUN VIOLENCE
ITALIAN SOCCER FANS ATTACK PUB
MYSTERY OF SOCCER FAN'S DEATH PLUNGE
STABBING BLOW FOR SOCCER STAR'S BROTHER
SOCCER TRIBUTE TO TRAGIC TEENAGER
SIX-YEAR SOCCER BAN FOR JAILED THUGS
SOCCER PLAYER STABBED IN THE STREET
SOCCER THUGS WRECK PUB AND CARS
SOCCER STRAIGHT
2011
A LONDON PICTURE
IT'S WRITTEN ALL OVER THEM

SOCCER STRAIGHT. 2011. 226 x 190 cm

TEENAGE STAB VICTIM FIGHTS FOR LIFE
PARK STAB VICTIM FIGHTS FOR LIFE
ROBBERS STAB MAN IN STREET
STAB VICTIM FIGHTS FOR HIS LIFE
STORE STAB VICTIM: MUM'S HORROR
HEATWAVE STAB HORROR
GANG'S THREAT TO STAB GIRLS
MYSTERY MURAL TRIBUTE TO STAB VICTIM
FINSBURY MAN ON STAB MURDER CHARGE
STAB VICTIM SCHOOL TRIBUTE
STAB VICTIM'S MOTHER SPEAKS OUT
CCTV MAY HOLD KEY TO STAB TEEN'S KILLERS
GIRLFRIEND TELLS OF STAB DEATH HORROR
N7 TEEN HAILED AS STAB ATTACK HERO
STAB VICTIM RESCUED BY STORE STAFF
EC1
COURAGE OF POLICE STAB ATTACK HEROES
YOUTH FACES 'STAB' CHARGE
STAB
2011
A LONDON PICTURE
IT'S WRITTEN ALL OVER THEM

STAB. 2011. 226 x 381 cm

NEWINGTON GREEN STAB DEATH HORROR
TRAGEDY OF DAD'S STAB DEATH
CANDLE-LIT VIGIL FOR STAB DEATH TEEN
STAB DEATH TEEN TRIBUTE BANNED
STAB DEATH GUARD WAS "MISLED"
STAB DEATH WITNESSES TURN "BLIND EYE"
BEN
SHOCK AND OUTRAGE AT STAB DEATH
TRAGEDY OF BOY'S STAB DEATH
STAB DEATH FATHER: FAMILY'S HEARTACHE
NEW DAD IS SIXTH STAB DEATH VICTIM
PAL'S TRIBUTE TO STAB DEATH VICTIM
STAB DEATH
2011
A LONDON PICTURE
IT'S WRITTEN ALL OVER THEM

STAB DEATH. 2011. 226 x 254 cm

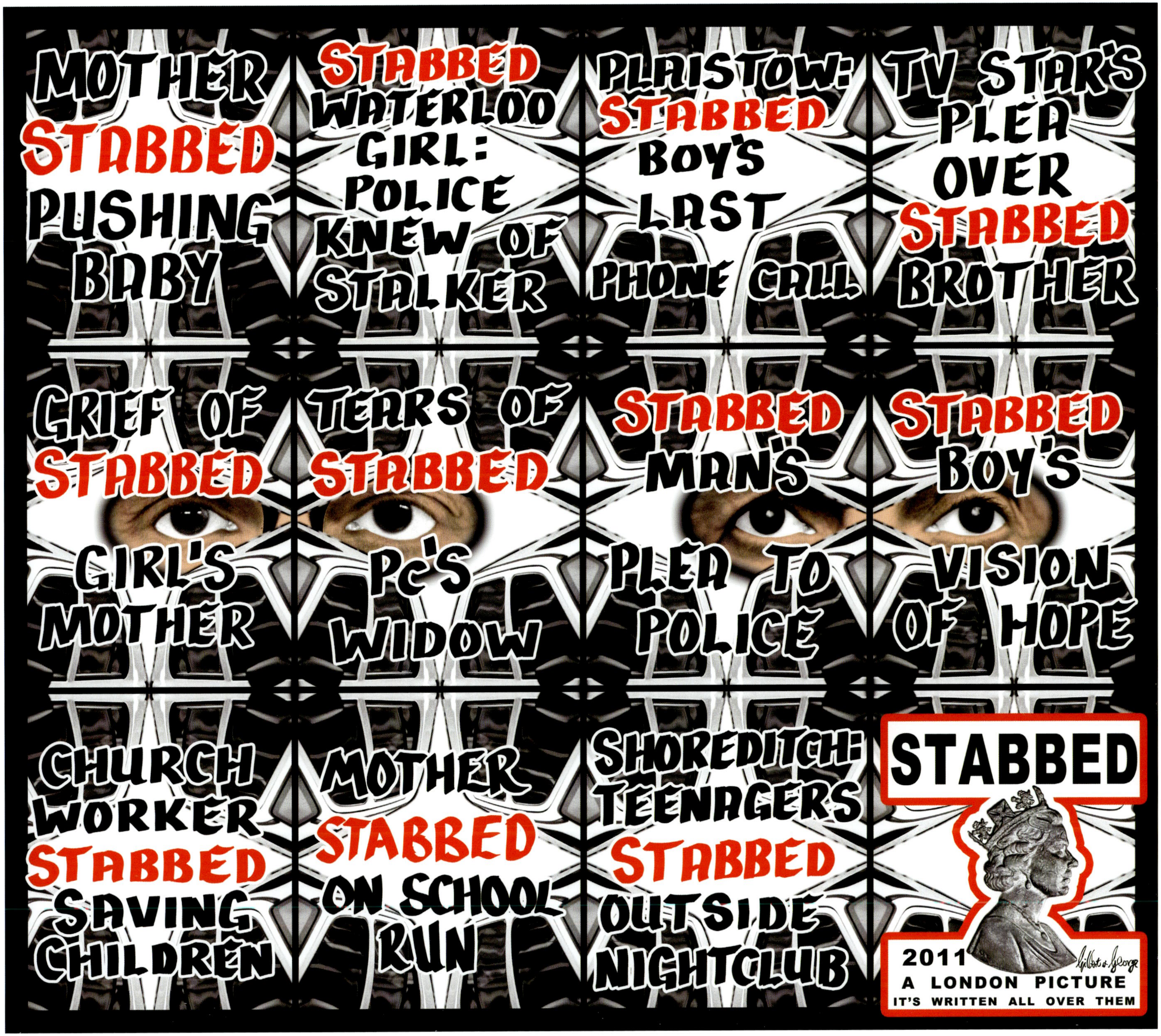
MOTHER STABBED PUSHING BABY
STABBED WATERLOO GIRL: POLICE KNEW OF STALKER
PLAISTOW: STABBED BOY'S LAST PHONE CALL
TV STAR'S PLEA OVER STABBED BROTHER
GRIEF OF STABBED GIRL'S MOTHER
TEARS OF STABBED PC'S WIDOW
STABBED MAN'S PLEA TO POLICE
STABBED BOY'S VISION OF HOPE
CHURCH WORKER STABBED SAVING CHILDREN
MOTHER STABBED ON SCHOOL RUN
SHOREDITCH: TEENAGERS STABBED OUTSIDE NIGHTCLUB
STABBED
2011
A LONDON PICTURE
IT'S WRITTEN ALL OVER THEM

STABBED. 2011. 226 x 254 cm

STABBED ARCHWAY MUM – THE LAST HOURS
STABBED BEN WAS 'BLAMELESS' – KINSELLA COURT TOLD
THREE STABBED IN STREET BATTLES
THREE STABBED IN BARNSBURY GANG ATTACK
MAN STABBED IN N4 STREET FIGHT
STABBED TEENAGER FIGHTS FOR LIFE
TEENAGERS STABBED IN HOLLOWAY BATTLE
HOLLOWAY TEENAGER STABBED
MAN IS STABBED 26 TIMES
MAN IS STABBED IN CHIP SHOP
STABBED MAN IN FIGHT OVER SISTER
TWO STABBED AT PUB PARTY
STABBED MUM FIGHTS FOR LIFE
PUB BOSS STABBED 14 TIMES
TWO STABBED ON CANAL TOWPATH
STUDENTS STABBED IN RIVAL SCHOOL FEUD
STABBED COPS: MAN IN COURT
THREE STABBED IN STREET BRAWL
COMMUNITY TRIBUTE TO STABBED MARTIN
STABBED BOY'S LAST PHONE CALL
YOUNG ACTOR STABBED AFTER AUDITION
TEENAGER STABBED IN HEAD
DRINKER STABBED IN STREET
MAN IS STABBED FOR HIS WATCH
MAN STABBED IN FRENZIED ATTACK
MAN STABBED IN BUS STOP ROW
TWO STABBED IN BROAD DAYLIGHT
HIGHBURY WOMAN STABBED
TEENAGER STABBED AS GUN IS FIRED AT HOUSE
ALGERIAN STABBED IN BUS STOP ATTACK
FOUR STABBED IN PARK CLASH
STABBED STRAIGHT
2011 A LONDON PICTURE
IT'S WRITTEN ALL OVER THEM

STABBED STRAIGHT. 2011. 302 x 508 cm

HACKNEY FATHER STABBED TO DEATH
LONDON TEACHER'S SON STABBED TO DEATH
'MODEL PUPIL' STABBED TO DEATH
HACKNEY: WOMAN STUDENT STABBED TO DEATH
BOY, 8, STABBED TO DEATH
HACKNEY WOMAN STABBED TO DEATH
TEENAGED GIRL STABBED TO DEATH
BETHNAL GREEN: MAN, 21, STABBED TO DEATH
CASINO WOMAN STABBED TO DEATH
LONDON BOY, 16 STABBED TO DEATH
MODEL, 18, STABBED TO DEATH
LONDON CHARITY CHIEF STABBED TO DEATH
PLAISTOW: 'MODEL PUPIL' STABBED TO DEATH
SCHOOLBOY STABBED TO DEATH
HORROR OF GIRL, 15, STABBED TO DEATH
STABBED TO DEATH
2011
A LONDON PICTURE
IT'S WRITTEN ALL OVER THEM

STABBED TO DEATH

2011

302 x 254 cm

MAN STABBED TO DEATH IN FACTORY
MAN STABBED TO DEATH IN GANG CHASE
MAN 'STABBED TO DEATH IN PHONE ROW'
MAN STABBED TO DEATH BY FORMER WORKMATE
DRINKING BUDDY STABBED TO DEATH
ISLINGTON WIFE STABBED TO DEATH
FATHER OF FOUR STABBED TO DEATH
TEENAGER STABBED TO DEATH
FATHER OF FIVE STABBED TO DEATH
LONDON BOY, 14, STABBED TO DEATH
MOTHER STABBED TO DEATH
DJ IS STABBED TO DEATH IN STREET
MOTHER, 100, STABBED TO DEATH
ANOTHER TEENAGER STABBED TO DEATH
MAN STABBED TO DEATH
STABBED TO DEATH STRAIGHT
2011
A LONDON PICTURE
IT'S WRITTEN ALL OVER THEM

STABBED TO
DEATH STRAIGHT

2011

302 x 254 cm

STABBING: DRAMATIC PICTURE APPEAL
HACKNEY STABBING: FAMILY SPEAK OUT
TUBE STABBING HORROR -DETAILS
STABBING: FOUR 13 YEAR OLDS HELD
LONDON SHOP STABBING HORROR
ABIGAIL STABBING -LATEST
CHELSEA STABBING HORROR
EDMONTON STABBING VICTIM'S GANGLAND LIFESTYLE
STABBING: WOMAN AND MAN HUNTED
Pc DIES IN 999 STABBING
ABIGAIL STABBING: COUPLE ARRESTED
STABBING
2011
A LONDON PICTURE
IT'S WRITTEN ALL OVER THEM

STABBING. 2011. 226 x 254 cm

RENEWED PALACE PAVILLION STABBING APPEAL
PARENTS APPEAL OVER FATAL STABBING
SIXTH CHARGED OVER SHAQUILLE STABBING
TWO CHARGED AFTER FATAL STABBING
FOUR CHARGED OVER STREET STABBING
ENGINEER JAILED FOR STABBING HIS BEST FRIEND
RECORD STUDIO DEATH STABBING
MOTHER'S PLEA OVER SON'S DEATH STABBING
NEWINGTON GREEN STABBING – FOUR IN COURT
MAN IS FINED £80 FOR STABBING HIMSELF
BLOODBATH FEAR AFTER SHOOTING AND STABBING
OXFORD STREET STABBING: MAN CHARGED
FATAL STABBING: COUPLE IN COURT
FINSBURY PARK STABBING HORROR
'BITCH FIGHT' STABBING WOMAN JAILED
CROWD WATCHES N5 DEATH STABBING
FATAL STABBING AT FLATS: LATEST
KILLER JAILED 25 YEARS AFTER STABBING
POLICE PROBE DOUBLE STABBING
MUM'S STABBING DEATH: SON CHARGED
SHAQUILLE STABBING LATEST
HOXTON STABBING MAN CHARGED
STABBING VICTIM'S RETURN TO LIFE'
STABBING STRAIGHT
2011 A LONDON PICTURE
IT'S WRITTEN ALL OVER THEM

STABBING STRAIGHT. 2011. 302 x 381 cm

HACKNEY
STABBINGS
HORROR
MAYFAIR
NIGHTCLUB
STABBINGS
COVENT
GARDEN:
PARTY
STABBINGS
HORROR
STABBINGS
2011
A LONDON PICTURE
IT'S WRITTEN ALL OVER THEM

STABBINGS. 2011. 151 x 127 cm

STAR
STUDENTS
RELIED
ON AXED
GRANT
RAP STAR
FACES
JAIL OVER
KNIFE
DRUG
SMUGGLE
STAR IS
JAILED
POP
STAR
DRUGS
SHAME
CHART
STAR ON
N1 RAPE
CHARGE
STAR
2011
A LONDON PICTURE
IT'S WRITTEN ALL OVER THEM

STAR. 2011. 151 x 190 cm

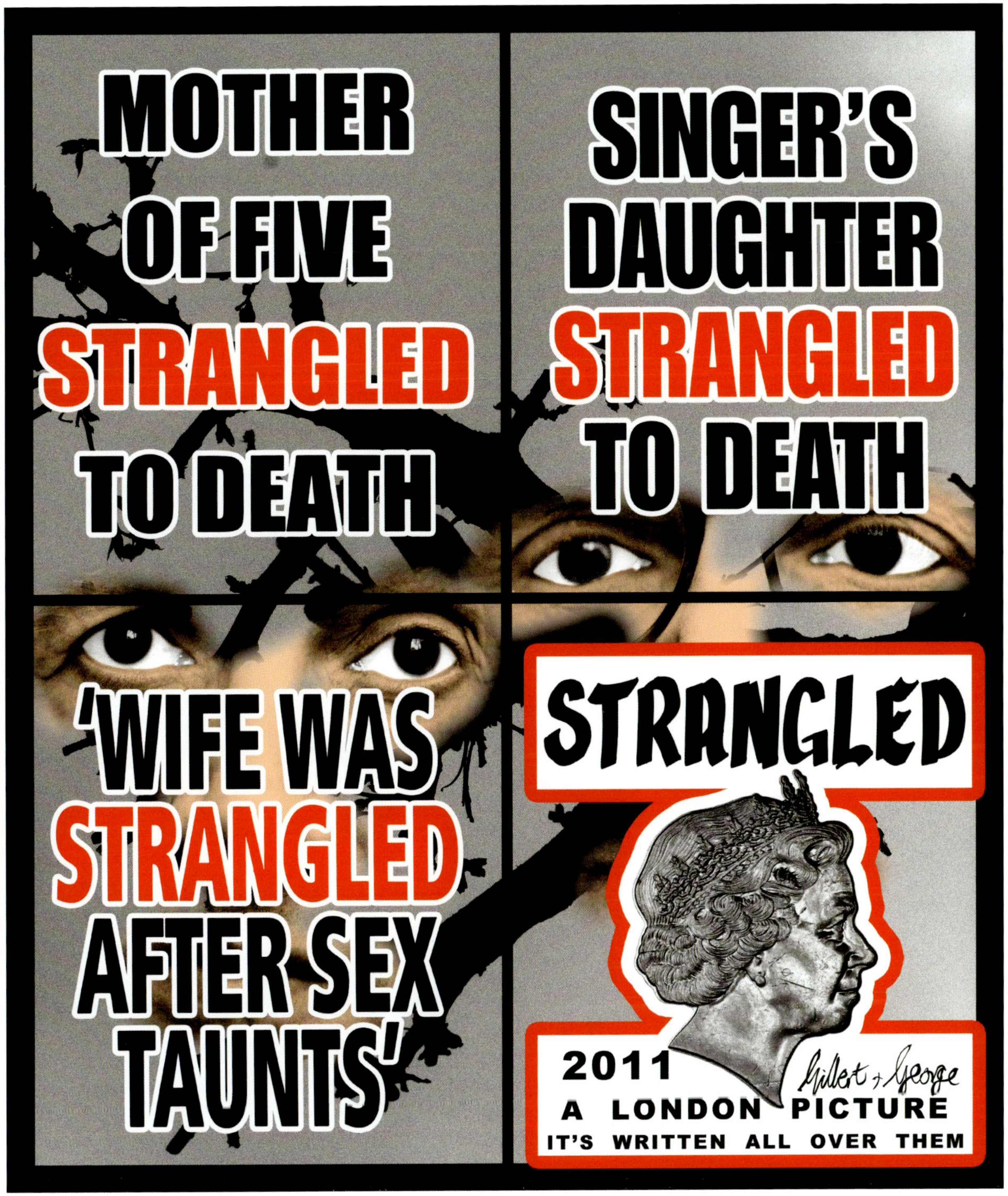
MOTHER
OF FIVE
STRANGLED
TO DEATH
SINGER'S
DAUGHTER
STRANGLED
TO DEATH
'WIFE WAS
STRANGLED
AFTER SEX
TAUNTS'
STRANGLED
2011
Gilbert & George
A LONDON PICTURE
IT'S WRITTEN ALL OVER THEM

STRANGLED. 2011. 151 x 127 cm

CRICKET COACH STRANGLER MYSTERY
STRANGLER: KEY SUSPECT HELD
STRANGLER: FORMER PC HELD
STRANGLER
2011
A LONDON PICTURE
IT'S WRITTEN ALL OVER THEM

STRANGLER. 2011. 151 x 127 cm

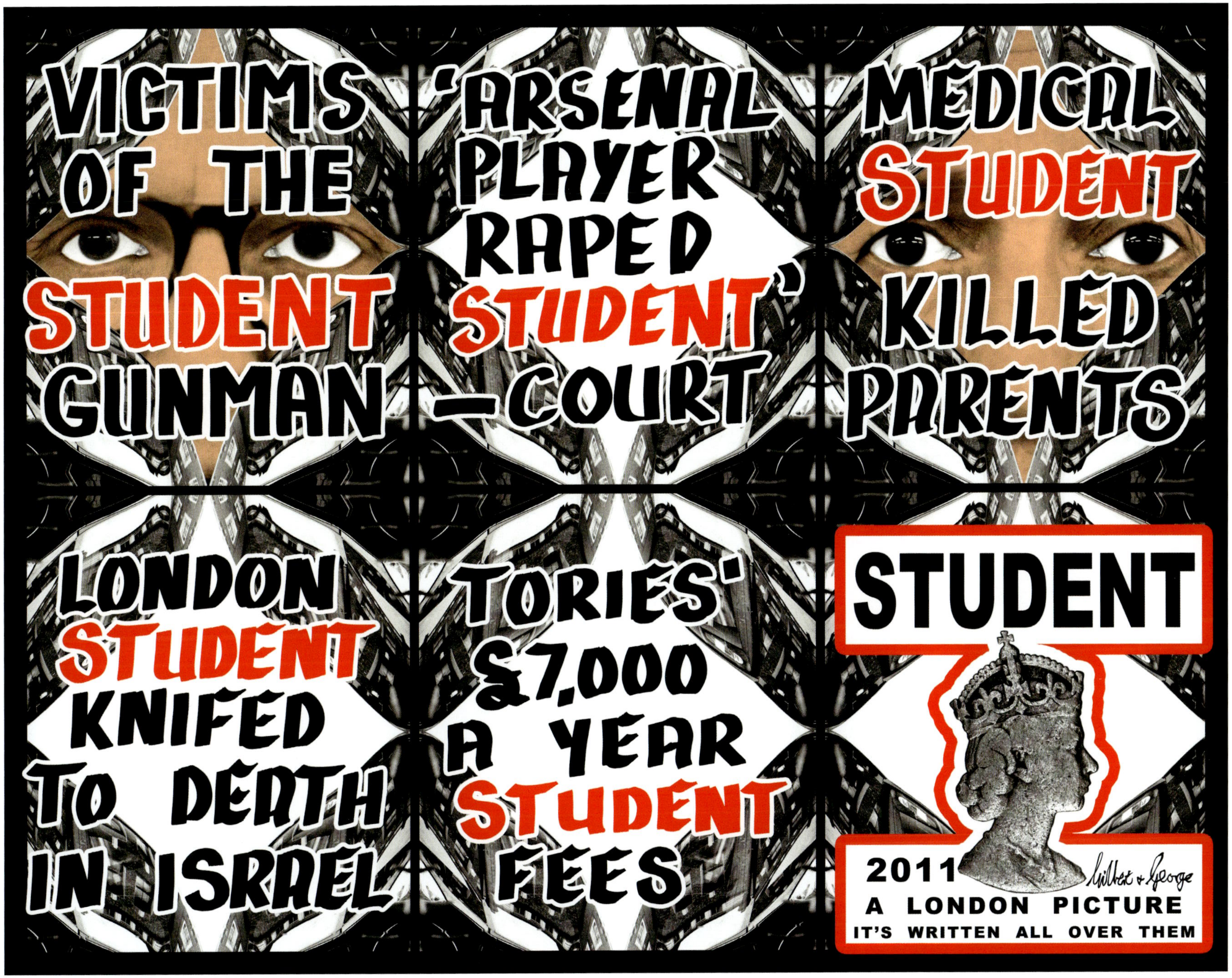
VICTIMS OF THE STUDENT GUNMAN
'ARSENAL PLAYER RAPED STUDENT' —COURT
MEDICAL STUDENT KILLED PARENTS
LONDON STUDENT KNIFED TO DEATH IN ISRAEL
TORIES' £7,000 A YEAR STUDENT FEES
STUDENT
2011
A LONDON PICTURE
IT'S WRITTEN ALL OVER THEM

STUDENT. 2011. 151 x 190 cm

STUDENT CLEARED OF TRYING TO JOIN TALIBAN
'TERROR BOMB PLOT' STUDENT IN COURT
STUDENT DEATH FALL TRAGEDY
ESSEX RD STUDENT STABBED IN BACK
STUDENT JAILED FOR PART IN KILLING FATHER
MURDERED STUDENT IN TORTURE ORDEAL
N7 STREET GANG BEAT STUDENT WITH GUN
STUDENT PLANNED TO BE A GAP-YEAR TERRORIST
STUDENT DIES IN ROAD CRASH
STUDENT FACING CERTAIN DEATH CLAIM
MY RAPE HORROR – BY N1 STUDENT
STUDENT RAIL DEATH HORROR
STUDENT MISSING FOR TWO WEEKS FOUND SAFE
FRENCH STUDENT KILLER'S SENTENCE QUASHED
PEACE MARCH STUDENT JAILED
ASDA ATTACK STUDENT 'LEFT FOR DEAD'
STUDENT DEATH MYSTERY
STUDENT HID GUN INSIDE COMPUTER
STUDENT EAR BITTEN OFF IN ROW
PLANS FOR 475 STUDENT HOMES REJECTED
STUDENT TOWER BLOCK TO HAVE 650 FLATS
FEARS OVER STUDENT 'GHETTO'
FEARS OVER STUDENT HOMES EXPLOSION
STUDENT STRAIGHT
2011
A LONDON PICTURE
IT'S WRITTEN ALL OVER THEM

STUDENT STRAIGHT. 2011. 302 x 381 cm

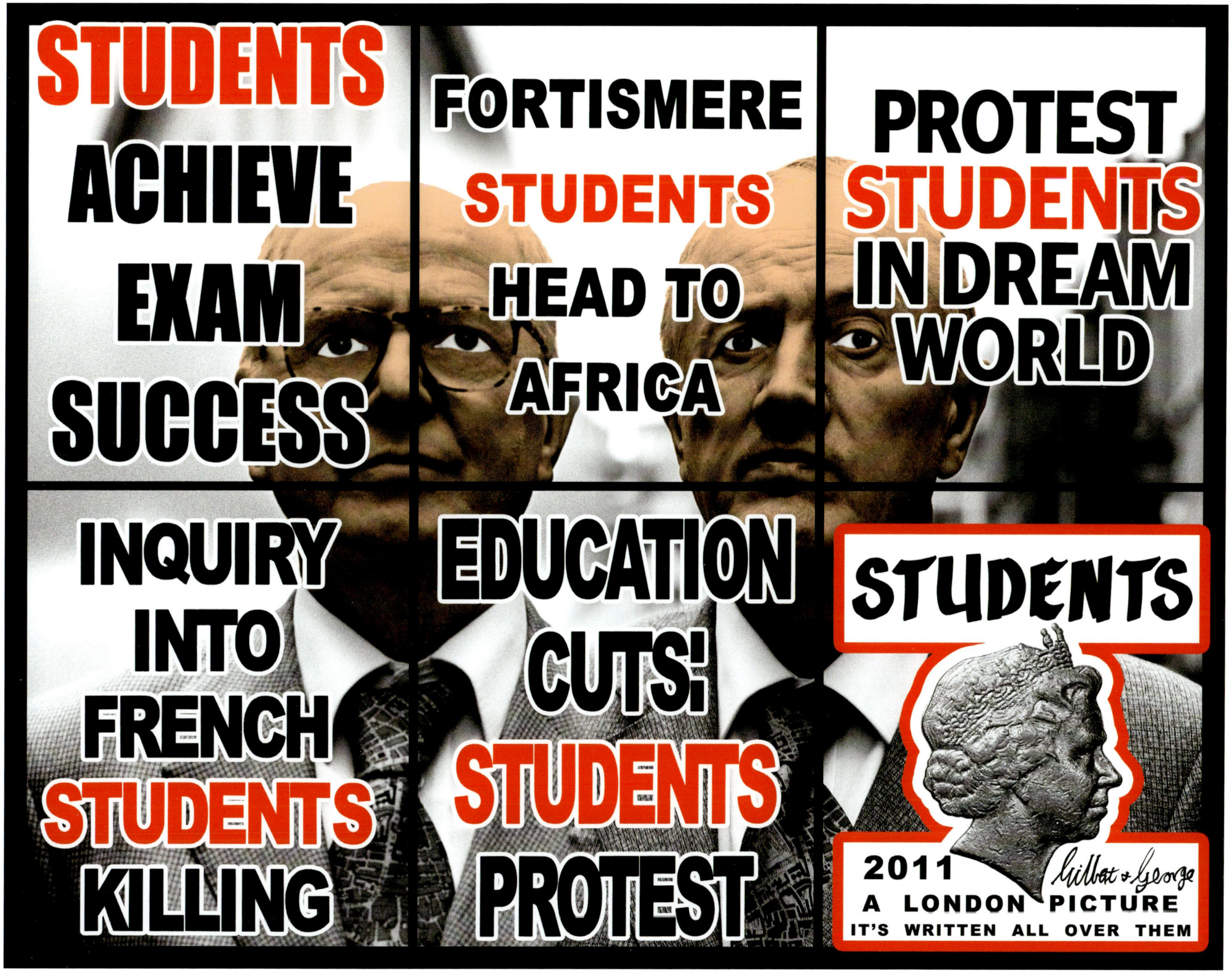
STUDENTS
ACHIEVE
EXAM
SUCCESS
FORTISMERE
STUDENTS
HEAD TO
AFRICA
PROTEST
STUDENTS
IN DREAM
WORLD
INQUIRY
INTO
FRENCH
STUDENTS
KILLING
EDUCATION
CUTS!
STUDENTS
PROTEST
STUDENTS
2011
A LONDON PICTURE
IT'S WRITTEN ALL OVER THEM

STUDENTS. 2011. 151 x 190 cm

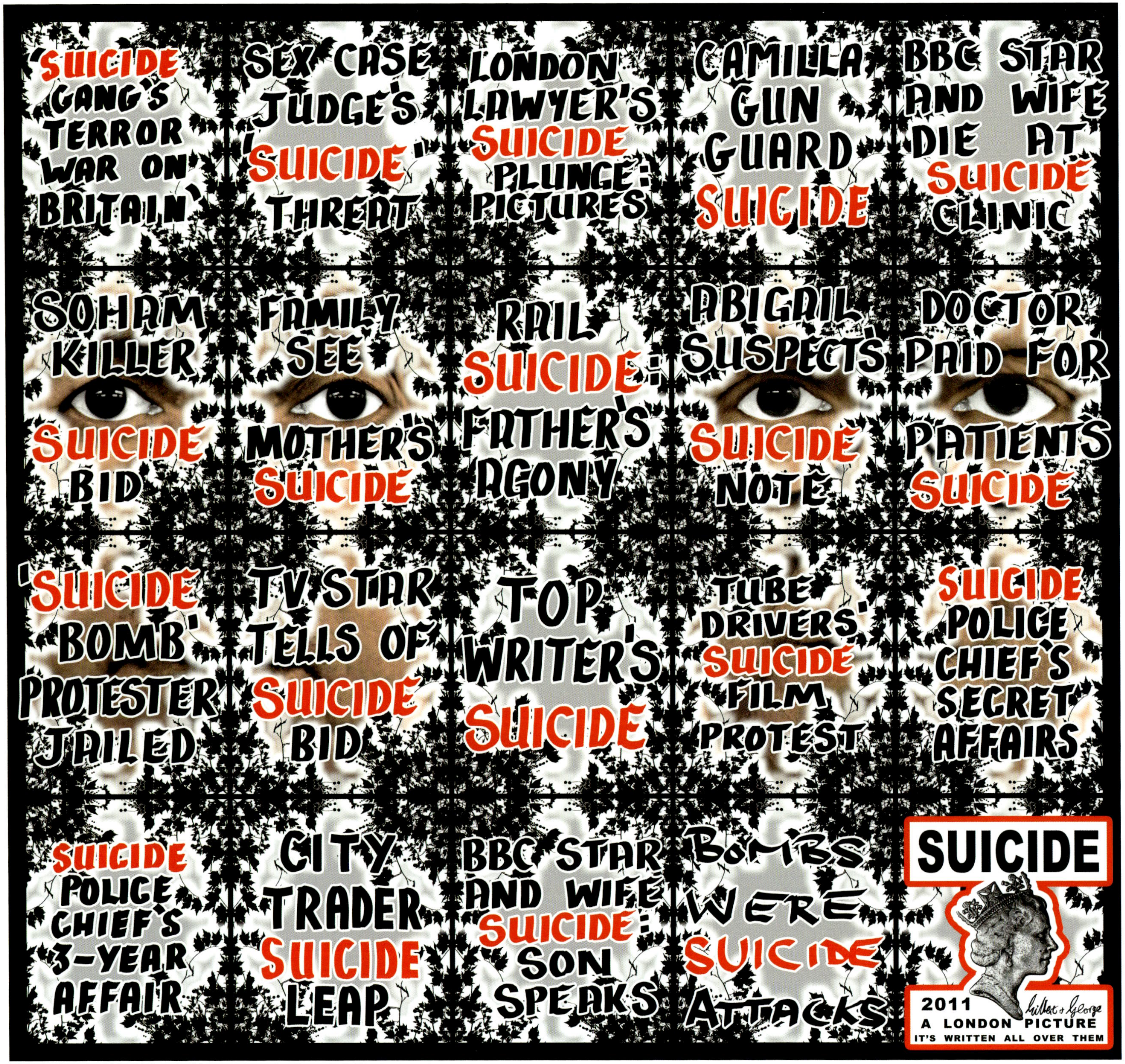
'SUICIDE GANG'S TERROR WAR ON BRITAIN'
SEX CASE JUDGE'S 'SUICIDE' THREAT
LONDON LAWYER'S SUICIDE PLUNGE: PICTURES
CAMILLA GUN GUARD SUICIDE
BBC STAR AND WIFE DIE AT SUICIDE CLINIC
SOHAM KILLER SUICIDE BID
FAMILY SEE MOTHER'S SUICIDE
RAIL SUICIDE: FATHER'S AGONY
ABIGAIL SUSPECT'S SUICIDE NOTE
DOCTOR PAID FOR PATIENT'S SUICIDE
'SUICIDE BOMB' PROTESTER JAILED
TV STAR TELLS OF SUICIDE BID
TOP WRITER'S SUICIDE
TUBE DRIVERS' SUICIDE FILM PROTEST
SUICIDE POLICE CHIEF'S SECRET AFFAIRS
SUICIDE POLICE CHIEF'S 3-YEAR AFFAIR
CITY TRADER SUICIDE LEAP
BBC STAR AND WIFE SUICIDE: SON SPEAKS
BOMBS WERE SUICIDE ATTACKS
SUICIDE
2011 A LONDON PICTURE
IT'S WRITTEN ALL OVER THEM

SUICIDE. 2011. 302 x 317 cm

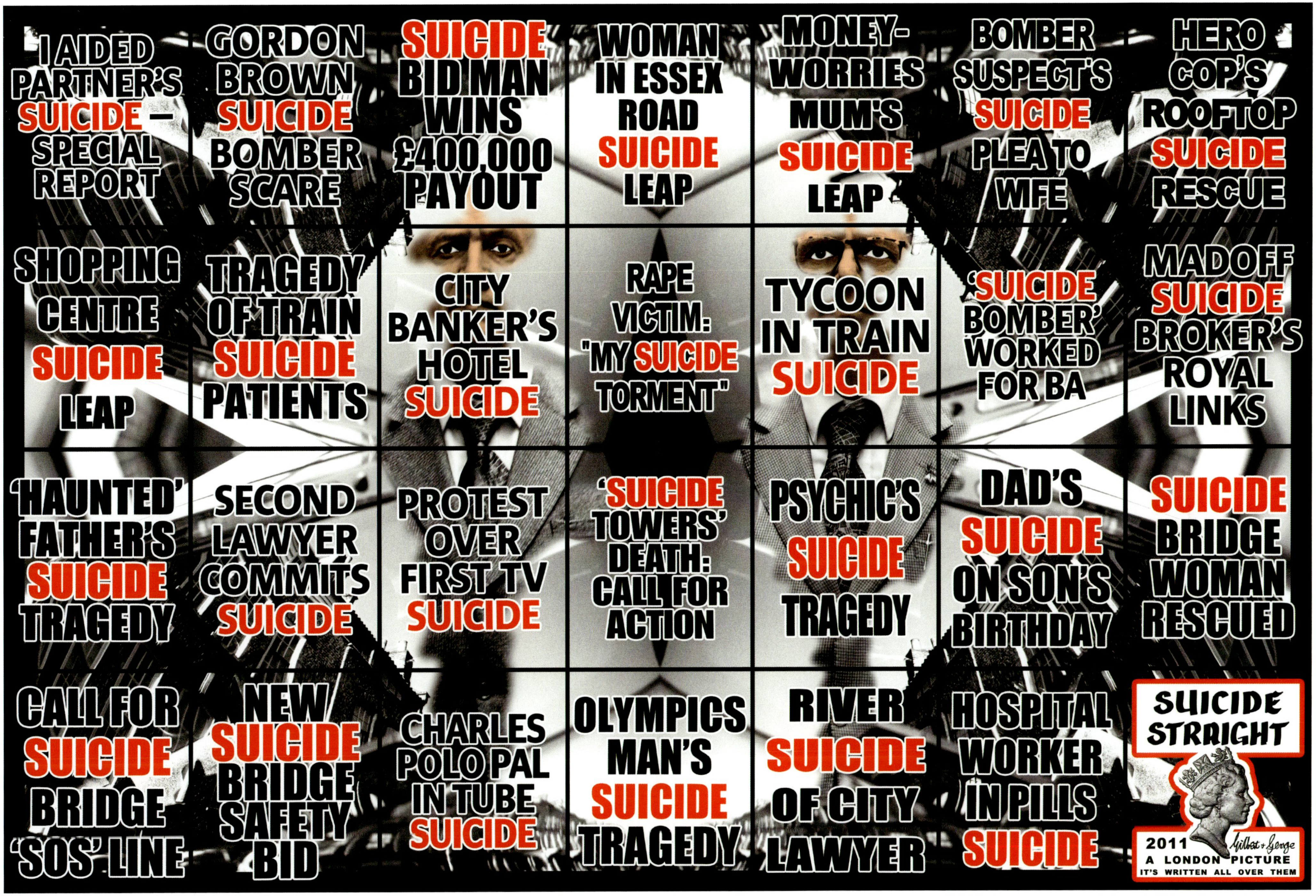
I AIDED PARTNER'S SUICIDE – SPECIAL REPORT
GORDON BROWN SUICIDE BOMBER SCARE
SUICIDE BID MAN WINS £400,000 PAYOUT
WOMAN IN ESSEX ROAD SUICIDE LEAP
MONEY-WORRIES MUM'S SUICIDE LEAP
BOMBER SUSPECT'S SUICIDE PLEA TO WIFE
HERO COP'S ROOFTOP SUICIDE RESCUE
SHOPPING CENTRE SUICIDE LEAP
TRAGEDY OF TRAIN SUICIDE PATIENTS
CITY BANKER'S HOTEL SUICIDE
RAPE VICTIM: "MY SUICIDE TORMENT"
TYCOON IN TRAIN SUICIDE
'SUICIDE BOMBER' WORKED FOR BA
MADOFF SUICIDE BROKER'S ROYAL LINKS
'HAUNTED' FATHER'S SUICIDE TRAGEDY
SECOND LAWYER COMMITS SUICIDE
PROTEST OVER FIRST TV SUICIDE
'SUICIDE TOWERS' DEATH: CALL FOR ACTION
PSYCHIC'S SUICIDE TRAGEDY
DAD'S SUICIDE ON SON'S BIRTHDAY
SUICIDE BRIDGE WOMAN RESCUED
CALL FOR SUICIDE BRIDGE 'SOS' LINE
NEW SUICIDE BRIDGE SAFETY BID
CHARLES POLO PAL IN TUBE SUICIDE
OLYMPICS MAN'S SUICIDE TRAGEDY
RIVER SUICIDE OF CITY LAWYER
HOSPITAL WORKER IN PILLS SUICIDE
SUICIDE STRAIGHT
2011
A LONDON PICTURE
IT'S WRITTEN ALL OVER THEM

SUICIDE STRAIGHT. 2011. 302 x 444 cm

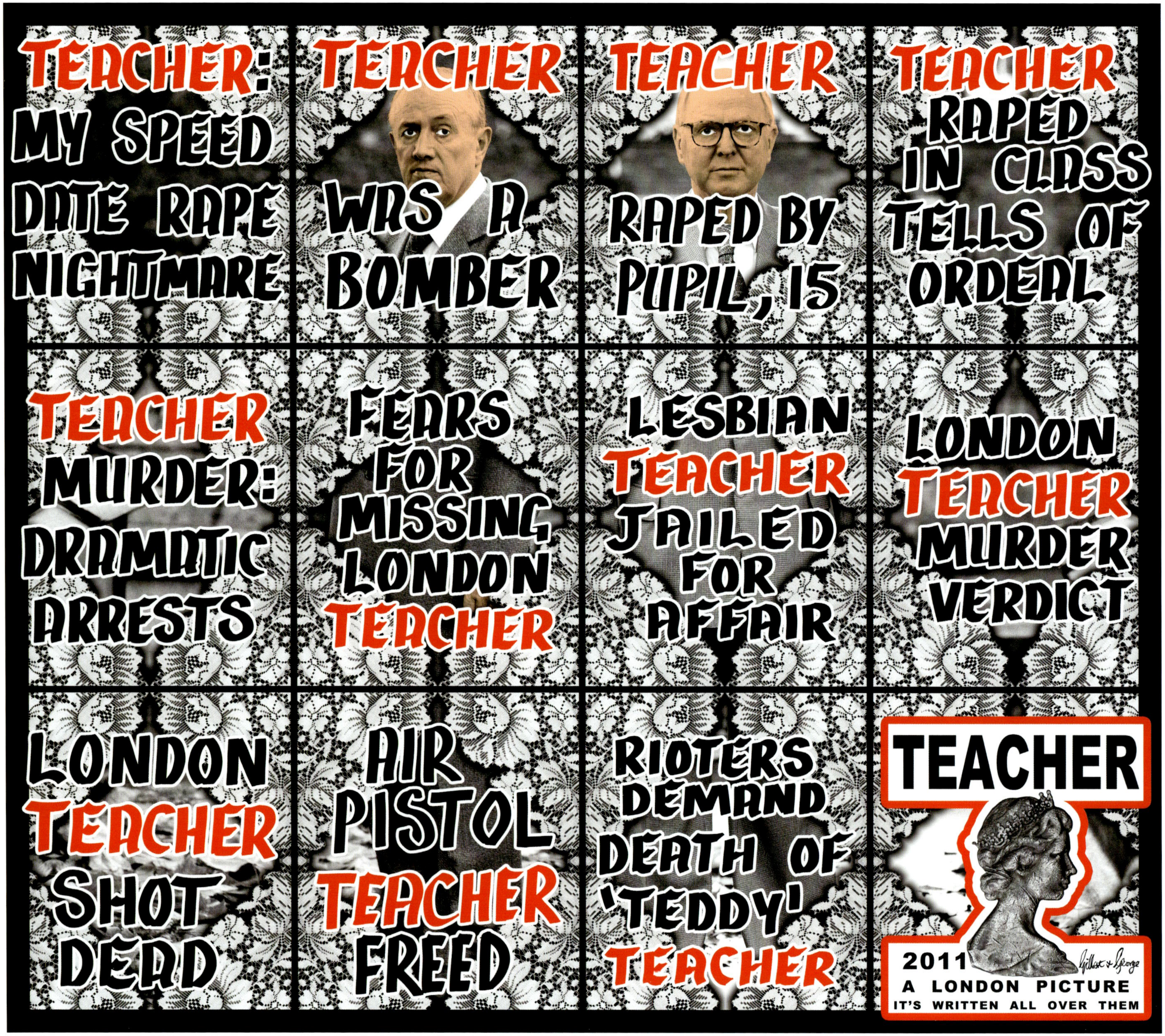
TEACHER: MY SPEED DATE RAPE NIGHTMARE
TEACHER WAS A BOMBER
TEACHER RAPED BY PUPIL, 15
TEACHER RAPED IN CLASS TELLS OF ORDEAL
TEACHER MURDER: DRAMATIC ARRESTS
FEARS FOR MISSING LONDON TEACHER
LESBIAN TEACHER JAILED FOR AFFAIR
LONDON TEACHER MURDER VERDICT
LONDON TEACHER SHOT DEAD
AIR PISTOL TEACHER FREED
RIOTERS DEMAND DEATH OF 'TEDDY' TEACHER
TEACHER
2011
A LONDON PICTURE
IT'S WRITTEN ALL OVER THEM

TEACHER. 2011. 226 x 254 cm

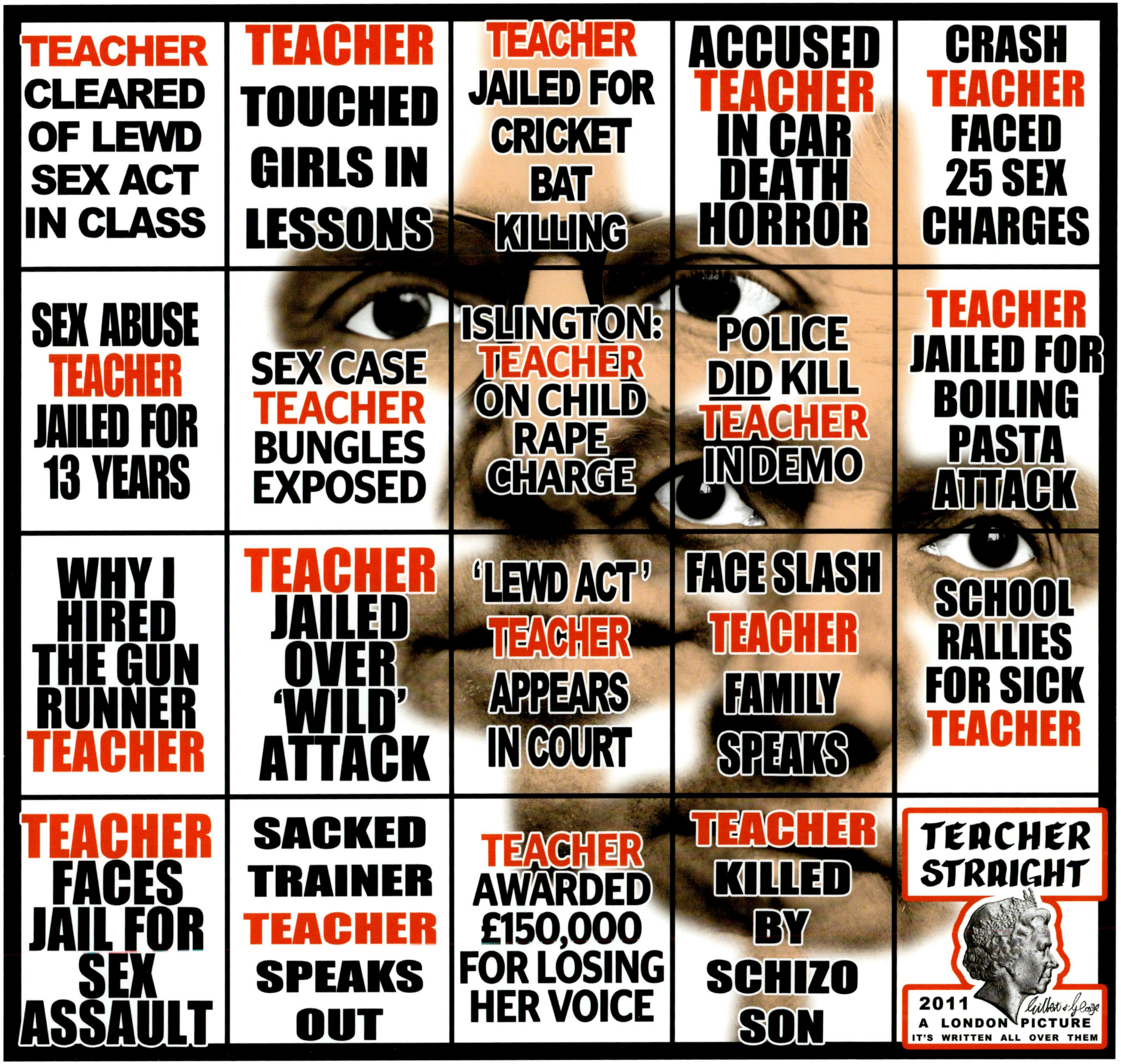
TEACHER CLEARED OF LEWD SEX ACT IN CLASS
TEACHER TOUCHED GIRLS IN LESSONS
TEACHER JAILED FOR CRICKET BAT KILLING
ACCUSED TEACHER IN CAR DEATH HORROR
CRASH TEACHER FACED 25 SEX CHARGES
SEX ABUSE TEACHER JAILED FOR 13 YEARS
SEX CASE TEACHER BUNGLES EXPOSED
ISLINGTON: TEACHER ON CHILD RAPE CHARGE
POLICE DID KILL TEACHER IN DEMO
TEACHER JAILED FOR BOILING PASTA ATTACK
WHY I HIRED THE GUN RUNNER TEACHER
TEACHER JAILED OVER 'WILD' ATTACK
'LEWD ACT' TEACHER APPEARS IN COURT
FACE SLASH TEACHER FAMILY SPEAKS
SCHOOL RALLIES FOR SICK TEACHER
TEACHER FACES JAIL FOR SEX ASSAULT
SACKED TRAINER TEACHER SPEAKS OUT
TEACHER AWARDED £150,000 FOR LOSING HER VOICE
TEACHER KILLED BY SCHIZO SON
TEACHER STRAIGHT
2011
A LONDON PICTURE
IT'S WRITTEN ALL OVER THEM

TEACHER STRAIGHT. 2011. 302 x 317 cm

MILE END: STABBED TEEN FIGHTS FOR LIFE
LONDON'S 21st TEEN KNIFE VICTIM
MOTHER HELD OVER MURDER OF TEEN DAUGHTERS
ZERO ALCOHOL FOR TEEN DRIVERS
GANGS TSAR: HOW I'LL BEAT TEEN CRIME
TEEN
2011
A LONDON PICTURE
IT'S WRITTEN ALL OVER THEM
Gilbert & George

TEEN. 2011. 151 x 190 cm

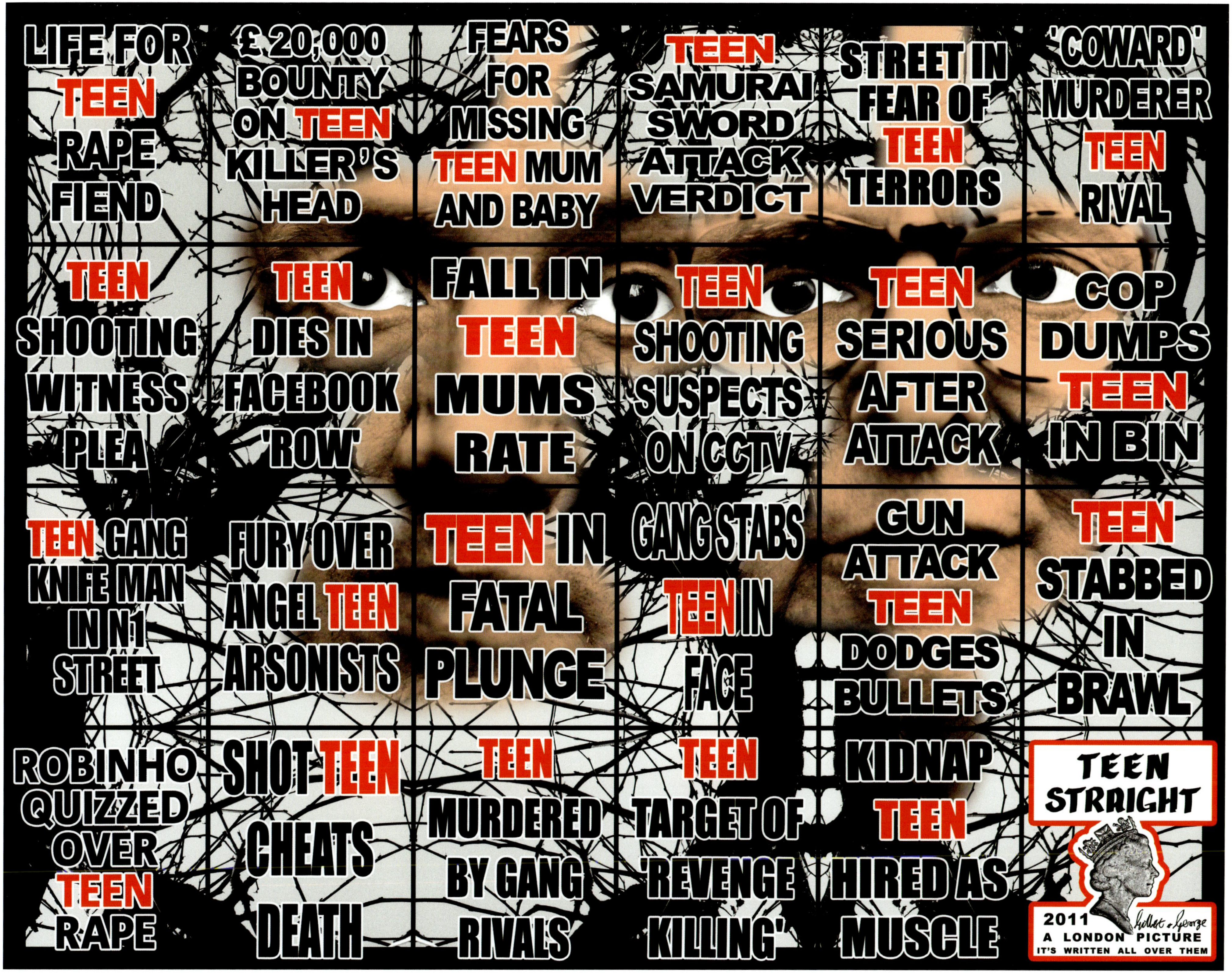
LIFE FOR TEEN RAPE FIEND
£ 20,000 BOUNTY ON TEEN KILLER'S HEAD
FEARS FOR MISSING TEEN MUM AND BABY
TEEN SAMURAI SWORD ATTACK VERDICT
STREET IN FEAR OF TEEN TERRORS
'COWARD' MURDERER TEEN RIVAL
TEEN SHOOTING WITNESS PLEA
TEEN DIES IN FACEBOOK 'ROW'
FALL IN TEEN MUMS RATE
TEEN SHOOTING SUSPECTS ON CCTV
TEEN SERIOUS AFTER ATTACK
COP DUMPS TEEN IN BIN
TEEN GANG KNIFE MAN IN N1 STREET
FURY OVER ANGEL TEEN ARSONISTS
TEEN IN FATAL PLUNGE
GANG STABS TEEN IN FACE
GUN ATTACK TEEN DODGES BULLETS
TEEN STABBED IN BRAWL
ROBINHO QUIZZED OVER TEEN RAPE
SHOT TEEN CHEATS DEATH
TEEN MURDERED BY GANG RIVALS
TEEN TARGET OF 'REVENGE KILLING'
KIDNAP TEEN HIRED AS MUSCLE
TEEN STRAIGHT
2011
A LONDON PICTURE
IT'S WRITTEN ALL OVER THEM

TEEN STRAIGHT. 2011. 302 x 381 cm

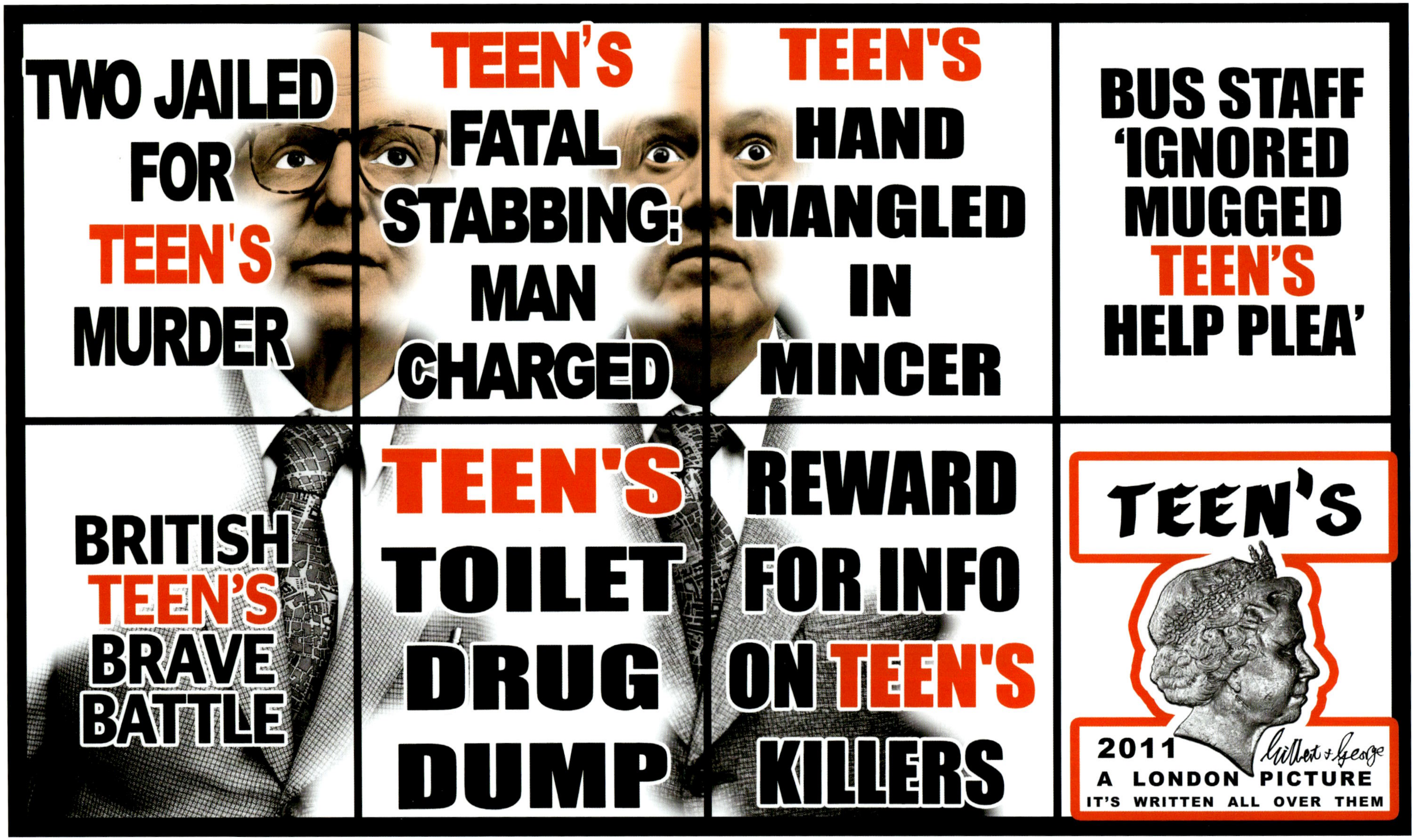

TWO JAILED FOR TEEN'S MURDER
TEEN'S FATAL STABBING: MAN CHARGED
TEEN'S HAND MANGLED IN MINCER
BUS STAFF 'IGNORED MUGGED TEEN'S HELP PLEA'
BRITISH TEEN'S BRAVE BATTLE
TEEN'S TOILET DRUG DUMP
REWARD FOR INFO ON TEEN'S KILLERS
TEEN'S
2011
A LONDON PICTURE
IT'S WRITTEN ALL OVER THEM
Gilbert & George

TEEN'S. 2011. 151 x 254 cm

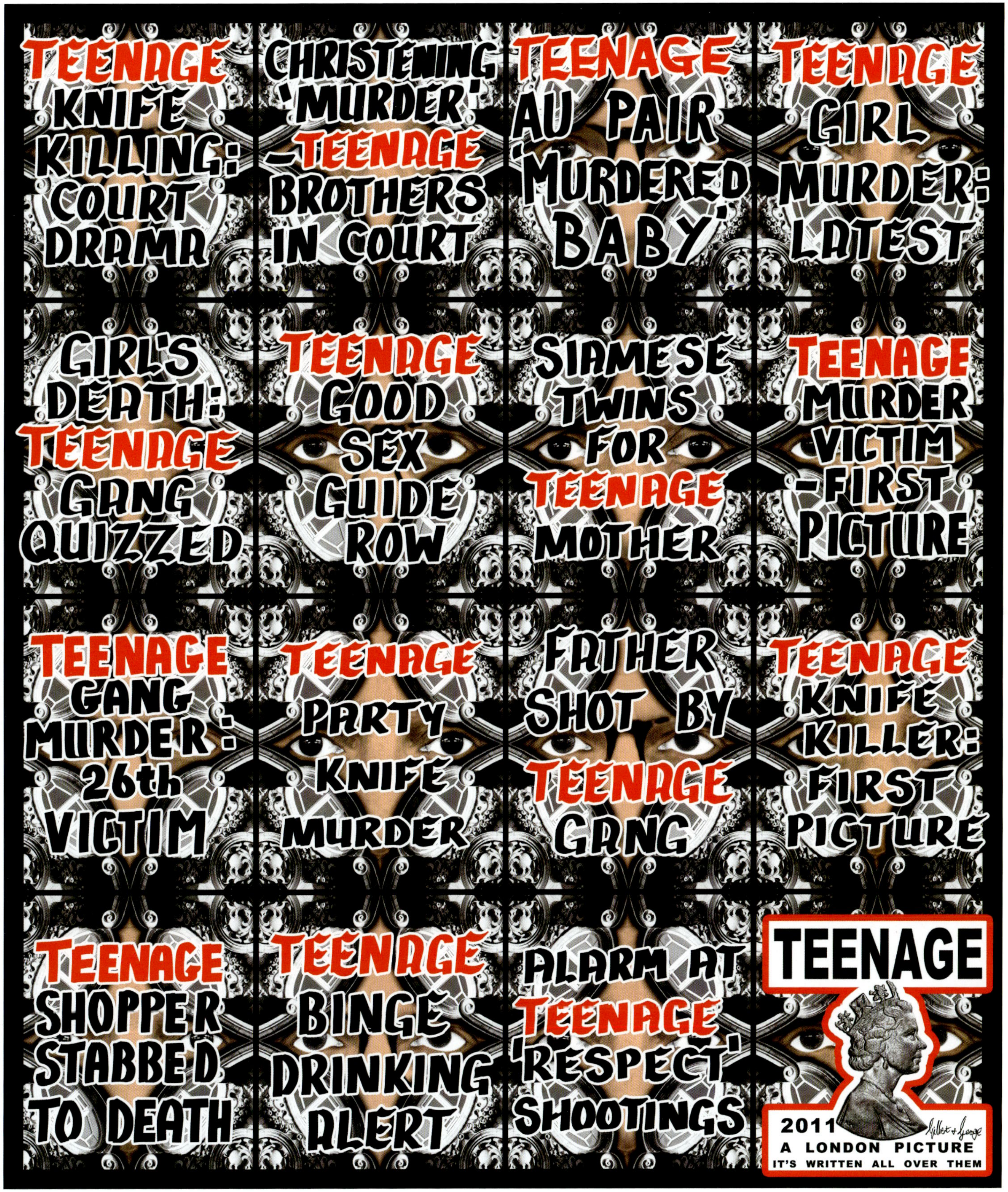
TEENAGE KNIFE KILLING: COURT DRAMA
CHRISTENING 'MURDER' – TEENAGE BROTHERS IN COURT
TEENAGE AU PAIR 'MURDERED' BABY'
TEENAGE GIRL MURDER: LATEST
GIRL'S DEATH: TEENAGE GANG QUIZZED
TEENAGE GOOD SEX GUIDE ROW
SIAMESE TWINS FOR TEENAGE MOTHER
TEENAGE MURDER VICTIM – FIRST PICTURE
TEENAGE GANG MURDER: 26th VICTIM
TEENAGE PARTY KNIFE MURDER
FATHER SHOT BY TEENAGE GANG
TEENAGE KNIFE KILLER: FIRST PICTURE
TEENAGE SHOPPER STABBED TO DEATH
TEENAGE BINGE DRINKING ALERT
ALARM AT TEENAGE 'RESPECT' SHOOTINGS
TEENAGE
2011
A LONDON PICTURE
IT'S WRITTEN ALL OVER THEM

TEENAGE

2011

302 x 254 cm

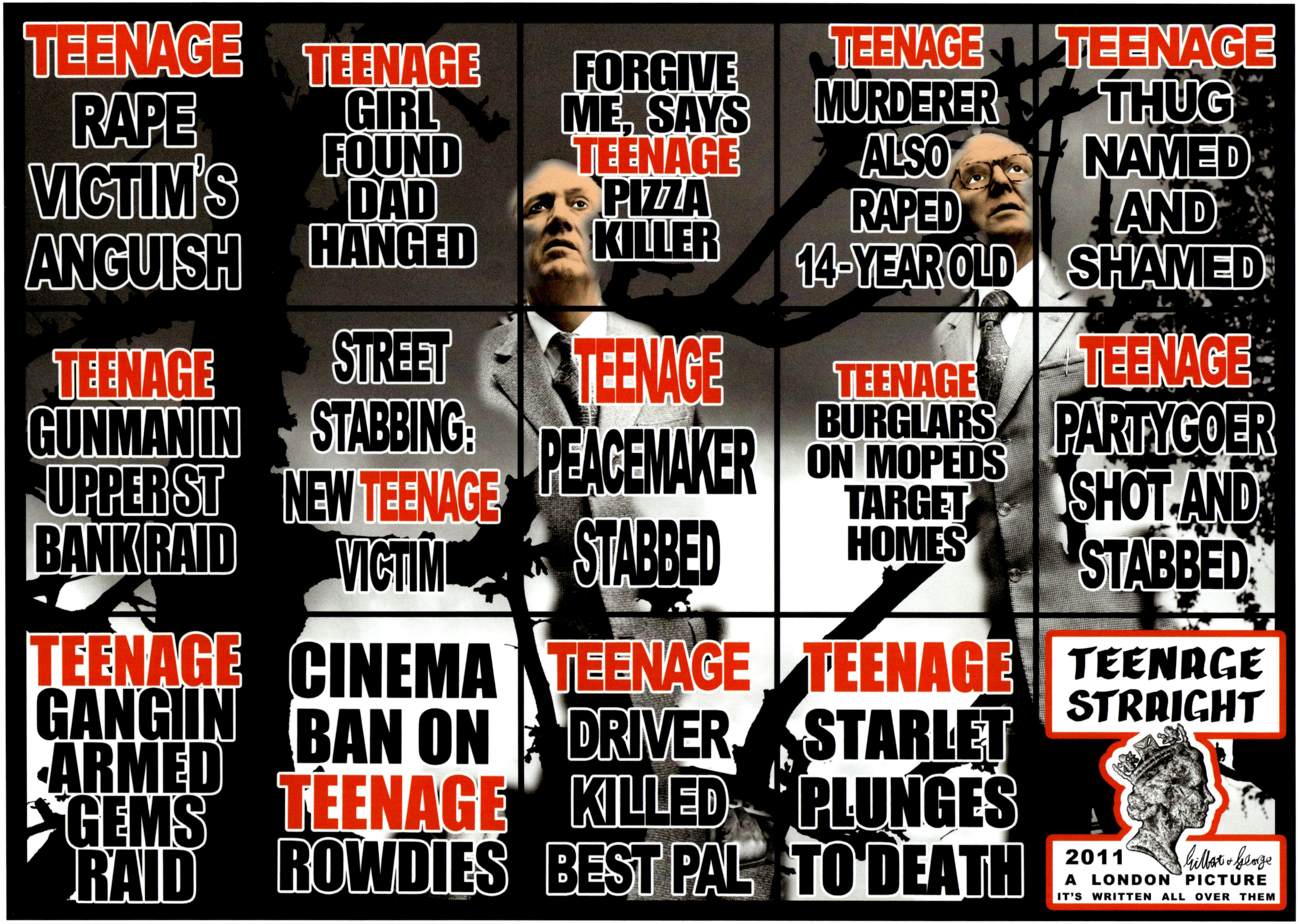
TEENAGE RAPE VICTIM'S ANGUISH
TEENAGE GIRL FOUND DAD HANGED
FORGIVE ME, SAYS TEENAGE PIZZA KILLER
TEENAGE MURDERER ALSO RAPED 14-YEAR OLD
TEENAGE THUG NAMED AND SHAMED
TEENAGE GUNMAN IN UPPER ST BANK RAID
STREET STABBING: NEW TEENAGE VICTIM
TEENAGE PEACEMAKER STABBED
TEENAGE BURGLARS ON MOPEDS TARGET HOMES
TEENAGE PARTYGOER SHOT AND STABBED
TEENAGE GANG IN ARMED GEMS RAID
CINEMA BAN ON TEENAGE ROWDIES
TEENAGE DRIVER KILLED BEST PAL
TEENAGE STARLET PLUNGES TO DEATH
TEENAGE STRAIGHT
2011
A LONDON PICTURE
IT'S WRITTEN ALL OVER THEM
Gilbert & George

TEENAGE STRAIGHT. 2011. 226 x 317 cm

CLAPTON TEENAGER KILLED IN 'POSTCODE' GANG WAR
FEARS FOR MISSING INTERNET TEENAGER
REGIS KILLING: TEENAGER ARRESTED
TEENAGER MURDERED OUTSIDE TUBE
MUSWELL HILL BACKPACK TEENAGER IS FOUND ALIVE
SWINE FLU KILLS LONDON TEENAGER
TEENAGER DIES IN 'RACIST' ATTACK
BACKPACK TEENAGER BACK FROM THE DEAD
TEENAGER KILLED IN 'POSTCODE' GANG WAR
TEENAGER SHOT DEAD AT SHOP
N. LONDON: TEENAGER STABBED TO DEATH
TEENAGER
2011
A LONDON PICTURE
IT'S WRITTEN ALL OVER THEM

TEENAGER. 2011. 226 x 254 cm

TEENAGER STABBED AS GANG STORMS NIGHTCLUB
TEENAGER CHARGED OVER STOLEN PUPPY
TEENAGER SURVIVES FIVE STOREY PLUNGE
KILLER TEENAGER FACES LIFE BEHIND BARS
FAKE GUN TEENAGER IS PUT BEHIND BARS
CRAZED CANNABIS SMOKER KILLED TEENAGER
TEENAGER SLASHED DRUG DEALER'S THROAT
'TINKER' KILLING: TEENAGER ARRESTED
STABBING: TEENAGER CHARGED
TEENAGER IS JAILED FOR BUS STABBING
TEENAGER KILLING: SIX IN COURT
TEENAGER CHARGED WITH BUS STABBING
NIGHTCLUB TEENAGER SHOT DEAD
TEENAGER STABBED IN GANG ATTACK
TEENAGER DIES IN CAR CRASH 'CARNAGE'
TEENAGER KILLED IN RAID ON TIFFANY'S
TEENAGER KEPT LOADED MACHINE GUN UNDER HIS BED
TEENAGER WAS USED AS A SEX SLAVE
TEENAGER JAILED FOR STATION ATTACK
TEENAGER CHARGED WITH DJ MURDER
GANG KILLING: TEENAGER JAILED
FINSBURY PARK TEENAGER STABBED
TEENAGER SET FOR X FACTOR STARDOM
£8.5 MILLION AWARD TO CRIPPLED TEENAGER
TEENAGER HELD AFTER GANG MURDER
TEENAGER KILLED IN HOUSE OF HORROR
'LAUGHING KILLER STABBED TEENAGER TO DEATH'
TEENAGER STRAIGHT
2011
A LONDON PICTURE
IT'S WRITTEN ALL OVER THEM

TEENAGER STRAIGHT. 2011. 302 x 444 cm

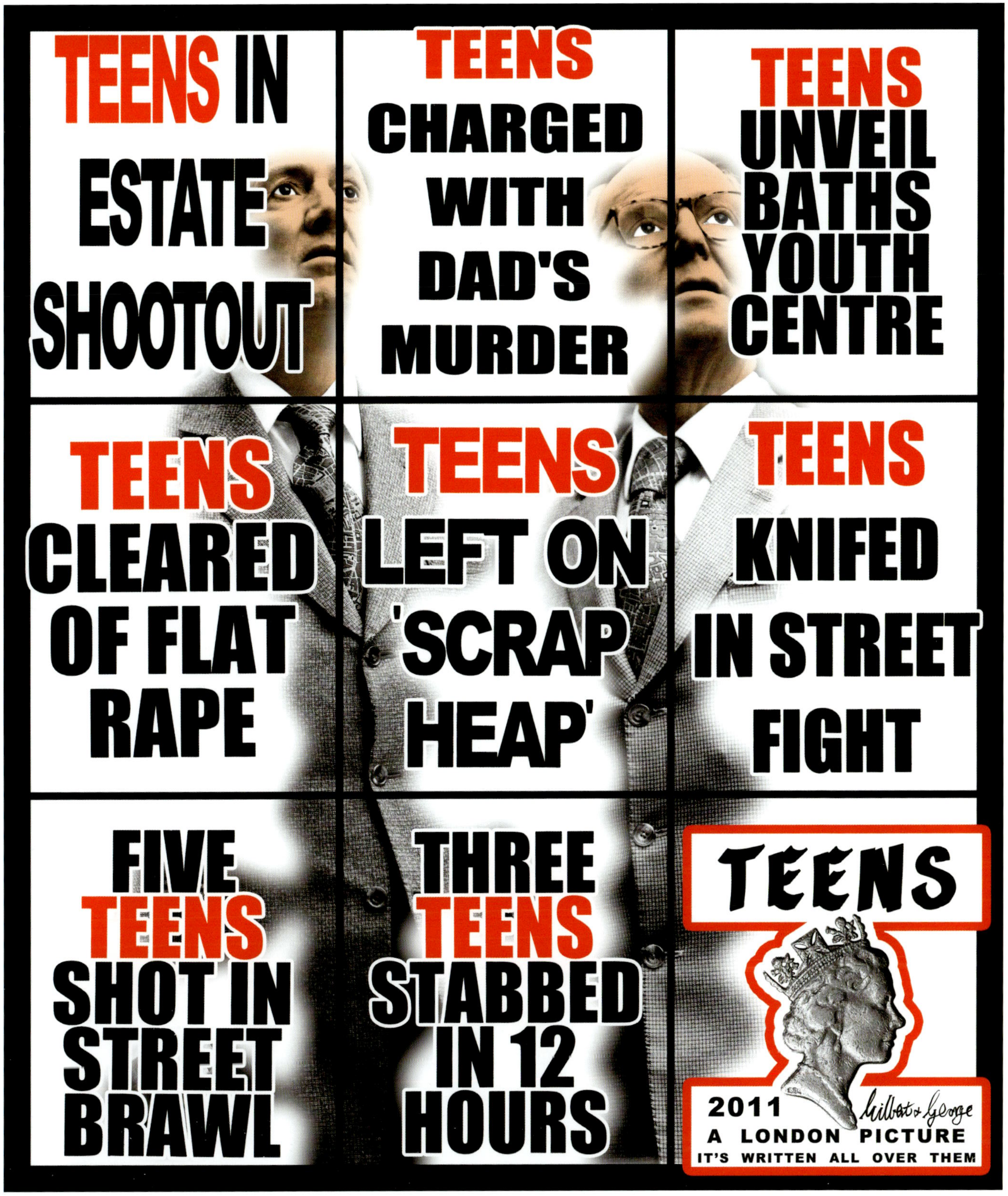
TEENS IN ESTATE SHOOTOUT
TEENS CHARGED WITH DAD'S MURDER
TEENS UNVEIL BATHS YOUTH CENTRE
TEENS CLEARED OF FLAT RAPE
TEENS LEFT ON 'SCRAP HEAP'
TEENS KNIFED IN STREET FIGHT
FIVE TEENS SHOT IN STREET BRAWL
THREE TEENS STABBED IN 12 HOURS
TEENS
2011
A LONDON PICTURE
IT'S WRITTEN ALL OVER THEM

TEENS. 2011. 226 x 190 cm

FASHION HEIRESS RAID TERROR
BRITISH TYCOON DEAD IN MUMBAI TERROR
LONDON WOMAN'S £10,000 CARJACK TERROR
TERROR TRIAL JUROR'S AMAZING STORY
REVEALED: TERROR CHIEF'S CYBER HQ IN W12
TERROR ATTACK ON U.S. EMBASSY
EXPENSES ROW TERROR CHIEF QUITS
MET: 15 TERROR PLOTS FOILED
2,000 TERROR SUSPECTS IN UK
HOTEL TERROR SURVIVORS' STORIES
KIDNAP TERROR SUSPECT: PICTURE
TERROR DOCTOR: CASE DROPPED
LONDON 21/7 TERROR TRIAL VERDICTS
'TERROR DOCTORS' NHS VISA FIASCO
TERROR CHECKS TO HIT AIRPORTS
TERROR: MORE DOCTORS QUIZZED
EUROSTAR LIVE CABLE TERROR
BRITISH HOSTAGES IN MUMBAI TERROR
BLUNDERS OF TERROR DOCTOR INQUIRY
MUSLIMS ON TERROR HIT LIST
TERROR RECRUITS IN OUR SCHOOLS
TERROR BOMBS: NEW APPEAL
HOLIDAY BRITS IN TERROR BOMBING
TERROR
2011
A LONDON PICTURE
IT'S WRITTEN ALL OVER THEM

TERROR. 2011. 302 x 381 cm

BOMB POLICE HOLD 'DR TERROR'
MAN UTD TERROR BOMB DRAMA
TERROR CHIEF TOLD ME TO BOMB LONDON
TERROR BOMB
2011
A LONDON PICTURE
IT'S WRITTEN ALL OVER THEM

TERROR BOMB. 2011. 151 x 127 cm

JUDGES FREE FOUR TERROR SUSPECTS
WEDDING EMAILS SPARKED TERROR SWOOP
MARQUESS ESTATE FAMILY LIVING IN TERROR
FEARS AFTER
CAMERON: PAKISTAN EXPORTING TERROR
TERROR PAIR TO STAY IN BRITAIN
TERROR ORDEAL ON NIGHT BUS
TERROR
TERROR AS JET'S ENGINE EXPLODES
ESCAPED SNAKE SPARKS TERROR
CYBER TERROR THREAT TO 2012 GAMES
YORK HALL BOXING EVENT TERROR
FEWER TERROR STOPS BY COPS
IRA TERROR: VICTIM'S NEW FIGHT
MOB IN TESCO TERROR

TERROR STRAIGHT. 2011. 302 x 571 cm

GANG MENACE OF LITTLE TERROR AGED 9
HACKNEY PLANE TERROR RAIDS DUO CHARGED
FIVE HELD IN JET PLANE TERROR RAIDS
'TERROR LINK' DAD BANNED FROM UK
LONDON TERROR BOMBS: DOCTOR GUILTY
TOWN HALL TERROR TARGET FEARS
TWELVE TERROR SUSPECTS IN NHS
SUMMIT TERROR SWOOP: 5 HELD
'TERROR REIGN OF NIGHT STALKER'
COMMUTER TERROR GANG'S 100 VICTIMS
UNIVERSITY LINKS TO TERROR SUSPECTS
ST PAUL'S ROAD TERROR RAID
TERROR STRATEGY UNDER FIRE
FOILED CHRISTMAS TERROR PLOT: 12 HELD
TERROR TRIAL LATEST
TERROR TRIAL TRIO VERDICT
WHITECHAPEL TERRER ECHOES IN EAST END
TERROR SUSPECTS VERDICT
BETTING SHOP REIGN OF TERROR
TERROR STRAIGHT
2011
A LONDON PICTURE
IT'S WRITTEN ALL OVER THEM

AIRLINE TERROR PLOT 'RETRIAL'
MASSIVE 9/11 TERROR PLOT
FIVE ON TERROR PLOT CHARGES
LONDON TERROR PLOT VERDICTS
MASS MURDER TERROR PLOT- DETAILS
TERROR PLOT: NEW DETAILS
LONDON 9/11 TERROR PLOT
BRITISH 'TERROR KIDNAP PLOT' SMASHED
TERROR PLOT
2011
A LONDON PICTURE
IT'S WRITTEN ALL OVER THEM

TERROR PLOT. 2011. 226 x 190 cm

CASH MACHINE THIEF GRABS £6 000
WHEEL-CHAIR THIEF IS JAILED
TEENAGER STABBED IN BACK BY BIKE THIEF
THIEF
2011
A LONDON PICTURE
IT'S WRITTEN ALL OVER THEM

THIEF. 2011. 151 x 127 cm

THIEVES THREATEN TO KILL KID'S PET
PASSENGERS ATTACKED BY BUS THIEVES
SAT NAV THIEVES BLAMED FOR CABBIE'S DEATH
SPRAY THIEVES GRAB £60,000 RINGS
CCTV SHAME OF TEEN THIEVES
N7 GAS TERROR AS COPPER THIEVES STRIKE
THIEVES TARGET SUPER BIKES
EC1 COMPUTER THIEVES TUNNEL INTO CENTRE
THIEVES
2011
Gilbert & George
A LONDON PICTURE
IT'S WRITTEN ALL OVER THEM

THIEVES. 2011. 226 x 190 cm

SINK PLUNGER THUG ATTACKS COPS
THUG WHO STAMPED ON HEAD GETS LIFE
HAMMER ATTACK THUG JAILED
STABBED HERO COPS SEE THUG JAILED
SCHOOLKIDS HELP CAGE GUN THUG
THUG
2011
Gilbert & George
A LONDON PICTURE
IT'S WRITTEN ALL OVER THEM

THUG. 2011. 151 x 190 cm

FOOTBALL
THUGS'
BLOODY
BATTLE:
PICTURES
'NURSERIES
'TURN
TODDLERS
INTO
THUGS'
POLICE
HUNT
200
SOCCER
THUGS
THUGS
2011
A LONDON PICTURE
IT'S WRITTEN ALL OVER THEM

THUGS. 2011. 151 x 127 cm

POLICE RAIDS NAB VIOLENT THUGS
HUNT FOR BUS THUGS
THUGS SMASH HERO PC GRAVE
THUGS MOW DOWN BIKE COP
HIGHBURY BARMEN SLASHED BY THUGS
THUGS JAILED OVER GANG ATTACK
HOSPITAL ROBOCAM TACKLES THUGS
CARJACK THUGS DRAG DAD FROM VEHICLE
THUGS STRAIGHT
2011
A LONDON PICTURE
IT'S WRITTEN ALL OVER THEM

THUGS STRAIGHT. 2011. 226 x 190 cm

MUM'S FIGHT IN VAIN TO SAVE TODDLER
TODDLER KILLED IN BUS TRAGEDY
COUNCIL WORKER SAVES CHOKING TODDLER
TODDLER SAVED FROM CHOKING
TODDLER POISONED IN DRUGS BLUNDER
TODDLER SURVIVES STUN GUN ATTACK
TODDLER SHOOTING TRIO JAILED
TODDLER DROWNS: FATHER MISSING
DAD FINDS TODDLER 'CHEWING COCAINE'
MUM JAILED OVER DEATH OF TODDLER
TODDLER KILLED BY 'BADLY BUILT' WALL
TODDLER
2011
A LONDON PICTURE
IT'S WRITTEN ALL OVER THEM

TODDLER. A young child beginning to walk. 2011. 226 x 254 cm

TOP TOTS
COMPETITION
AT SOMERFIED
CHRISP ST E14
UNTIL SAT 12TH
R.I.P VOTE R.I.P
FOR YOUR
TOP
TOTS
TOP TOTS
R.I.P – THE
WINNERS!
TOP TOTS R.I.P –
THE PRIZE
WINNERS
TIOP
TOTS:
CAST
YOUR
VOTES
Top Tots
HERE TODAY
AND UNTIL
28TH AUGUST
FREE ENTRY FORM
IN THE PAPER
TOP TOTS
WINNERS
REVEALED
R.I.P R.I.P
YOUR
'TOP TOTS'
FINAL:
PICTURES
TOP TOTS
2011
A LONDON PICTURE
IT'S WRITTEN ALL OVER THEM

TOP TOTS. Annual competition of very young children. 2011. 226 x 190 cm

MUM AND TOT IN GUN TERROR
MUM KILLED TOT WITH PILLS
HOSPITAL PAYOUT OVER SICK TOT
ROW OVER RETURN OF TOT DEATH FUNFAIR
CONTEST: IS YOUR CHILD A TOP TOT?
TOT
2011
A LONDON PICTURE
IT'S WRITTEN ALL OVER THEM

TOT. A very young child. 2011. 151 x 190 cm

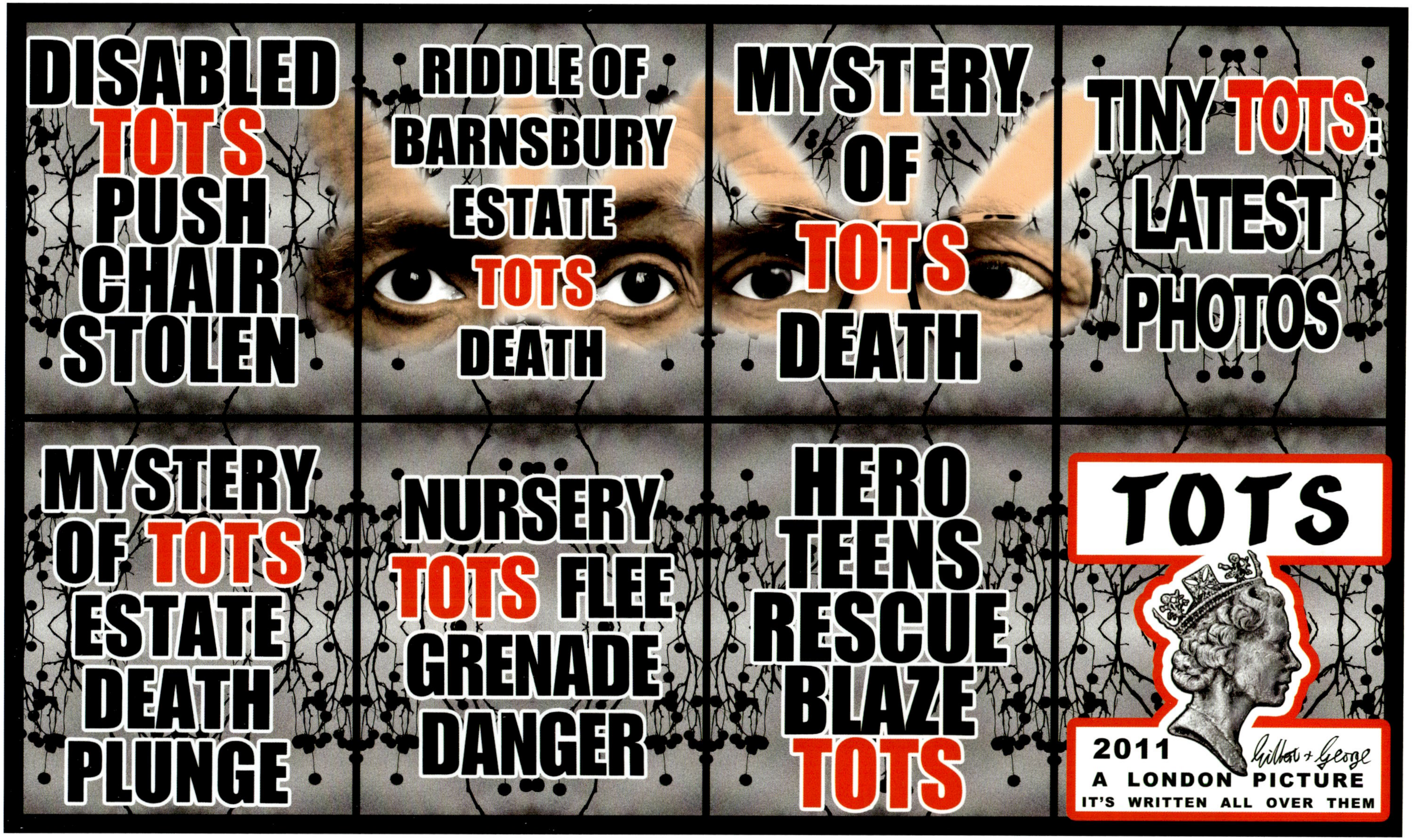
DISABLED TOTS PUSH CHAIR STOLEN
RIDDLE OF BARNSBURY ESTATE TOTS DEATH
MYSTERY OF TOTS DEATH
TINY TOTS: LATEST PHOTOS
MYSTERY OF TOTS ESTATE DEATH PLUNGE
NURSERY TOTS FLEE GRENADE DANGER
HERO TEENS RESCUE BLAZE TOTS
TOTS
2011
Gilbert + George
A LONDON PICTURE
IT'S WRITTEN ALL OVER THEM

TOTS. Very young children. 2011. 151 x 254 cm

HUNT FOR HIGHBURY RED PAINT VANDALS
VANDALS TIP OVER WOMAN'S SMART CAR
'BRAINLESS' VANDALS DESTROY TREES
VANDALS TARGET JEWISH GRAVES
TREE VANDALS OFFERED AMNESTY
N19 PARK IN BATTLE AGAINST VANDALS
CAMERAS AID HUNT FOR BUS VANDALS
PINT-SIZED GRAFFITI VANDALS NABBED
VANDALS
2011
A LONDON PICTURE
IT'S WRITTEN ALL OVER THEM

VANDALS. 2011. 226 x 190 cm

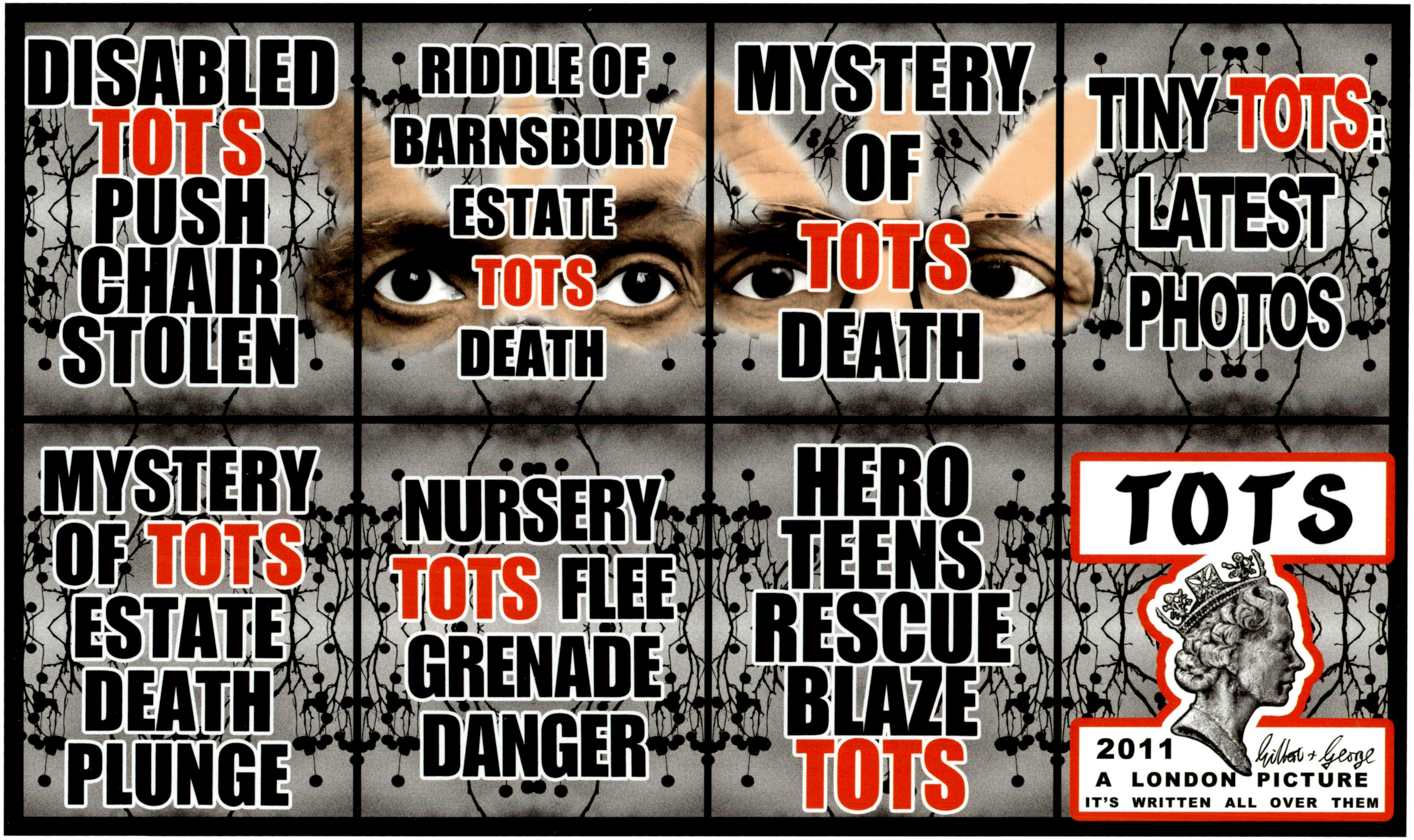
DISABLED TOTS PUSH CHAIR STOLEN
RIDDLE OF BARNSBURY ESTATE TOTS DEATH
MYSTERY OF TOTS DEATH
TINY TOTS: LATEST PHOTOS
MYSTERY OF TOTS ESTATE DEATH PLUNGE
NURSERY TOTS FLEE GRENADE DANGER
HERO TEENS RESCUE BLAZE TOTS
TOTS
2011
Gilbert + George
A LONDON PICTURE
IT'S WRITTEN ALL OVER THEM

TOTS. Very young children. 2011. 151 x 254 cm

TUBE CRIME: EVERY STATION'S RECORD
DRUNKEN VIOLENCE SOARS ON TUBE AND TRAINS
TUBE VIOLENCE SOARS: FULL DETAILS
TUBE STATION VIOLENCE -LIST OF SHAME
TUBE BOMB STILL UNSAFE
TUBE RAMPAGE GANG JAILED
TUBE TORTURE GANG JAILED
TUBE BOMB TRAVEL CHAOS
SNIFFER DOGS TO PATROL TUBE
TUBE CRIME SOARS
VANDALS SPARK TUBE STRIKE THREAT
MOMENT I FACED 21/7 TUBE 'BOMBER'
BLOODY KILLER HELD ON TUBE
STOP AND SEARCH PLAN ON TUBE
TERRORIST GIVEN JOB ON TUBE
TUBE
2011
A LONDON PICTURE
IT'S WRITTEN ALL OVER THEM

TUBE

2011

302 x 254 cm

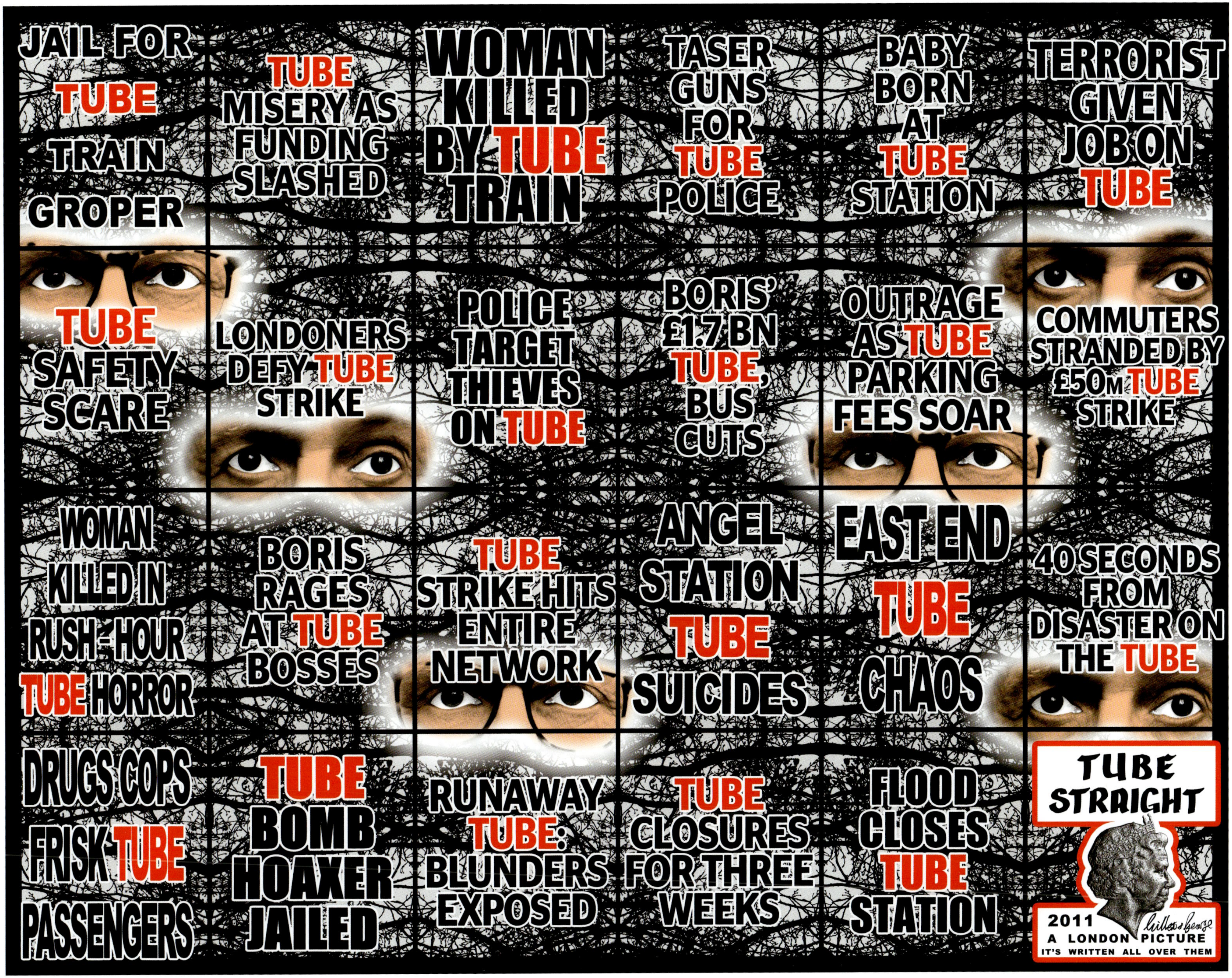
JAIL FOR TUBE TRAIN GROPER
TUBE MISERY AS FUNDING SLASHED
WOMAN KILLED BY TUBE TRAIN
TASER GUNS FOR TUBE POLICE
BABY BORN AT TUBE STATION
TERRORIST GIVEN JOB ON TUBE
TUBE SAFETY SCARE
LONDONERS DEFY TUBE STRIKE
POLICE TARGET THIEVES ON TUBE
BORIS' £1.7BN TUBE, BUS CUTS
OUTRAGE AS TUBE PARKING FEES SOAR
COMMUTERS STRANDED BY £50M TUBE STRIKE
WOMAN KILLED IN RUSH-HOUR TUBE HORROR
BORIS RAGES AT TUBE BOSSES
TUBE STRIKE HITS ENTIRE NETWORK
ANGEL STATION TUBE SUICIDES
EAST END TUBE CHAOS
40 SECONDS FROM DISASTER ON THE TUBE
DRUGS COPS FRISK TUBE PASSENGERS
TUBE BOMB HOAXER JAILED
RUNAWAY TUBE: BLUNDERS EXPOSED
TUBE CLOSURES FOR THREE WEEKS
FLOOD CLOSES TUBE STATION
TUBE STRAIGHT
2011
A LONDON PICTURE
IT'S WRITTEN ALL OVER THEM

TUBE STRAIGHT. 2011. 302 x 381 cm

HUNT FOR HIGHBURY RED PAINT VANDALS
VANDALS TIP OVER WOMAN'S SMART CAR
'BRAINLESS' VANDALS DESTROY TREES
VANDALS TARGET JEWISH GRAVES
TREE VANDALS OFFERED AMNESTY
N19 PARK IN BATTLE AGAINST VANDALS
CAMERAS AID HUNT FOR BUS VANDALS
PINT-SIZED GRAFFITI VANDALS NABBED
VANDALS
2011
A LONDON PICTURE
IT'S WRITTEN ALL OVER THEM

VANDALS. 2011. 226 x 190 cm

VICE
ZONE
BLITZ
VICE RING
ASYLUM
SEEKER
JAILED
£20,000
REWARD
IN VICE GIRL
KILLING
MULTIPLE
ARRESTS
IN VICE
ZONE
BLITZ
DOZENS
NABBED
IN VICE
PURGE
UPPER
STREET
VICE GIRL
FEARS
'CANNIBAL'
CLAIM BY
VICE-GIRL
MURDER
SUSPECT
VICE
2011
A LONDON PICTURE
IT'S WRITTEN ALL OVER THEM

VICE. 2011. 151 x 254 cm

WEDDING
COURAGE
OF 7/7
VICTIM
NEW
RUSSIAN
POISON
VICTIM
CANNING
TOWN
GANG'S
NEW
VICTIM
VICTIM
2011
A LONDON PICTURE
IT'S WRITTEN ALL OVER THEM

VICTIM. 2011. 151 x 127 cm

VICTIM STRAIGHT. 2011. 151 x 254 cm

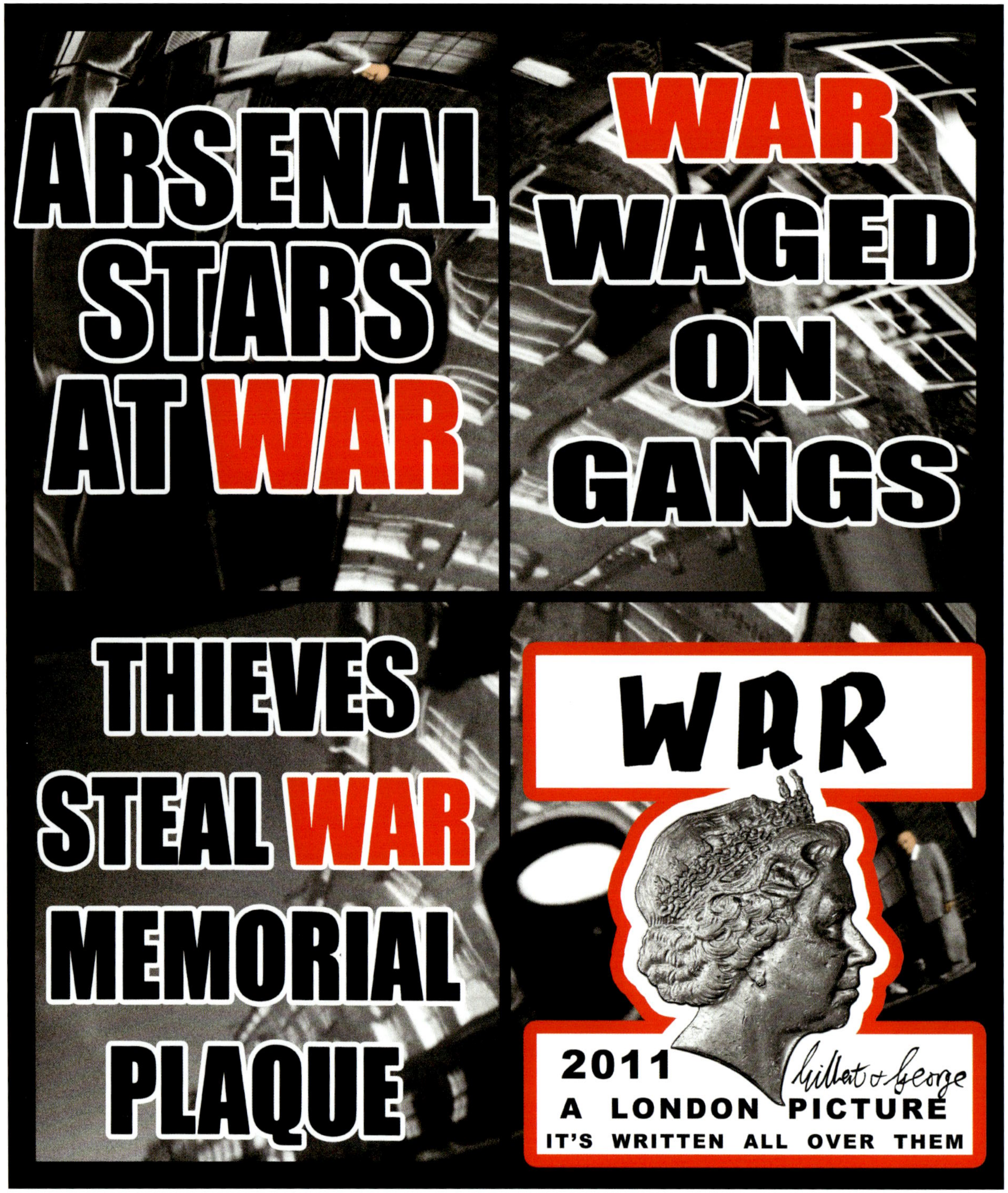
ARSENAL STARS AT WAR
WAR WAGED ON GANGS
THIEVES STEAL WAR MEMORIAL PLAQUE
WAR
2011
A LONDON PICTURE
IT'S WRITTEN ALL OVER THEM

WAR. 2011. 151 x 127 cm

ARSENAL FAN SPAT AT WOMAN IN VEIL
RIPPER: FOURTH WOMAN MISSING
WOMAN KILLED BY HER DAUGHTER
WOMAN SOLDIER KILLED IN IRAQ -PICTURE
BRITISH WOMAN KILLED IN IRAQ -PICTURE
WOMAN PUSHED ON TRACK- DRAMATIC PICTURES
FIRST BRITISH WOMAN KILLED BY TALIBAN
POLICE WOMAN MURDER- VERDICT
WOMAN HURLED ONTO RAIL TRACK
WOMAN KILLED ON SAS MISSION
WOMAN BANKER'S £15m SEX CASE VICTORY
WOMAN
2011
A LONDON PICTURE
IT'S WRITTEN ALL OVER THEM

WOMAN. 2011. 226 x 254 cm

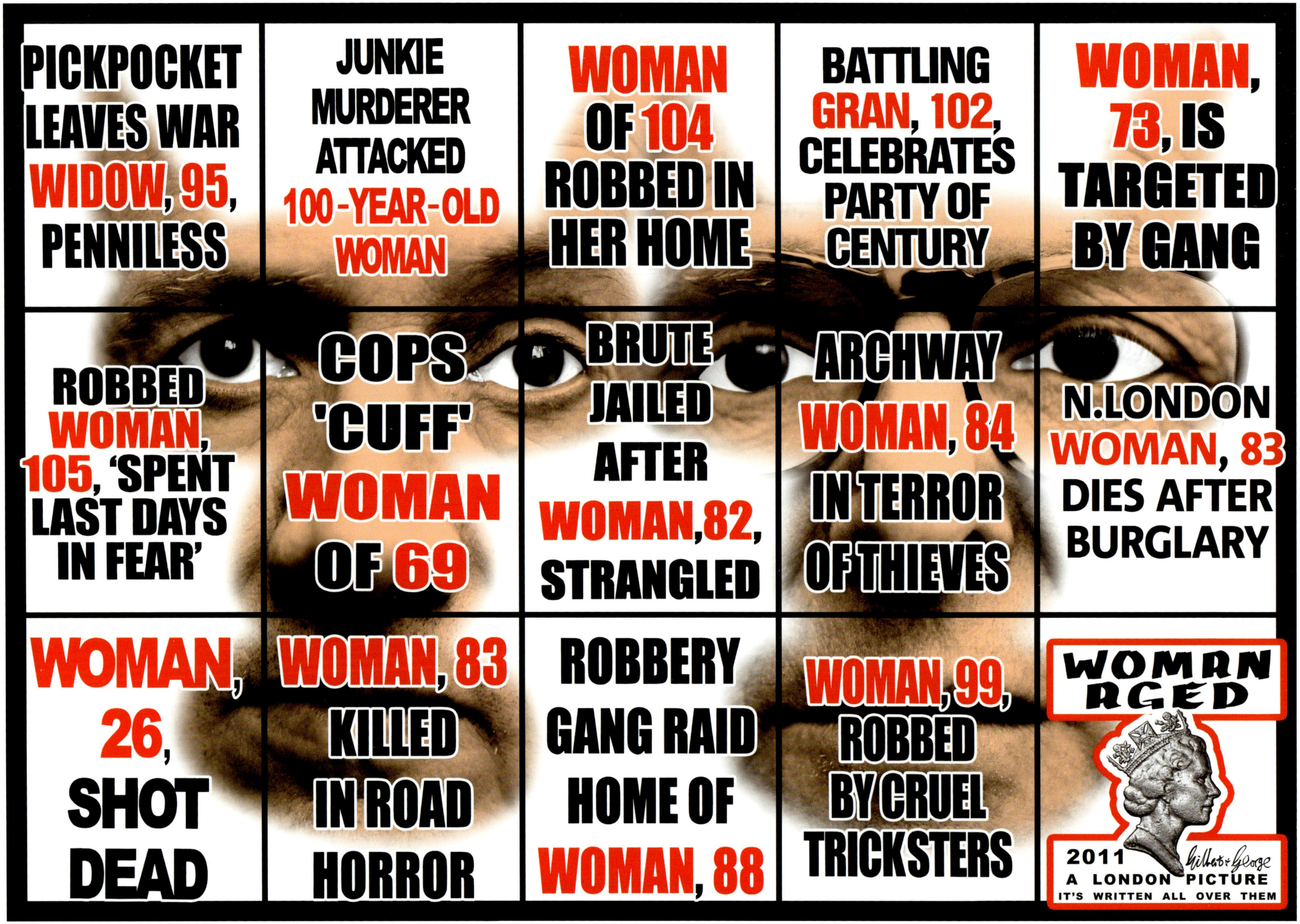
PICKPOCKET LEAVES WAR WIDOW, 95, PENNILESS
JUNKIE MURDERER ATTACKED 100-YEAR-OLD WOMAN
WOMAN OF 104 ROBBED IN HER HOME
BATTLING GRAN, 102, CELEBRATES PARTY OF CENTURY
WOMAN, 73, IS TARGETED BY GANG
ROBBED WOMAN, 105, 'SPENT LAST DAYS IN FEAR'
COPS 'CUFF' WOMAN OF 69
BRUTE JAILED AFTER WOMAN,82, STRANGLED
ARCHWAY WOMAN, 84 IN TERROR OF THIEVES
N.LONDON WOMAN, 83 DIES AFTER BURGLARY
WOMAN, 26, SHOT DEAD
WOMAN, 83 KILLED IN ROAD HORROR
ROBBERY GANG RAID HOME OF WOMAN, 88
WOMAN, 99, ROBBED BY CRUEL TRICKSTERS
WOMAN AGED
2011
A LONDON PICTURE
IT'S WRITTEN ALL OVER THEM

WOMAN AGED. 2011. 226 x 317 cm

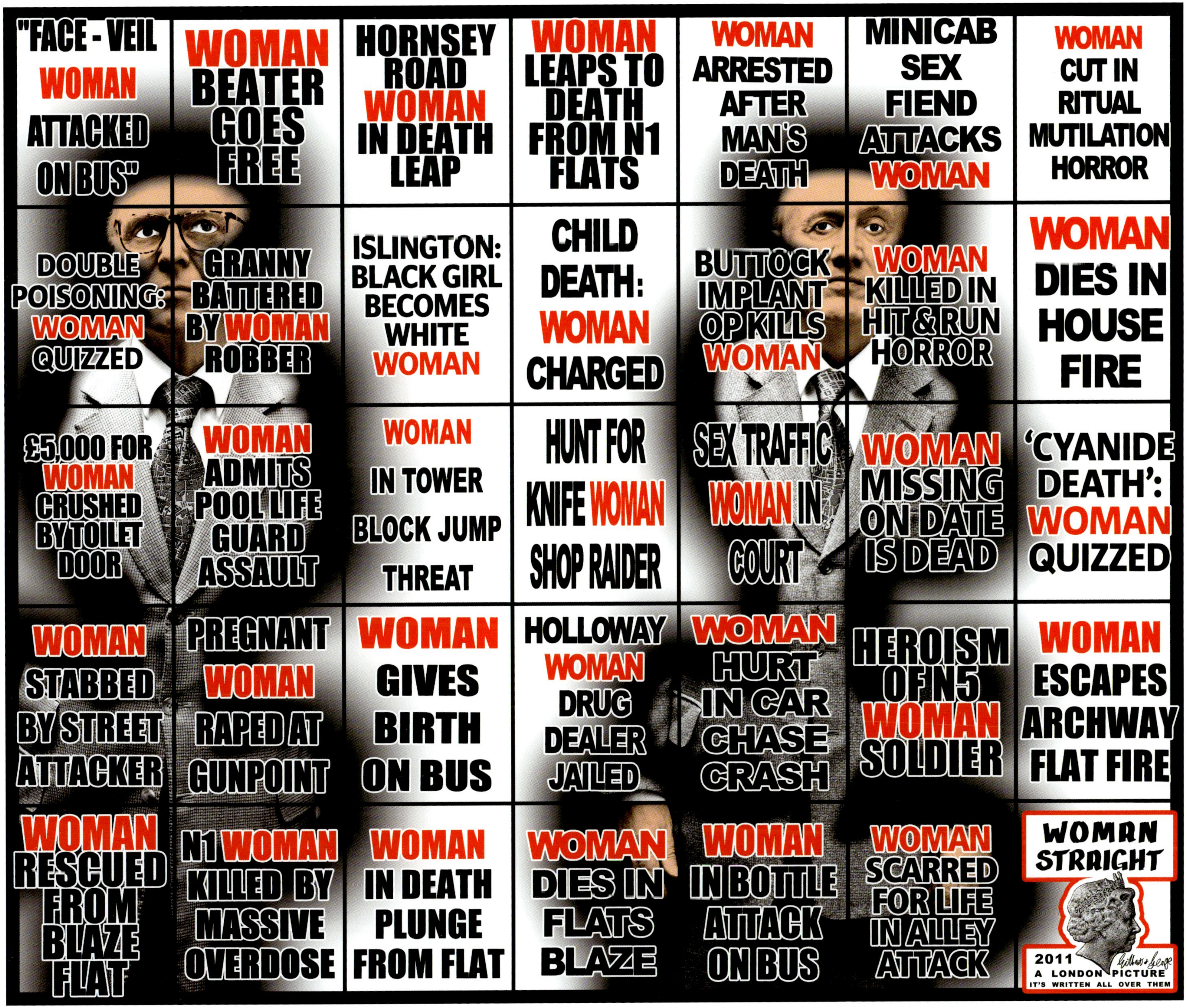
"FACE - VEIL WOMAN ATTACKED ON BUS"
WOMAN BEATER GOES FREE
HORNSEY ROAD WOMAN IN DEATH LEAP
WOMAN LEAPS TO DEATH FROM N1 FLATS
WOMAN ARRESTED AFTER MAN'S DEATH
MINICAB SEX FIEND ATTACKS WOMAN
WOMAN CUT IN RITUAL MUTILATION HORROR
DOUBLE POISONING: WOMAN QUIZZED
GRANNY BATTERED BY WOMAN ROBBER
ISLINGTON: BLACK GIRL BECOMES WHITE WOMAN
CHILD DEATH: WOMAN CHARGED
BUTTOCK IMPLANT OP KILLS WOMAN
WOMAN KILLED IN HIT & RUN HORROR
WOMAN DIES IN HOUSE FIRE
£5,000 FOR WOMAN CRUSHED BY TOILET DOOR
WOMAN ADMITS POOL LIFE GUARD ASSAULT
WOMAN IN TOWER BLOCK JUMP THREAT
HUNT FOR KNIFE WOMAN SHOP RAIDER
SEX TRAFFIC WOMAN IN COURT
WOMAN MISSING ON DATE IS DEAD
'CYANIDE DEATH': WOMAN QUIZZED
WOMAN STABBED BY STREET ATTACKER
PREGNANT WOMAN RAPED AT GUNPOINT
WOMAN GIVES BIRTH ON BUS
HOLLOWAY WOMAN DRUG DEALER JAILED
WOMAN HURT IN CAR CHASE CRASH
HEROISM OF N5 WOMAN SOLDIER
WOMAN ESCAPES ARCHWAY FLAT FIRE
WOMAN RESCUED FROM BLAZE FLAT
N1 WOMAN KILLED BY MASSIVE OVERDOSE
WOMAN IN DEATH PLUNGE FROM FLAT
WOMAN DIES IN FLATS BLAZE
WOMAN IN BOTTLE ATTACK ON BUS
WOMAN SCARRED FOR LIFE IN ALLEY ATTACK
WOMAN STRAIGHT
2011 A LONDON PICTURE
IT'S WRITTEN ALL OVER THEM

WOMAN STRAIGHT. 2011. 377 x 444 cm

WOMEN. 2011. 151 x 127 cm

NURSERY CARE 'CREATES YOB CHILDREN'
COPS FACE YOB TERROR
YOB GANGS TARGET US BECAUSE WE ARE CHRISTIAN
ANTI-YOB HOTLINE LAUNCH
N1 YOB FAMILIES TO BE EVICTED FROM ESTATE
YOB
2011
A LONDON PICTURE
IT'S WRITTEN ALL OVER THEM

YOB. A rude and aggresive young male. Back slang for boy. 2011. 151 x 190 cm

GRADUATE DIES TAKING ON YOBS
ULTASOUND WEAPON TACKLES YOBS
FIREWORK YOBS IN SHOCKING ATTACK
LASER YOBS ENDANGERED 'COPTER PILOT
TV FLAT IS FIRE BOMBED BY YOBS
POLICE SLAM MINIBIKE YOBS
BONFIRE NIGHT YOBS ON RAMPAGE
ESTATE YOBS IN POLICE ATTACK THREAT
CAMERAS TO BEAT ESTATE YOBS
HORROR MOVIE ESTATE YOBS ARE CAUGHT ON FILM
YOBS CAUGHT ON CAMERA
RABBIT IS SET ALIGHT BY YOBS
YOBS PICTURED ROBBING 104-YEAR-OLD
BOOZE BAN TARGETS UNRULY YOBS
YOBS SLASHED TEACHER'S FACE
YOBS
2011
A LONDON PICTURE
IT'S WRITTEN ALL OVER THEM

YOBS
Rude and aggresive
young males.

2011

302 x 254 cm

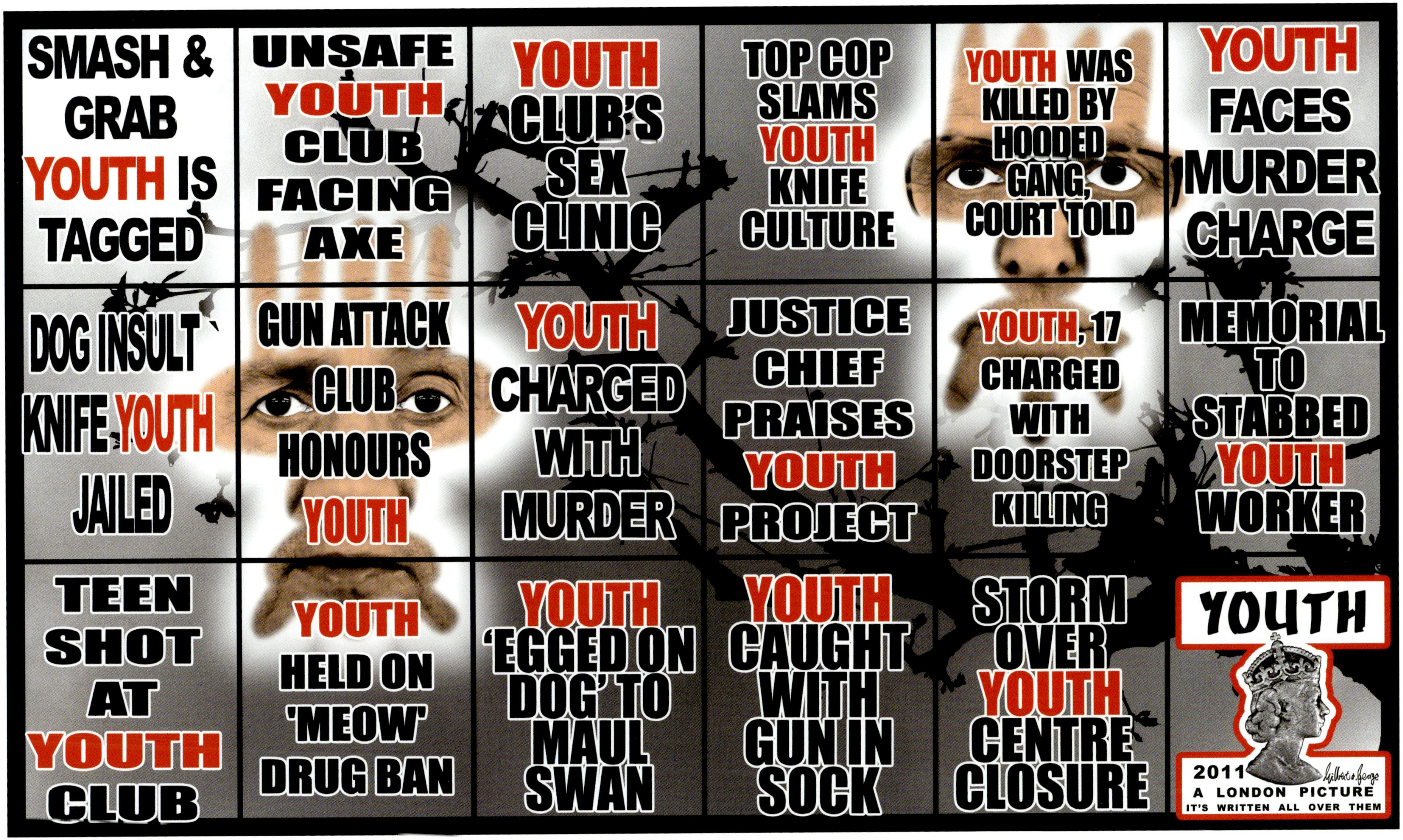
SMASH & GRAB YOUTH IS TAGGED
UNSAFE YOUTH CLUB FACING AXE
YOUTH CLUB'S SEX CLINIC
TOP COP SLAMS YOUTH KNIFE CULTURE
YOUTH WAS KILLED BY HOODED GANG, COURT TOLD
YOUTH FACES MURDER CHARGE
DOG INSULT KNIFE YOUTH JAILED
GUN ATTACK CLUB HONOURS YOUTH
YOUTH CHARGED WITH MURDER
JUSTICE CHIEF PRAISES YOUTH PROJECT
YOUTH, 17 CHARGED WITH DOORSTEP KILLING
MEMORIAL TO STABBED YOUTH WORKER
TEEN SHOT AT YOUTH CLUB
YOUTH HELD ON 'MEOW' DRUG BAN
YOUTH 'EGGED ON DOG' TO MAUL SWAN
YOUTH CAUGHT WITH GUN IN SOCK
STORM OVER YOUTH CENTRE CLOSURE
YOUTH
2011
A LONDON PICTURE
IT'S WRITTEN ALL OVER THEM

YOUTH. 2011. 226 x 381 cm

INDEX TO PICTURE TITLES

ACCUSED ... 17
ADDICT ... 18
ADDICTS ... 19
ANGEL ... 20
ARMED ... 21
ARREST ... 22
ARREST STRAIGHT ... 23
ARRESTED ... 24
ARRESTED STRAIGHT ... 25
ARSON ... 26
ATTACK ... 27
ATTACK STRAIGHT ... 28
ATTACKER ... 29
ATTACKS ... 30
ATTACKS STRAIGHT ... 31
AXE ... 32
BABIES ... 33
BABY ... 34
BABY STRAIGHT ... 35
BANKER ... 36
BATTERED ... 37
BATTLE ... 38
BATTLE STRAIGHT ... 39
BEATEN TO DEATH ... 40
BEATEN TO DEATH STRAIGHT ... 41
BIKER ... 42
BLAZE ... 43
BODY ... 44
BOMB ... 45
BOMB STRAIGHT ... 46
BOMBEY ... 47
BOMBEY STRAIGHT ... 48
BOY ... 49
BOY AGED ... 50
BOY AGED STRAIGHT ... 51
BOY STRAIGHT ... 52
BOYS ... 53
BRAWL ... 54
BROTHEL ... 55
BURGLAR ... 56
BURGLAR STRAIGHT ... 57
BURGLARY ... 58
CABBIE ... 59
CAGED ... 60
CEMETERY ... 61
CHILD ... 62
CHILD STRAIGHT ... 63
CHILDREN ... 64
CHILDREN STRAIGHT ... 65
CHURCH ... 66
CITY ... 67
CITY MONEY ... 68
CITY STRAIGHT ... 69
CRACK ... 70
CRIME ... 71
CUTE KIDS ... 72
CYCLIST ... 73
CYCLIST STRAIGHT ... 74
DEAD ... 75
DEAD STRAIGHT ... 76
DEATH ... 84
DEATH CRASH ... 77
DEATH LEAP ... 78
DEATH PLUNGE ... 79
DEATH PLUNGE STRAIGHT ... 80
DEATH SOMETHING ... 81
DEATH STRAIGHT ... 82
DEATHS ... 85
DEATHS STRAIGHT ... 86
DIE ... 87
DIE STRAIGHT ... 88
DIED ... 89
DIED STRAIGHT ... 90
DIES ... 91
DIES STRAIGHT ... 92
DOG ... 93
DRIVER ... 94
DRUG ... 95
DRUG STRAIGHT ... 96
DRUGS ... 97
DRUGS STRAIGHT ... 98
DRUNK ... 99
DYING ... 100
FAMILY ... 101
FAMILY STRAIGHT ... 102
FOUND ... 104
FURY ... 105
GANG ... 108
GANG STRAIGHT ... 106
GANGS ... 109
GANGS STRAIGHT ... 110
GAY ... 111
GAY STRAIGHT ... 112
GIRL ... 113
GIRL AGED ... 114
GIRL AGED STRAIGHT ... 115
GIRL STRAIGHT ... 116
GRANDAD ... 117
GUN ... 118
GUN STRAIGHT ... 119
GUNMAN ... 120
GUNMAN STRAIGHT ... 121
GUNMEN ... 122
GUNNED DOWN ... 123
GUNPOINT ... 124
GUNS ... 125
HANGED ... 126
HANGING ... 127
HATE ... 128
HELL ... 129
HOLIDAY ... 130
HOODIES ... 131
HOOKER ... 132
HORROR ... 133
HUNT ... 134
HUNTED ... 135
HURT ... 136
ISLAM ... 137
ISLAM STRAIGHT ... 138
JAIL ... 139
JAIL STRAIGHT ... 140
JAILED ... 141
JAILED STRAIGHT ... 142
KERB ... 144
KIDNAP ... 145
KIDS ... 146
KILL ... 147
KILL STRAIGHT ... 148
KILLED ... 149
KILLED STRAIGHT ... 150
KILLER ... 151
KILLER STRAIGHT ... 152
KILLERS ... 154
KILLERS STRAIGHT ... 155
KILLING ... 156
KILLING STRAIGHT ... 157
KILLINGS ... 158
KILLS ... 159
KILLS STRAIGHT ... 160
KNIFE ... 161
KNIFE MURDER ... 162
KNIFE STRAIGHT ... 163
KNIFED ... 164
KNIFED TO DEATH ... 165
KNIFEMAN ... 166
LADPALMATE ... 167
LIFE ... 168
LIFE STRAIGHT ... 169

LONDON....170
LONDON BOMB....171
LONDON CRIME....174
LONDON CRIME STRAIGHT....172
LONDON STRAIGHT....175
LONDON'S....176
LOVER....177
MACHETE....178
MAN....179
MAN AGED....180
MAN DIES....181
MAN STABBED....182
MAN STRAIGHT....183
MISSING....184
MONEY....186
MONEY FIRST....185
MONEY LAST....190
MONEY STRAIGHT....188
MOSQUE....191
MOTHER....192
MOTHER STRAIGHT....193
MUGGER....194
MUGGER STRAIGHT....195
MUGGERS....196
MUGGING....197
MUGGY....198
MUM....199
MURDER....200
MURDER STRAIGHT....202
MURDERED....204
MURDERED STRAIGHT....205
MURDERS....206
MUSLIM....207
MUSLIM STRAIGHT....208
MYSTERY....209
OAP....210
OAPS....211
PAEDO....212
PARK....213
PENSIONER....214
PERVERT....215
PLAYBOY....216
PLOT....217
PLUNGE....218
POLICE....219
POLICE STRAIGHT....220
PORN....222
PREACHER....223
PRISON....224
PUPIL....225
PUPILS....226
RACE....227
RACE HATE....228
RACIST....229
RAID....230
RAID STRAIGHT....231
RAIDERS....232
RAPE....233
RAPE STRAIGHT....234
RAPED....235
RAPIST....236
RAPIST STRAIGHT....237
RAT....238
ROBBED....239
ROBBER....240
ROBBERS....241
ROBBERY....242
ROBBERY STRAIGHT....243
SCHOOL....246
SCHOOL STRAIGHT....244
SCHOOLBOY....247
SCHOOLS....248
SEX....249
SEX & MONEY....250
SEX ATTACKER....251
SEX BEAST....252
SEX PEST....253
SEX STRAIGHT....254
SHOOT OUT....255
SHOOTING....256
SHOOTING STRAIGHT....257
SHOOTINGS....258
SHOP....259
SHOT....260
SHOT DEAD....261
SHOT GUN....262
SHOT STRAIGHT....263
SHOTS....264
SOCCER....265
SOCCER STRAIGHT....266
STAB....267
STAB DEATH....268
STABBED....269
STABBED STRAIGHT....270
STABBED TO DEATH....271
STABBED TO DEATH STRAIGHT. 272
STABBING....273
STABBING STRAIGHT....274
STABBINGS....275
STAR....276
STRANGLED....277
STRANGLER....278
STUDENT....279
STUDENT STRAIGHT....280
STUDENTS....281
SUICIDE....282
SUICIDE STRAIGHT....283
TEACHER....284
TEACHER STRAIGHT....285
TEEN....286
TEEN STRAIGHT....287
TEEN'S....288
TEENAGE....289
TEENAGE STRAIGHT....290
TEENAGER....291
TEENAGER STRAIGHT....292
TEENS....293
TERROR....294
TERROR BOMB....295
TERROR PLOT....298
TERROR STRAIGHT....296
THIEF....299
THIEVES....300
THUG....301
THUGS....302
THUGS STRAIGHT....303
TODDLER....304
TOP TOTS....305
TOT....306
TOTS....307
TUBE....308
TUBE STRAIGHT....309
VANDALS....310
VICE....311
VICTIM....312
VICTIM STRAIGHT....313
WAR....314
WOMAN....315
WOMAN AGED....316
WOMAN STRAIGHT....317
WOMEN....318
YOB....319
YOBS....320
YOUTH....321

First published by Hurtwood Press in 2012 in conjunction with the exhibition
GILBERT & GEORGE: **LONDON PICTURES**

Hurtwood Press 31 Station Road West, Oxted, Surrey RH8 9EE Great Britain

ISBN 978-0-903696-45-6 (Hardback)
ISBN 978-0-903696-31-9 (Softback)